The 1.5 Generation Korean Diaspora

Korean Communities across the World

Series Editor: Joong-Hwan Oh, Hunter College, CUNY

Korean Communities across the World publishes works that address aspects of (a) the Korean American community, (b) Korean society, (c) the Korean communities in other foreign lands, or (d) transnational Korean communities. In the field of (a) the Korean American community, this series welcomes contributions involving concepts such as Americanization, pluralism, social mobility, migration/immigration, social networks, social institutions, social capital, racism/discrimination, settlement, identity, or politics, as well as a specific topic related to family/marriage, gender roles, generations, work, education, culture, citizenship, health, ethnic community, housing, ethnic identity, racial relations, social justice, social policy, and political views, among others. In the field of (b) Korean society, this series embraces scholarship on current issues such as gender roles, age/aging, low fertility, immigration, urbanization, gentrification, economic inequality, high youth unemployment, sexuality, democracy, political power, social injustice, the nation's educational problems, social welfare, capitalism, consumerism, labor, health, housing, crime, environmental degradation, and the social life in the digital age and its impacts, among others. Contributors in the field of (c) Korean communities in other foreign lands are encouraged to submit works that expand our understanding about the formation, vicissitudes, and major issues of an ethnic Korean community outside of South Korea and the Unites States, such as cultural or linguistic retention, ethnic identity, assimilation, settlement patterns, citizenship, economic activities, family relations, social mobility, and racism/discrimination. Lastly, contributions relating to (d) transnational Korean communities may touch upon transnational connectivity in family, economy/finance, politics, culture, technology, social institutions, and people.

The 1.5 Generation Korean Diaspora

A Comparative Understanding of Identity, Culture, and Transnationalism

Edited by Jane Yeonjae Lee and Minjin Kim

LEXINGTON BOOKS

Lanham • Boulder • New York • London

Published by Lexington Books
An imprint of The Rowman & Littlefield Publishing Group, Inc.
4501 Forbes Boulevard, Suite 200, Lanham, Maryland 20706
www.rowman.com

6 Tinworth Street, London SE11 5AL, United Kingdom

British Library Cataloguing in Publication Information Available

Library of Congress Cataloging-in-Publication Data

Library of Congress Control Number: 2020943845

For all 1.5 generation sojourners

Contents

List of Figures and Tables

FIGURES

TABLES

Acknowledgments

We would like to thank the publishing team at Lexington Books, and in particular Joong-Hwan Oh, Courtney Morales, and Shelby Russell, for their tremendous support and continuous help with the production of this book.

On March 2019, we first announced our "Call for papers: 1.5 generation Korean immigrants across the world" in various email lists and relevant research websites. We were both excited and nervous at the same time, and did not know what to expect. After several weeks of anticipation, we were extremely pleased to compile these excellent papers from our contributors and we would like to thank them for their wonderful contributions and commitments. All of their work has been critical and incredibly insightful within their own fields. We felt our work was meaningful in combining these diverse disciplines to tell a shared narrative about the 1.5 generation Koreans.

We must thank our wonderful reviewers who spent their precious time to read our individual chapters and give critical feedback. We would like to thank Allen Bartley, Jin Jun, Peter Nien-chu Kiang, Jihye Kim, Paul Watanabe, Stephanie L. Young, and other anonymous reviewers for giving the most helpful feedback and comments to our contributors. We were truly lucky to have their input and support in improving our work.

We would also like to give special thanks to Insu Kim for his willingness to design the cover page of our book. The illustration was inspired by the 1.5 generation's chameleon-like ability to adapt and thrive in a globalized society. We are certain that our readers will enjoy this design as much as we do.

Our heartfelt gratitude goes out to our family members and friends for their continuous encouragement and support throughout the preparation of this volume.

Finally, the production of this book has been the product of the editors coming together with a shared vision and understanding about the 1.5 generation migrant scholarship within a transnational context. Being 1.5 generation immigrants ourselves, but coming from very different migration trajectories, we wanted to showcase the very complexities, temporalities, and spatialities of being a 1.5 generation Korean migrant. Compiling this collection has been a truly enjoyable and meaningful process!

Jane Yeonjae Lee
Minjin Kim

1

Introduction

Jane Yeonjae Lee and Minjin Kim

This edited collection builds from a standpoint that there is a need to revisit and re-theorize the 1.5 generation migrant group as we enter the third decade of the twenty-first century. We contend that the 1.5 generation's strategies and experiences are greatly inconsistent with the historical experiences of earlier migrants, especially within the context of the continuing growth of information and communication technology (ICT) and the transnational social field. We would also like to highlight that there has not been a single edited collection that specifically examines the 1.5 generation Korean immigrants living in diverse host country settings from the past and the present. In this volume, we illustrate that as we begin to compare different 1.5 generation Korean diasporas across various host countries that are situated within the landscape of particular policies, cultures, norms, communities, power dynamics, and societal expectations, we begin to see similarities and unique elements of 1.5 generation Korean identities across all nations. In this volume, we explore questions such as: What is a Korean identity? What does it mean to be a 1.5 generation Korean immigrant? How do gender, family relationships, different stages of life, and religion shape the identities of the 1.5 generation? What is particular about Koreanness that is different from other ethnic 1.5 generation immigrants? How has the development of Korean identity in general over the past few decades contributed to the 1.5 generation immigrants' experiences now? What shapes the Korean 1.5 generation's imagination of their homeland? What is unique within the 1.5 generation's health and health behaviors? How are 1.5 generation immigrants different from other generation groups? What does it mean to be a "Korean" today? What does the future look like for the 1.5 generation Korean immigrants?

CONCEPTUALIZING THE 1.5
GENERATION KOREAN DIASPORA

There is not a universal definition of who is considered to be a 1.5 generation (im)migrant. The term 1.5 generation is mostly used to differentiate those who immigrated as the children of their first-generation parents, but who were nonetheless born in their home country. Most importantly, it refers to the children of the first-generation immigrants who have spent most of their adolescent years and some of their formative socialization in their host countries (Lee, 2019a). Bartley and Spoonley (2008: 68) broadly define the 1.5 generation immigrant as "children, aged between six and 18 years, who migrate as part of a family unit, but who have experienced at least some of their formative socialization in the country of origin," while others define the 1.5 generation as those who spent their pre-teen years and schooling in their home country (Oh and Min, 2011; Park, 2004; Shin, 2016). In a more descriptive term, and without specifying a certain age, Park (1999) defines the 1.5 generation group as those who experience biculturalism or multiculturalism involving both home and host cultures, and often with conflict. More recently, scholars have expanded the usage of the term 1.5 generation to refer to international students who end up staying in their host countries until their adulthood (Collins, 2010) or return to their homeland with overseas experiences and bicultural identities (Bartley and Spoonley, 2008). Indeed, international students who move to a new country without their families as children or adolescents should also be considered as a 1.5 generation group, as they also spend their adolescent years in the host society and may experience biculturalism. This particular group may arguably experience higher acculturative distress, loneliness, and depression due to long periods of family separation without adequate support (Son, 2013). Moreover, they are often not included in the studies of 1.5 generation Koreans, as they are neither immigrants nor citizens of their host countries.

Starting in the mid-1960s, particularly following the American Immigration Reform Act of 1965, a large number of Koreanse migrated to America, with the hope of achieving "American dreams," and in the pursuit of better economic opportunities and education. Similarly, the reform of Canadian immigration policy in 1966 stimulated movement to Canada (Kwak and Berry, 2001). The most recent emigration destinations for Koreans are Australia and New Zealand, which increased dramatically in the early 1990s also after the lenient migration policy reforms of those countries (Friesen, 2008). As of 2019, the Korean diaspora—the overseas Korean population—consists of approximately 7.5 million people, including descendants of early emigrants and recent emigrants from Korea. It is estimated that the Korean diaspora lives in more than 170 countries around the world. Of these, about 85 percent of the overseas Koreans are concentrated in five countries—the United States, China, Japan, Canada, and Uzbekistan (Ministry of Foreign Affairs, Republic of Korean, n.d.). The Korean diaspora continues to expand as more Koreans migrate to other countries for education, jobs, and business opportunities. Interestingly, wherever they maybe, Korean immigrants usually arrive in a new country with a strong sense of cultural origin and collective Korean identity (Kim, 2004).

Korean diaspora communities have been very active in forming Korean community associations and continuing to maintain their collective ethnic identity. These activities serve as a cornerstone that brings people together and maintains a collective ethnic identity, Korean language, and culture. Different types of agencies, institutions, and structures shape and maintain the 1.5 generation identities, yet access to those agencies may significantly differ by class, gender, religion, or ethnicity. For instance, having access to Korean churches and language schools has been documented in many studies as an important type of social capital among Korean immigrants, and this is especially the case for the 1.5 generation immigrants to sustain their Korean culture and identity (Lee, 2019b; Min, 2013; Kim, 1996). However, not all 1.5 generation individuals have access to this social and cultural capital. They may not grow up in a town where there are enough co-ethnic communities to belong to, or there may be other individual difficulties that prevent belonging. For instance, the 1.5 generation Korean Americans who grew up in Hawaii often had different experiences depending on whether they were from a working-class family or a middle-class family (Danico, 2004). The 1.5 generation Korean Americans from middle-class families had better access to language schools, cultural capital, and their homeland of Korea itself and felt more free to express their Korean identity to others. In comparison, the 1.5 generation Korean Americans from working-class families often wanted to hide their Korean identity among their Korean peers, had much more complicated and difficult identity-building experiences and felt a weaker sense of belonging to the wider Korean American community (Danico, 2004). These different identity dynamics and experiences of the 1.5 generation need to be further explored on a class, gender, and racial basis. Additionally, ideologies of a shared Korean identity, language, and cultural values and practices among the Korean diaspora continue to attract scholarly interests that seek for further conceptualization and understanding as each of the migration destinations and communities matures and as the new wave of Korean migrations continue to arrive. This volume reflects our interest in theorizing and understanding the 1.5 generation migrant group.

Identities are not fixed, but performative, relational, and always under construction throughout one's life course and changing circumstances (Hall, 1996; Kroger, 2007; Sarup, 1996). We often refer to identity construction as an ongoing process, noting that we all carry "contradictory selves." However, there is also the "stable self" within us, which does not change despite all other identities developing over time. It is the "collective or true self hiding inside the many other, more superficial or artificially imposed 'selves' which people with a shared history and ancestry hold in common and which can stabilize, fix or guarantee an unchanging 'oneness' or cultural belongingness underlying all the other superficial differences" (Hall, 1996:4). Indeed, one's own ethnic or national identity, although also being socially and historically constructed, remain as one's relatively "stable self" compared to all other social identities we carry throughout our lives. For a 1.5 generation immigrant, sustaining such a "stable" identity has been documented as a conflicting process by many scholars (Kim et al., 2003; Kim and Agee, 2018; Yoon, 2018).

"Home" is a key element in the development of one's identity, as it gives a sense of belonging (McDowell, 1999; Tuan, 1977). Often, the search for a sense of belonging is explored in relation to how the 1.5 generation defines where "home" is. Living as a migrant, one is often situated in a minority position where belonging to mainstream society is always contested through policy or social stigma, and hence many immigrants remain in a position where they always feel away from their "home." For immigrants, "home" can both be a "nostalgic past or a utopian future" (Blunt, 2005), as they live with the memories of their "home" or imagine the future of visiting or returning to their homeland. However, for a 1.5 generation immigrant, such a sense of belonging to one's "home" is often a difficult question to answer. For instance, a study of 1.5 generation Korean New Zealander returnees found that they have expressed the desire to return to their homeland to find a sense of belonging. However, the study argues that their sense of "home" is never fully found as they also navigate their longing for a "New Zealand home" once they return to their original homeland (Lee, 2018). Lee (2018) argues that such ambiguity over where their "home" is stems from the 1.5 generation's teenage years having been spent in their host society, where they acquired a New Zealander's sense of identity and home without even realizing it. It is only once they physically return "home" that these individuals begin to recognize their dual identities. Further, it is the "transnational connectivities" (Kivisto, 2005) that allowed the returnees to hold stronger sentiments toward their original homeland.

There is a particular "in-betweenness" about the 1.5 generation Koreans' migratory experiences that makes them unique and different from their parents' experiences, as well as from the experiences of second- and third-generation immigrants who are born in the host destination (Yoon, 2018). Unlike the first-generation immigrants, who are less likely to fully adapt to their host country, the 1.5 generation immigrants often adapt quickly to their new environment by attending local schools and interacting with local classmates, while maintaining their national traditions at home and in their communities (Lee, 2012; Lee et al., 2015). In navigating both worlds, this group often faces conflict, especially during their early adaptation phase in their host country as they interact between their old and new cultures in their everyday lives. Research has suggested that Korean immigrant adolescents and young adults experience more negative psychological symptoms such as depression and other psychological distress due to language barriers, cultural conflicts, and high academic pressure (Hwang & Ting, 2008; Kim, Suh, Heo, 2012; Thomas & Choi, 2006). Furthermore, Korean immigrant children experience a high level of parent-child conflict due to the acculturation discrepancy (Kim & Wolpin, 2008; Thomas & Choi, 2006; Yang & Rettig, 2003; Yeh, 2003). This pattern is a particularly significant concern during the transition from adolescence to adulthood, a time when the likelihood of depressive symptoms and other forms of psychological distress may be increased (Vannucci, Flannery, & Ohannessian, 2018).

Hybridity is the most prominent feature of the group's identity (Ang, 2001). Gaining a sense of tolerance for unsettling identities can be difficult for young adults, especially while growing up as part of an ethnic minority within a larger mainstream group. As they migrate overseas as children, the process of navigating their home and host cultures may come into conflict during their teenage years, a period that is already difficult, with questions about various identities. During their late teens and twenties, individuals are often self-focused, exploring multiple possibilities, and they experience identity exploration, instability, and feeling "in-between" (Arnett, 2000). The 1.5 generation's identities are perhaps the most ambiguous in terms of how they identify themselves and where they find their sense of belonging. Kim and Agee (2018) illustrate through their case study of the 1.5 generation Korean New Zealanders that they often face ambiguity and confusion as they are usually perceived by the first generation as second-generation, or seen as first-generation by the second generation, and they are identified as only Koreans by the non-Koreans and locals in their host countries (Kim and Agee, 2018). Such perception developed via others is referred to as having "double consciousness" by other scholars (Park, 1999). Having to deal with such hybridity can be more crucial during their teenage years, as these are known to be the most significant identity development phase (Erikson, 1997) that affects the psychological development and well-being of adolescents and young adults. A less well-developed identity or role confusion could lead to low self-esteem, low self-efficacy, and greater psychological distress such as depression and anxiety (Arseth, Kroger, Martinussen, Marcia, 2009).

Research has shown that the first-generation immigrants often face downward social mobility once they move to their host country and engage in service sector jobs (Lee, 2016; Min, 1990). On the other hand, the 1.5 generation and second-generation immigrants often illustrate upward social mobility from their parents and become successful in their careers by attaining highly skilled jobs (Kim, 2006; Park, 1996; Oh and Min, 2011). Korean culture places a high value on education, and the pursuit of children's higher academic attainment is one of the most important goals for Korean parents (Kim & Bang, 2016; Jung, Stang, Ferko, & Han, 2011). Consequently, Korean parents set high expectations for their children. This is also seen in 1.5 generation Korean parents as well, which Park illustrates in detail in chapter 2. The Korean parents' most common reason for immigrating to English-speaking countries is to provide better educational opportunities for their children (Jung, Stang, Ferko, & Han, 2011). This cultural value on education has caused many parents to put intense pressure on their children to achieve academically, which may explain why there is upward social mobility.

Members of the 1.5 generation often act as the "middling migrants" helping their first-generation parents ease into the host society and growing up with the cultural and social capital to "mix" their diverse culture in various settings. However, studies have also shown that the 1.5 generation group who immigrates with family often faces stresses by taking on the role of translator, interpreter, and general cultural intermediary for their non-English-speaking parents (Choi & Dancy, 2012, Son, 2013). The changes in roles and responsibilities in the family may disorient 1.5

generation children's developing sense of identity and belonging, as the power relationship between parents and children changes. Moreover, a less well-developed identity or role confusion can lead to low self-esteem, low self-efficacy, and greater psychological distress such as depression and anxiety (Arseth, Kroger, Martinussen, Marcia, 2009). Studies suggest that the cultural experience in changing roles and responsibilities in the family among this group could be challenging during their adolescence; however, it can also mitigate some of the growing pains of living in a new country, strengthen resilience, and maximize the development potential of the 1.5 generation (Bhang, 2019; Choi et al., 2016). The intersecting factors that explain the resilience experiences of 1.5 generation Koreans are crucial areas that need to be investigated, especially as they relate to their health and well-being, yet this has seldom been previously explored.

Having a hybrid or dual identity does not always involve a negative experience. The hybridity has often been associated with cultural flexibility and strategies. For instance, Bhang (2019) states that in their emerging young adulthood, these individuals begin to acknowledge and understand their 1.5 generation cultural experiences more, appreciate their bicultural and bilingual experiences, and see the in-between space as "positive," "privilege," and "advantageous" (Bhang, 2019). Further, a study on 1.5 generation Asian migrants in New Zealand showed that despite the non-white status, which often creates social distance in these intergenerational youth experiences, their middle-class backgrounds often motivate the Asian migrants to pursue higher education and skilled occupations with their bilingual abilities and cultural flexibility (Bartley and Spoonley, 2008). Wang and Collins (2016) argue that the contemporary 1.5 generation Chinese migrants in New Zealand are capable of "blocking out" unpleasant experiences of being an ethnic minority; rather, they utilize their cross-cultural identity capital and knowledge to become cosmopolitan young adults who are freely open to differences. Recognizing those cosmopolitan values within 1.5 generation immigrants is important in understanding this group and especially encourages us to avoid overgeneralization of 1.5 generation's being hybrid in the sense of "not belonging." Indeed, 1.5 generation immigrants can cross back and forth between their home and host cultures, and they are able to choose and assemble their own identities depending on the circumstances. The unprecedented dynamism of the 1.5 generation makes it possible to live in both cultures, in sequence or simultaneously. In this sense, the 1.5 generation identity is a radical departure from the identities found in both the first generation and the second generation, as their lives are capable of becoming more fluid and mobile.

The sociocultural, linguistic, and historical assets of the 1.5 generation are framed much more positively in relation to community-based issues and needs. Sometimes, the success stories of the 1.5 generation migrants can only be fully seen once they have returned to their home country. For instance, studies have shown that the 1.5 generation, skilled return migrants can be effective "cross-border brokers" and help to transfer the skills gained overseas to their home countries if they are fully/equally embedded in both their home and host societies (Wang, 2015; Lee, 2019a; Conway and Potter, 2009). Indeed, 1.5 generation immigrants are considered to be an ideal type of global talent who can aid in the home country's development through the use of their cultural and social capital, global and local tacit knowledge, bicultural and bilingual skills, and a commitment to their home nation (Jones, 2011; Shin and Choi, 2015; Lee, 2019a). Scholars have contended that the recent transnational 1.5 generation's strategies differ greatly from the historical experiences of earlier migrants (Bartley and Spoonley, 2008), and such strategies provide much more positive experiences and opportunities for them to acquire better jobs and careers once they enter adulthood. Although the study mainly refers to 1.5 generation migrant groups from middle-class families, this gives a somewhat realistic contextualization to the recent Korean 1.5 generation diaspora, as their parents mostly moved overseas as the result of a point system which requires some levels of education and income.

The "New" Korean 1.5 Generation: Identities, Spatialities, and Temporalities

In our edited collection, we are concerned with the changing and complex nature of being a 1.5 generation Korean immigrant through divergent spatialities and temporalities, while also focusing on redefining what it means to be a Korean nowadays and how the shared Korean identity shapes the experiences of overseas Koreans. So far, we have attempted to theorize and conceptualize what it means to be a 1.5 generation Korean immigrant overseas and to consider how the 1.5 generation's hybrid identities may at times cause difficulties as well as opportunities once fully embraced and strategically utilized. This important work on the 1.5 generation has also highlighted the significance of taking a life course approach in understanding migratory experiences, as individuals' identities evolve as they move from one phase to another. We have also contended that although the term 1.5 generation is used universally across all immigrant groups to refer to the generational differences, the particular experiences and identities of individuals are complicated by different individual factors such as ethnicities, culture, religion, education, family situation, income, and so on. Trying to define and conceptualize the 1.5 generation Korean identity is an almost impossible task, as the 1.5 generation Korean diaspora is a heterogeneous group with varied experiences and situations, and they are bound to change and evolve over time and space. In our edited collection, we attempt to explore the inherent complexities of being a 1.5 generation Korean migrant by (1) redefining what it means to be a Korean in current times and considering how the new imaginations of being a Korean may affect the identities and experiences of overseas Koreans, (2) recognizing the importance of the contexts of different host societies by examining the Korean diaspora of various host country settings, and (3) developing a fuller picture of the past, present, and future of the 1.5 generation Korean diaspora by understanding the importance of an individual's life course as well as the changing nature of international migration itself through time. We discuss them below.

The "New" Korean Identity

While it is important to discuss the complexities and development of the 1.5 genera-tion's "hybrid" identities in their host society's setting, one first needs to understand what it means to be a "Korean." Earlier, we discussed how members of the Korean diaspora attempt to maintain their Korean culture and identity as they settle in their new societies, the 1.5 generation migrants' in-between identities and "middling" situations, and how a sense of belonging to a wider Korean ethnic community helps them maintain their original culture and social capital. We have also discussed how Korean parents generally hold high expectations for their children, and Korean migrants place importance on education, family affiliation, and the Korean heritage. However, what has not been fully discussed is: What is a Korean identity anyway? Is being a "Korean" always the same, or does it also change and evolve? If so, how may the "new" Korean identity today affect the value system and identity-building for the 1.5 generations overseas?

The economic status and political situations of a migrant's original home nation (in)directly affect the immigrants' identity and everyday struggle. Demonstrations of xenophobia toward Middle Eastern immigrants after the 911 attack in the United States, and racism toward Asians during the emergence of COVID-19 are just a few examples of how the global knowledge about immigrants' original countries forms certain stereotypes and shapes their everyday experiences as minorities overseas. Even without the extreme examples, one could argue that the general economic status and political situations of the original home country form certain power dynamics and important background for an immigrant's identity-building experiences. For instance, studies have documented the different treatment of skilled and unskilled migrants by the host nations and how they may produce divergent realities and regulations for the immigrants' uneven settlements and experiences (Collins, 2016; Nugroho et al., 2018; Tsuda, 2010). In the context of South Korea and the Korean diaspora overseas, it is certain that the way the dominant groups of the host society viewed South Koreans in the 1960s and 1970s is vastly different from how Koreans are perceived today—and this is mainly due to the economic growth of Korea itself.

South Korea grew economically at a very fast pace during its industrial period in the 1970s, and now it is the twelfth largest economy in the world and the fourth largest economy in Asia in 2018 (World Bank, 2018), and it is the leading ICT country. In addition, due to Hallyu, the "Korean wave," and the increasing popular-ity of K-pop, K-dramas, and Korean celebrities in general, Korea itself has become a popular country among teenagers and young adults, and Seoul is a top tourist destination (Anderson et al., 2014). Korea is now a global economy, and this led to increased national pride for South Koreans (Chung and Choe, 2008). We want to emphasize that the global context of South Korea may lead to a more positive identity-building situation and different power dynamics for Korean immigrants overseas, as has already been explored by a few scholars (Yook et al., 2014; Jang and Paik, 2012). The changes in the national economy of South Korea would ultimately affect the 1.5 generation Korean diaspora's everyday experiences in their interactions with the locals in their host countries and how they can associate with their own culture in front of others.

More importantly, the improved socioeconomic situation in South Korea means that there are more social and economic capitals for the 1.5 generation Koreans as they may seek jobs and other opportunities in their homeland as they enter adulthood. As presented by a number of chapters in our volume, the transnational linkages that the 1.5 generation Koreans build between their home and host nations often bring more economic and social opportunities. For instance, in chapter 10, the story about a female Korean American entrepreneur who built an online fashion platform illustrates that she was able to reach out to a wider market overseas because Korean fashion has generally become popular worldwide. Also, because of the growing economy, overseas Korean entrepreneurs are able to gain funding from various venture capital sources in South Korea, which leads to a stronger transnational entrepreneurship between the home and host countries. We hope that in this book, we are able to showcase these newly emerging cosmopolitan identities of overseas Koreans and the need for a continuous reconceptualization of the "new" Korean 1.5 generation immigrants to reflect the increasing diversity and globalizing of Korea.

Spatialities

Through different "spatialities," meaning different contexts and spaces of where the migration originally happened, the 1.5 generation's experiences can be quite different depending on the societal and political situations of both home and host countries. As we have discussed so far in this introduction, the current literature about the 1.5 generation Korean diaspora is predominantly about Koreans from English-speaking countries, including the United States, Canada, Australia, and New Zealand. Further, it is hard to find studies about the differences within those nations as the migrant communities tend to concentrate in bigger cities. For example, it is more common to find studies about Korean New Zealanders in the city of Auckland or to find studies about Korean Americans in L.A. than in Iowa. Hence, it is often difficult to find more information about Korean migrants who grew up in rural communities where there may be less of a Korean community whose migrant narratives would be quite different and to find out about those Koreans who grew up in Europe, Africa, and other parts of South Asia, for instance.

In this edited volume, the authors write from various migration contexts, and they tell quite contradictory stories. Most importantly, they all share the message that different places make different people, and that every 1.5 generation identity is locally grown. For example, in chapter 3, Lee uses the story of a young boy who grew up in a very small town where there was a small Korean community and illustrates how difficult it is for non-Christian Korean Americans to find their own sense of belonging outside the Korean church. As for this boy, the church was the only means of having access to Korean culture, so despite his non-religious belief, his family forced him to attend the church. On the other hand, the same chapter shares the story of a young girl living in Boston and explores how she came to find her own circle of

Korean friends in college, which was possible due to the large number of Korean international students in the area. These spatialities are important in discussing the nature of the divergent infrastructure and the social and cultural capital that shape the 1.5 generation in multiple ways.

Earlier, we discussed the potential for the 1.5 generation Korean immigrants to become skilled transnational immigrants and global talents with their bilingual and bicultural skills. However, what has not been further discussed is that those success stories are only confined to certain groups of the 1.5 generation Korean diaspora with certain privilege that comes from the host society in which they grew up. Much of this should be examined from a spatial perspective. For instance, in chapter 10, the study argues that the Korean female transnational entrepreneurs in Silicon Valley often decided to become entrepreneurs and started their own businesses because of the "Silicon Valley atmosphere" and the "vibe" they have become accustomed to. Often referred to as the "Silicon Valley ecosystem," where there is a high concentration of venture capital and easily accessible workshops and seminars for new entrepreneurs, the place offered many windows for the 1.5 generation Korean Americans to become entrepreneurs. In contrast, the occupation trajectories shared by Korean Argentinians in chapter 3 illustrate somewhat different narratives. The Latin American culture, as discussed by one of the study participants, is somewhat more laid back compared to American and Korean culture. Along with this, because the occupations of Korean Argentinian parents are concentrated in the garment industry, and they are relatively less well off, among the 1.5 generation Korean Argentinians, having a college degree is considered a privilege, and not all 1.5 generations Korean Argentinians face upward social mobility and become involved in professional fields. In our edited volume, we showcase the importance of context through a number of different shared and distinct case studies. We illustrate that the 1.5 generation Korean identities and experiences are shaped by not only individual factors, but they are locally, socially, and spatially constructed.

Temporalities

The particular 1.5 generation experiences are also temporal in the sense that they come from a particular time, historical moments, and a distinct era of migration history, and they are always prone to change and evolve over time. We stated at the beginning of this book that there is a need to reconceptualize the recent 1.5 generation Korean diaspora's experiences, as they are bound to be inconsistent with the historical experiences of overseas Korean ancestors. One way to explain the current era of migration is through the increasing transnationalism of recent migrants, whose everyday lives are connected between their host and home societies due to the increase in ICT and mobility (Glick-Schiller et al., 1992; Kivisto, 2001). Indeed, transnational scholars have argued over the past two decades that recent immigrants should be examined from a transnational perspective, as they continuously engage in various social, economic, and political activities in their homeland and distinctively live in their transnational social field. Such characteristics of recent immigrants are now the norm and have become part of the mundane life with the increase in the usage of smart phones and better internet connections worldwide. Most of the chapters in our book illustrate the experiences of 1.5 generation Koreans born in the 1980s and 1990s who have fully or partially grown up in this recent migration era. For instance, in chapter 6, the 1.5 generation Korean New Zealander parents teach their second-generation children Korean culture through Korean TV sites and online webpages. Although everyone's access to the transnational linkages varies, it is important to note that these particular experiences of the 1.5 generation Koreans are part of the globalized era, and they are bound to change in the future.

The 1.5 generation's identities and experiences are also temporal within their personal circumstances and throughout the course of their lives. Many of the existing studies about the 1.5 generation migrants explore their adolescent years of struggles and findings; hence, they remain temporal in some ways. Yet, there are fewer studies about their identities and values changes in their later stages of life. The individual chapters in our book illustrate certain forms of life and identity transitions of 1.5 generation Koreans through the stories about their marriages, occupation trajectories, parenthood, and further movements in their future. In chapter 4, through the narrations of a Korean Canadian family, the chapter uses the 1.5 generation children's names as a symbol for change and solidarity in their identities over time. For example, the son suddenly likes his Korean name as an adult, which he did not want to use when he was growing up and used his English name in order to "fit in" to the host society. Such changes in their value, coming to terms with their Koreanness, and finding solidarity are common narratives shared in other chapters in this book. Through the illustrations of the diverse experiences of the 1.5 generation Koreans in various stages and moments of their lives, our book shows that every identity and migratory trajectory is temporal and always malleable to change over time. Such temporalities and spatialities are among the key themes of this edited volume, and we hope that you enjoy reading the different chapters and searching for the differences and similarities shared by the 1.5 generation Korean diaspora over space and time.

TOWARD A COMPARATIVE UNDERSTANDING OF THE 1.5 GENERATION: ABOUT THIS BOOK

In this special volume, the authors contribute to the understanding of 1.5 generation Korean immigrants from various empirical, theoretical, and methodological approaches. In doing so, we showcase work from diverse disciplines that take a macro, meso, and micro approach to studying immigrants. We have included contributors from different disciplines, including sociology, anthropology, geography, media studies, innovation, Asian studies, and health studies; they are informed by different study methods, including qualitative and quantitative approaches and theoretical text analysis. Our case studies of different types of 1.5 generation Korean immigrants are based on a number of different host country settings, including the United States, Argentina, Canada, and New Zealand. We believe this book is the first attempt at looking at the 1.5 generation group of Koreans from such multiple angles and contexts. All of the contributions aim to explore the inherent complexities of the term 1.5 generation, but also embrace the usefulness of this term, enhance understanding of 1.5 generation strategies and experiences, and show how the unique situation of being embedded in their two cultures helps shape an individual's migration trajectories and experiences.

We have chosen a conceptual approach to organize the collection to emphasize how the 1.5 generation migrant cohort can be researched from diverse angles. The book is organized around four research themes: (1) community, identity, and belonging, (2) family and gender, (3) health and well-being, and (4) transnationalism and entrepreneurship. The chapters are reflective of various methods and contexts connecting discussions of theory and practice by situating the 1.5 generation migratory experiences within a relevant conceptual framework. Given this conceptual framework, the reader can approach the book in various ways: conceptually, for example, by engaging with various chapters on hybrid identity; methodologically, by reading through various qualitative and quantitative approaches and thinking through the subtleties of how our research methods shape our findings; spatially, by examining the particular experiences of migrants from particular locations; or chronologically, by searching for migrant narratives from the past and the present.

Part I. Community, Identity, and Belonging

Identity is a major component of the psychological development and well-being of adolescents and young adults. It is a complicated process, especially when many factors, including gender, race, ethnicity, country of origin, class, language, and cultural background, intersect to shape the multiple dimensions of one's experience. These factors can confer either disadvantages or privileges to each individual, in relation to time and space. Among the various factors that shape an individual's identity, co-ethnic community has been considered a major component of a migrant's life that offers social and cultural capital, a sense of belonging, and in turn, an environment where the migrants can maintain the cultural identity of their original homeland. In this section, we have three chapters that investigate these complexities of the 1.5 generation identity-construction experiences through their explorative and original approaches and case studies.

Irene Park opens chapter 2 by illustrating the complexities of identity construction of 1.5 generation Koreans in Argentina by examining how they make sense of their lives and occupational choices in their 40s. As an insider researcher, she offers vivid narratives of how Korean Argentinian communities are characterized by both Argentinian and Korean culture and how the 1.5 generation Argentinian Koreans' identities are distinctive of this locally mixed culture. Through her stories of those who "fail" or "succeed" in their occupational trajectories, she illustrates how the notions of good life or success for the 1.5 generation are complicated by their relationships with their family, imaginations of their homeland, and personal growth. In chapter 3, Jane Lee explores the life trajectories and identity-building experiences of the 1.5 generation Korean Americans who are non-Christians. She examines this distinctive group's experiences in relation to the predominantly Christian Korean American community and illustrates how those non-Christian Korean Americans experience religious marginality. The chapter shows that the difficulty of obtaining a sense of belonging to a wider Korean American community does have a significant impact on the 1.5 generation's divergent identities over their life courses. The stories of identity construction and deconstruction are further complicated by Alicia Cort in chapter 4, which examines the 1.5 generation Korean Canadian experience in relation to Christian religion that is knitted to their family kinship. This chapter introduces some relevant concepts from performance theory and theater studies, such as liminality, social drama, and ritual performance to help further the understanding of the complexities of the 1.5 generation Korean diaspora living "between two worlds." Through the theatrical characters who are 1.5 generation Korean Canadians, the chapter illustrates how by being part of a Korean church community, the in-between experiences are further complicated by the different expectations held by their families, Korean church communities, and the Canadian society.

Part II. Family and Gender

The 1.5 generation's hybridity is further highlighted through the particular experiences and positionalities in relation to family and gender. Studies of the 1.5 generation cohort often show that they possess hybrid identities. By growing up as migrant children in their host countries with their first-generation Korean parents, they are influenced by various factors to acquire hybrid norms, identities, and perceptions. The chapters in this section entail strong narratives of such hybridity, especially in relation to family dynamics and gender roles. The chapters tell stories of identities caught between the past and present, tradition and modernity, homeland and host country, and East and West. Yet, they also show that these binary oppositions are inadequate to illustrate the complexities of their hybrid normativities, and that further discussion is necessary to fully grasp what it means to acquire a hybrid identity, especially in relation to family and gender roles. In chapter 5, Su Cho examines the complicated relationships between the Korean American first-generation mothers (who got married in Korea through arranged marriages in the 1970s and 1980s) and their 1.5 generation daughters who grew up in America after migration, and how they share different perceptions of love and marriage. The study shows that despite the distinct narratives of tradition and modernity between the mothers and daughters, their current views and perceptions about love and marriage are complicated by their migration trajectories where the family power dynamics and gender roles change. In chapter 6, Hyeeun Kim explores the 1.5 generation Koreans' parenthood in New Zealand, illustrating their experiences of cultural tension, in-betweenness, and everyday negotiations in parental norms and expectations for their children. The chapter illustrates that due to the close family kinship among Koreans, the 1.5 generation Korean New Zealander ("Kowi") parents receive help from their parents, in-laws, and their extended families, yet they all come with certain conflicts and generational differences in norms and value. While the chapter shows the difficulties and complexities, the study also argues that the 1.5 generation parents are better positioned to teach their children about both home and host cultures, as they are capable of knowing both worlds because they have already experienced the cultural dynamics by growing up as immigrant children.

Part III. Health and Well-being

Korean family and cultural values tend to be deeply rooted in collectivism, where the self is interdependent with collective goals and close relationships. This emphasis on cultural and social relationships and group membership also means that behavioral expressions of filial piety, family obligation, family recognition through achievement, emotional self-control, and humility are valued in this culture. This contrasts with one of the core cultural values of the West, individualism, which emphasizes individual goals over collective goals, and places value on self-reliance and individuality. The 1.5 generation often falls in between these two opposing cultural orientations of individualism and collectivism, which may impact their health and well-being. This is one of the ways the experiences of 1.5 generation Koreans are complex, unique, and distinct from those of the first- or second-generation groups, and illustrates why it is important to consider as many contexts and situations as possible to understand 1.5 generation Koreans and their unique experiences. There is a growing recognition around the role of culture, gender, identity, language, socialization, and immigration as social determinants of health and health behavior among Korean immigrants and their offspring. However, minimal studies have specifically focused on the links between 1.5 generation Koreans' health experiences and health practices and their ethnic and cultural identities. This section highlights a little-explored aspect of the unique health experiences and needs of 1.5 generation Koreans. In chapter 7, Sou Hyun Jang provides valuable insights into the context of 1.5 generation Korean Americans' health utilization and how their behavior differs from first- and second-generation Korean Americans and other 1.5 generation Asian American subgroups. This chapter highlights that although 1.5 generation Korean Americans have the highest educational attainment and employment rates in general, they have lower health care utilization than first-generation Koreans and other 1.5 generation Asian subgroups (i.e., Chinese, Filipino, Japanese). In chapter 8, Minjin Kim and Chris Hahm further illustrate the intersection of acculturation and generational status on 1.5 and second-generation Korean American women's sexual health, health risk behaviors, and health utilization. This chapter concludes that changes in cultural values, attitudes, and practices can impact 1.5 generation Korean women's health and health behaviors in a way that differs from second-generation Korean women. The findings of these two chapters inform the need for the development of tailored interventions and specific public health policy implementation for different generational groups.

Part IV. Transnationalism and Entrepreneurship

Studies affirm that skilled migrants play a key role in contributing to their original home country's globalization and economic development with their skills gained from overseas, often providing innovation and entrepreneurship. Hence, sending countries are often interested in pulling back their overseas skilled co-ethnic population through lenient policy toward them. Also, within the host society context, transnational entrepreneurship has gained huge interest among migration scholars as they continue to contribute to the globalizing local economy. In this section, we showcase two distinct yet interrelated chapters about Korean American transnational entrepreneurs who started their own businesses, mostly in the high-tech industry in Silicon Valley. In chapter 9, June Lee and Edison Tse illustrate the recent trajectories of 1.5 generation Korean entrepreneurs in Silicon Valley who share unique entrepreneurial skills, motives, and strategies based on their middling and in-between situations. The chapter shows that these transnational 1.5 generation entrepreneurs are able to use their connections back home and open their second offices in South Korea and gain funding from the South Korean venture capital. There is also a sense of "homebound" internationalization of their firms, as the decision to extend their companies to South Korea is not just about having more connections and opportunities, but they are complemented by their familiarities with the Korean culture and longings for their home. In the final chapter, June Lee and Jane Lee further complicate the entrepreneurial trajectories of the Korean American transnational entrepreneurs in Silicon Valley, as their study distinctively focuses on female participants. The chapter illustrates fascinating and vivid narratives about the first- and 1.5 generation Korean American transnational entrepreneurs' entrepreneurial motivations, organizations, and experiences, which are further complicated by their gender roles, family relationships, and having attachments to both home and host societies. Both chapters illustrate somewhat successful stories of the study participants who are able to make transnational connections and aid in economic growth in both worlds. However, in chapter 9, the authors pose an important question of whether this ability to build transnational firms between the host and home countries is only capable through the 1.5 generation group, who are culturally and linguistically competent in both societies, and whether such transnational linkages can be continued by the second- and third-generation Koreans overseas.

REFERENCES

Anderson, C. S., Balica, E., Balmain, C., Iadevito, P., Kida, P., Mazaná, V., ... & Yoon, S. (2014). *The Global Impact of South Korean Popular Culture: Hallyu Unbound.* Lexington Books.

Ang, I. (2001). *On Not Speaking Chinese: Living Between Asia and the West.* New York: Routledge.

Arnett, J. J. (2000). Emerging adulthood: A theory of development from the late teens through the twenties. *American Psychologist, 55*(5), 469–480. doi:10.1037/0003-066X.55.5.469

Årseth, A. K., Kroger, J., Martinussen, M., & Marcia, J. E. (2009). Meta-analytic studies of identity status and the relational issues of attachment and intimacy. *Identity: An International Journal of Theory and Research, 9*(1), 1–32. doi:10.1080/15283480802579532

Bartley, A., & Spoonley, P. (2008). Intergenerational transnationalism: 1.5 generation Asian migrants in New Zealand. *International Migration, 46*(4), 63–84.

Bhang, C. H. (2019). Resilience and 1.5 generation Korean American young/emerging adults in the U.S. (Order No. 13813002). Available from ProQuest Dissertations & Theses Global. (2321833427).

Blunt, A. (2005). *Domicile and Diaspora: Anglo-Indian Women and the Spatial Politics of Home.* Oxford: Blackwell Publishing.

Choi, Y., Tan, K. P., Yasui, M., & Hahm, H. C. (2016). Advancing understanding of acculturation for adolescents of Asian immigrants: Person-oriented analysis of acculturation strategy among Korean American youth. *Journal of Youth and Adolescence, 45*(7), 1380–1395. doi:10.1007/s10964-016-0496-0

Chung, K., & Choe, H. (2008). South Korean national pride: Determinants, changes, and suggestions. *Asian Perspective, 32*(1), 99.

Collins, F. L. (2010). International students as urban agents: International education and urban transformation in Auckland, New Zealand. *Geoforum, 41*(6), 940–950.

Collins, F. L. (2016). Labour and life in the global Asian city: The discrepant mobilities of migrant workers and English teachers in Seoul. *Journal of Ethnic and Migration Studies, 42*(14), 2309–2327.

Conway, D., & Potter, R. (2009). *Return Migration of the Next Generations: 21st Century Transnational Mobility.* Routledge.

Danico, M. (2004). *The 1.5 Generation: Becoming Korean American in Hawaii.* Los Angeles, CA: University of Hawaii Press.

Erikson, E. (1997). *The Life Cycle Completed.* New York: Norton.

Friesen, W. (2008). *Diverse Auckland: The Face of New Zealand in the 21st Century?* Auckland: Asia NZ Foundation.

Glick-Schiller, N., Basch, L., & Szanton-Blanc, C. (1992). Transnationalism: A new analytic framework for understanding migration. In N. Glick-Schiller, L. Basch & C. Blanc (eds.), *Towards a Transnational Perspective on Migration: Race, class, ethnicity, and Nationalism Reconsidered* (pp. 1–24). New York: New York Academy of Sciences.

Hall, S. (1996). Who needs 'identity'? In S. Hall & P. du Gay (eds.), *Questions of Cultural Identity* (pp. 1–17). London: Sage Publications.

Hwang, W.-C., & Ting, J. Y. (2008). Disaggregating the effects of acculturation and acculturative stress on the mental health of Asian Americans. *Cultural Diversity and Ethnic Minority Psychology, 14*(2), 147–154. doi:10.1037/1099-9809.14.2.147

Jang, G., & Paik, W. K. (2012). Korean Wave as tool for Korea's new cultural diplomacy. *Advances in Applied Sociology, 2*(03), 196.

Jones, R. (2011). The local economic imprint of return migrants in Bolivia. *Population, Space and Place, 17*(5), 435–453.

Jung, A. W., Stang, K., Ferko, D., & Han, S. (2011). A commentary on cultural influences impacting the education of Korean American adolescents. *American Secondary Education, 40*(1), 31–38. Retrieved from http://search.proquest.com.ezp-prod1.hul.harvard.edu/do cview/921231924?accountid=11311

Kim, A. (1996). *Women Struggling for a New Life: On the Role of Religion in the Cultural Passage from Korea to America.* Albany, NY: State University of New York Press.

Kim, B. S., Brenner, B. R., Liang, C. T., & Asay, P. A. (2003). A qualitative study of adaptation experiences of 1.5 generation Asian Americans. *Cultural Diversity and Ethnic Minority Psychology, 9*(2), 156.

Kim, D. (2006). Stepping-stone to intergenerational mobility? The springboard, safety net, or mobility trap functions of Korean immigrant entrepreneurship for the second generation. *International Migration Review, 40*(4), 927–962.

Kim, H., & Agee, M. (2019). 'Where are you from?' Identity as a key to parenting by 1.5 generation Korean-New Zealand migrants and implications for counselling. *British Journal of Guidance and Counselling, 47*(1), 35–49.

Kim, I. (ed). (2004). *Korean Americans: Past, Present, and Future.* Elizabeth, NJ: Hollym International Corp.

Kim, J., & Bang, H. (2017). Education fever: Korean parents' aspirations for their children's schooling and future career. *Pedagogy, Culture and Society, 25*(2), 207–224.

Kim, J., Suh, W., & Heo, J. (2014). Do Korean immigrant adolescents experience stress-related growth during stressful intergroup contact and acculturation? *Journal of Humanistic Psychology, 54*(1), 3–27. doi:10.1177/0022167812468614

Kivisto, P. (2001) Theorising transnational immigration: A critical review of current efforts. *Ethnic and Racial Studies, 24*(4), 549–577.

Kroger, J. (2007). *Identity Development: Adolescence through Adulthood.* Thousand Oaks, CA: Sage.

Kwak, K., & Berry, J. W. (2001). Generational differences in acculturation among Asian families in Canada: A comparison of Vietnamese, Korean, and East-Indian groups. *International Journal of Psychology, 36*(3), 152–162.

Lee, J. J. (2012). Ethnic identities: The role of institutions in the assimilation process. *International Journal of Interdisciplinary Social Sciences, 6*(11), 19–34. doi:10.18848/1833-1882/CGP/v06i11/52188

Lee, J. Y. (2016). Korean Americans: Entrepreneurship and religion. In I. Miyares, & C. Airriess, (eds.), *Contemporary Ethnic Geographies in America* (2nd edition, pp. 285–302). Rowman & Littlefield.

Lee, J. Y. (2018). *Transnational Return Migration of 1.5 Generation Korean New Zealanders: A Quest for Home.* Lanham, MD: Lexington Books.

Lee, J. Y. (2019a). The peripheral experiences and positionalities of Korean New Zealander returnees: Skilled return migrants and knowledge transfer. *Asian Survey, 59*(4), 653–672.

Lee, J. Y. (2019b). Living as a non-Christian in a Christian community: Experiences of religious marginalisation amongst young Korean Americans. *Journal of Ethnic and Migration Studies, 45*(11), 2062–2077. doi:10.1080/1369183X.2018.1427565

Lee, J. Y., Friesen, W., & Kearns, R. (2015). Return migration of 1.5 generation Korean New Zealanders: Short-term and long-term motives. *New Zealand Geographer, 71*(1), 34–44.

McDowell, L. (1999). *Gender, Identity and Place.* Minneapolis, MN: University of Minnesota Press.

Min, P. (2013). A comparison of Korean protestant, Catholic, and Buddhist religious institutions in New York. In Min, P. (ed.), *Koreans in North America: Their Experiences in the Twenty-First Century* (pp. 75–102). Lanham, MD: Lexington Books.

Min, P. G. (1990). Problems of Korean immigrant entrepreneurs. *International Migration Review, 24*(3), 436–455.

Ministry of Foreign Affairs, Republic of Korea, (n.d.). 다수거주국가: 재외동포정의및현황외교부. Retrieved from http://www.mofa.go.kr/www/wpge/m_21509/contents.do

Nugroho, S., Cho, Y., & Collins, F. L. (2018). Aspirations, ambivalence, and performances: The hyphenated identities of Indonesian worker-students in South Korea. *Discourse: Studies in the Cultural Politics of Education, 39*(5), 723–737.

Oh, S., & Min, P. (2011). Generation and earnings patterns among Chinese, Filipino, and Korean Americans in New York. *International Migration Review, 45*(4), 852–871.

Park, E. J. W. (1996). Asians matter: Asian Americans and the high technology industry in Silicon Valley. In B. O. Hing (ed.), *The State of Asian America: Immigration Policies* (pp. 155–177). Los Angeles, CA: LEAP Publications.

Park, J. (2004). Korean American youth and transnational flows of popular culture across the Pacific. *Amerasia Journal, 30*(1), 147–169.

Park, K. (1999). "I really do feel I'm 1.5": The construction of self and community by young Korean Americans. *Amerasia Journal, 25*(1), 139–163.

Sarup, M. (1996). *Identity, Culture and the Postmodern World.* Edinburgh: Edinburgh University Press.

Shin, G. W. & Choi, J. N. (2015). *Global Talent: Skilled Labor as Social Capital in Korea.* Stanford, CA: Stanford University Press.

Shin, J. (2016). Hyphenated identities of Korean heritage language learners: Marginalization, colonial discourses and internalized whiteness. *Journal of Language, Identity and Education, 15*(1), 32–43.

Son, J. (2013). Assimilation and health service utilization of Korean immigrant women. *Qualitative Health Research, 23*(11), 1528–1540. doi:10.1177/1049732313507142

Thomas, M., & Choi, J. (2006). Acculturative stress and social support among Korean and Indian immigrant adolescents in the United States. *Journal of Sociology and Social Welfare, 33*(2), 123–143.

Tsuda, T. (2010). Ethnic return migration and the nation-state: Encouraging the diaspora to return 'home.' *Nations and Nationalism, 16*(4), 616–636.

Tuan, Y. (1977). *Space and Place: The Perspective of Experience.* London: University of Minnesota Press.

Vannucci, A., Flannery, K. M., & Ohannessian, C. M. (2017). Social media use and anxiety in emerging adults. *Journal of Affective Disorders, 207*, 163–166. doi:10.1016/j.jad.2016.08.040

Wang, B., & Collins, F. L. (2016). Becoming cosmopolitan? Hybridity and intercultural encounters amongst 1.5 generation Chinese migrants in New Zealand. *Ethnic and Racial Studies, 39*(15), 2777–2795.

Wang, D. (2015). Activating cross-border brokerage: Interorganizational knowledge transfer through skilled return migration. *Administrative Science Quarterly, 60*(1), 133–176. doi:10.1177/0001839214551943

World Bank (2018). Gross domestic product 2018. Retrieved from https://databank.worldbank.org/data/download/GDP.pdf

Yeh, C. J. (2003). Age, acculturation, cultural adjustment, and mental health symptoms of Chinese, Korean, and Japanese immigrant youths. *Cultural Diversity and Ethnic Minority Psychology, 9*(1), 34–48. doi:10.1037/1099-9809.9.1.34

Yook, E. L., Yum, Y. O., & Kim, S. J. (2014). The effects of Hallyu (Korean wave) on Korean transnationals in the US. *Asian Communication Research, 11*(1–2), 5–21.

Yoon, K. (2018). Multicultural digital media practices of 1.5 generation Korean immigrants in Canada. *Asian and Pacific Migration Journal* (Sage Publications Inc.), *27*(2), 148–165. doi:10.1177/0117196818766906

I
COMMUNITY, IDENTITY, AND BELONGING

2

Making Sense of Migrant Life

Ethnicity among 1.5 Generation Koreans in Argentina

Irene Yung Park

INTRODUCTION

Many among the post-1962 Korean overseas populations are presently undergoing a generational shift, with its significance of historical sedimentation and identity change.[1] The Korean community in Argentina is no exception, and its 1.5 generation probably plays an important role in that transition. In effect, the age range and degree of acculturation of this cohort signals it as the main agent for the establishment and circulation of narratives about migrant experience, local insertion, group identity and relation to the host society, both within the ethnic boundaries and in the wider society.

The Korean communities of Latin America are smaller than their counterparts in the North, but they are significant as cases of successful economic insertion and accelerated upward mobility. Available data suggests that these groups have a high educational and economic level relative to comparable communities of overseas Koreans (Bae, 2014; Min, 2012), as well as a high degree of subjective identification with the homeland (Joo, 2010; Min, 2012). These characteristics make of them a valuable ethnic capital for both the sending and receiving societies (DeWind et al., 2012), but phenomena like remigration, return migration and delayed incorporation in the mainstream society pose questions about their stability and future standing (Kim, 2016).

This chapter aims at offering a prospect on these communities by examining how 1.5 generation Koreans of Buenos Aires make sense of their life in Argentina. Drawing on the tools of cultural sociology (Lamont, 2000; Lamont, Beljean and Clair, 2014) and counting on the personal experience of the researcher—herself a 1.5er from Argentina now back in her native country—it aims at identifying the narratives this generation Koreans in their midlife make use of to explain their lives as immigrants in a country that was not originally their own, they did not choose to come to, and that many of their coethnics left in search of a better destination.

The cultural approach intends to go beyond the external, objective, and macro approaches to host society incorporation and ethnicity reproduction that dominated previous research on overseas Koreans (Yoon et al., 2011). Instead, and as begged for by the ongoing generational shift, it sheds light on internal processes of identity construction and meaning-making unique to each community—especially to their locally grown generations—and the way these are shaping the group's future.

The main focus will be on the occupational trajectory of the subjects under study. The importance of the economic activity of immigrant communities for their mode of incorporation to the host society and identification is a well-established fact (Portes and Rumbaut, 2014). In the case of Koreans in Argentina, their strong concentration in the garment industry and weak presence in professional fields has already attracted scholarly attention (Kim, 2017; Mera, 2010) as a contrast to the trend in North America, where locally educated ethnic Koreans tend to abandon the small businesses many of their first-generation parents operated in order to enter the mainstream labor market as white-collar professionals (Yoon and Lim, 2008).

Up until now, explanations were provided in terms of economic motivations. Both in the United States and in Argentina, the first generation would have turned to self-employment or employment in coethnic businesses as the best alternative to overcome competitive disadvantage in the labor market and status inconsistency. But while in the United States this tendency was reverted in the following generation, the low pay in professional positions in Argentina would have held back their peers in this country, pushing them to remigrate or to stay in the ethnic garment business, where economic prospects are superior (Kim, 2017; Kim and Koo, 2017).

In this chapter I want to complement this type of explanation with the cultural perspective that places economic decisions within a more integral account of migrant life and identity. I will do this by connecting professional trajectories with processes of ethnic identification and notions of success or good life. Some questions are: Which perceptions, meanings, and justifications have provoked the occupational decisions of the 1.5 generation Koreans of Argentina or explain them? Whose agency they understand to have caused them? What constrictions did they perceive and where do they think they originated? How do 1.5 Koreans construct ethnic identity in relation to these choices? What retrospective evaluation do these choices deserve and how does it relate to notions of achievement, success, or good life?

Literature Review

Research on overseas Koreans is still in its beginning phase. In their homeland, these communities started to attract academic interest only as late as in the 1990s, when the country decidedly embraced a policy of globalization. Publications are thus limited in volume and diversity of approaches and regionally imbalanced in disfavor of Latin America due to the geographic distance and language and culture barriers

(Yoon et al., 2011). Existing studies on Argentina are mostly of historical descriptive character (Chae-a Han-in-hoe, 2016; Park, 2006; Suh, 2005) and, when cultural analysis is present, culture is seen as a function of the political more than as a proper dimension endowed with explanatory power (Han, 2016). More attention is paid to the subjective aspects of migrant identity construction by local scholars (Bialogorski, 2004; Mera, 1988, 2010), but their work is limited by the Korean community's reticence to be exposed to outsiders' eyes and by cultural and social distance.

The relatively advanced state of research on Korean-Americans makes of them a natural reference point, as comparable cases. But this body of research is also dominated by macro approaches to the socioeconomic status of these communities or by interest in the preservation of ethnicity (Kim, 2005; Min, 2006; Shinn, 1996; Yoon, 1996; Yoon and Lim, 2008). A few studies look into the subjective processes of identity construction at work among younger generations (Danico, 2004; Kibria, 2002; Paik, 1999). The caveat is that the perspectives commonly engaged in these studies strongly reflect the specificity of the American case, making them less suitable for analyzing the small-sized, geographically concentrated, not replenished Korean community in Argentina, with its unique context of reception. This confirms, once again, the need to engage in focused studies that highlight not the commonalities, but the particular traits in the process of identity construction of the different Korean communities.

Defining the 1.5 Generation in Argentina

The definition of migrant generations is not free of theoretical and operational complexities. To begin with, there is no scholarly consensus on the meaning and measurement of immigrant generations. The insufficiency of the most commonly used categories—first, second and 1.5 generations—to account for important differences in immigrant incorporation has been empirically proved (Rumbaut, 2004). Specifically, the notion of 1.5 immigrant generation based exclusively upon demographic data—place of birth (foreign born) and age of migration (18 or younger, 12 or younger, or 11–16, depending on the author)—cannot accurately capture the important sociological differences among migrant youth arrived at different life stages and equally important commonalities between foreign born children arrived at an early age and locally born children from just arrived parents. This presents us with the need to operationalize the generational cohorts in ways that make them significant to the specific migration experience that we are considering.

The Korean migration to Argentina started officially in 1965 and was characterized by the following traits: First, it was a family migration with strong endogamic propensities. Second, it took place in two distinct migratory waves, after which replenishment was virtually interrupted. The early wave corresponds to the steady inflow of immigrants in the 1970s, while the second wave refers to the boom experienced in the second half of the 1980s with the signing of an agreement by which Argentina opened its doors to investment immigration from Korea. The treaty was followed by an influx of families, usually with school age or younger children, during the years in which a migration peak was reached (1985–1988). Numbers started to drop after 1988, probably due to the improved political and economic conditions of the sending country, which was by then completing democratization and opening to the world.

The timing and demography of the Korean migration to Argentina brought up two results: First, a conflation between migrant generation and age range. Even if exact data is not available, it can be assumed that most children who followed their immigrant parents should now be in between their mid-30s and early 50s, constituting the bulk of the active population of the community and being parents to the second generation Koreans that are presently being schooled. Second, a sociological homogenization between immigrants of similar age that came in different waves and therefore at different life stages, facilitated by the small size of the community and the culture of age grouping. Concretely, the children of the early wave migrants, regardless of birthplace, were fused with the children of the second wave migrants that were of similar age by common socialization and marriage, with the consequent mutual cultural influence effect.

What the above implies is that, in Argentina, most Koreans in their mid-life, albeit personal differences depending on time of migration or place of birth, share in a generational consciousness that sets them apart from their first generation parents and from the younger native-born generation. For that reason, in this chapter we will operationalize the notion of 1.5 generation to indicate this specific group, that is, those Koreans presently in mid-life who have spent at least part of their teenage years in Argentina (13–18), regardless of place of birth. Apart from the fact that this approach seems to mirror better the actual social configuration of our case, it has the advantage of situating the settlement process in the larger social context, allowing to understand it as determined not only by the internal characteristics of the migrant cohort but also by the context of reception at every historical stage. Besides, the common socialization of this age group seems to condition the professional path of its members, regardless of differences in arrival time and language proficiency.

Methodology

The study is based on twenty-nine in-depth interviews with 1.5 generation Koreans, realized in the early months of 2019 during fieldwork in Buenos Aires. Interviewees were first recruited through personal contacts, expanded through snowball sampling and selected by diversity of migrant and professional trajectories and gender. For this chapter I opted to use a case study method because the level of empirical detail, completeness, and analytical depth it allows seemed best fit to capture the connections between micro level processes of individual meaning-making and the contingent and variable contexts in which they take place over time, as well as their relation to the multiple social spheres in which the agent is situated. Five cases were selected that were representative of the diverse trajectories and strategies of meaning-making encountered in the sample.

Results are also broadly based on long-term observational data secured during annual monthly stays in Buenos Aires for the last ten years, interviews with locals and Koreans of other generations, informal interactions, social media and documentary evidence. Table 2.1 serves as a basic presentation of the study cases. For privacy protection, aliases were used.

As the table shows, age similarity means migrants from the first wave moved to Argentina at primary school or pre-school age, while migrants from the second wave, in their teens. All participants married coethnics and have children of 6–26 years old. Interviews were mostly in Spanish, occasionally switching to Korean or to a mix of the two languages. Translations are mine.

PROFESSIONAL TRAJECTORIES

The Pull toward Productivity: Teresa and Yoonmi

A peculiarity of the 1.5 migrant experience is that it is strongly determined by parental decisions. For that reason, before focusing on the professional choices of the 1.5ers, we will deal with the heritage of the first generation as reflected in this cohort's narratives about childhood or teenage experiences.

Teresa arrived to Argentina via Bolivia with her grandmother. As in the case of many others, her house was also a sweat shop: "We all had factories. You came from school, put down your bag and had to sit to sew." Her childhood was socially quite secluded. "I used to go to church, to my house, to work and nothing else." She also keeps the memory of being bullied for looking different.

A generalized experience of the 1.5ers is that the limited capacity of adults to move within the local system led them to become their parents' bridge to the host society. An early development of self-sufficiency connected to the assumption of adult roles at a young age is thus recurrent. This is easily noticeable in matters related to schooling, even where parents were clearly concerned with their children's education. Teresa states: "I think that in those times adults were so busy trying to get ahead financially that, honestly, did not pay much attention to us. I looked for my own school."

Table 2.1   Presentation of Study Cases

Alias	Gender	Migratory Wave	Migration Age + Migrant Life = Present Age (in Years)	Occupation[a]
Liz	F	1	1 + 44 = 45	P
Sebastian	M	1	5 + 42 = 47	P
Teresa	F	1	8 + 41 = 49	C→P
Yoonmi	F	2	13 + 32 = 45	C
Hyunbin	M	2	16 + 29 = 45	P→C

[a]C = Clothing entrepreneur/P = Other profession.

Adult roles were generally assumed with naturalness by those who arrived at a young age. However, those who moved in their early teens experienced their new responsibilities as an abrupt coming of age. Yoonmi was thirteen when she landed in Argentina: "My experience was that of going from one extreme to the other. In Korea there was no need to work. And here they needed me, as interpreter. . . for everything."

Like many in her situation, Yoonmi had to face the challenges caused by transplantation at a delicate age on her own. She managed to adapt in academics but her socialization with locals was strongly curtailed: "In studies, all well. But I could not deepen the relationship with my friends because there was no *post-*. After school, I could not go hang around with them. . . . I had to come back home and work."

In the two cases just presented, there is a common pattern of school-home-church-reduced socialization that shows the impact on the children of the pressing importance making a living had for the first generation. Actually, the pull toward productivity set unsurmountable challenges for Teresa and Yoonmi to pursue a career path.

> I tried to study in the University but the economic situation of my grandmother did not allow me to only study. . . . I had to work from 9 to 6 pm. Sleep and at 5 am wake up, go to school . . . many times I fell asleep and missed the stop . . . and besides you arrived and understood nothing . . . I think the majority of the people around me, for example, Rosa she had started to study Pharmacy, but also, life did not give her that chance.

For Teresa, the shared migration experience of the 1.5ers meant curtailed occupational paths, where pursuing a college degree became a rare achievement or privilege. Not attending college, and against the backdrop of a secluded childhood, she had no social or cultural capital to count on in order to settle her life, with the exception of the ethnic one.

> It was either study and if you could not study, it [the clothing industry] was a means of survival . . . . I married very young with 21 and they [her Korean in-laws] set a sewing factory for us and I started. A little later was the shop and then we lost everything, then again the shop, as if there was no election. I don't know, I wouldn't have chosen that, maybe, but there was no other way. . . . For many people of my generation at least, that is what was there . . . the most accessible thing you had at that moment and yes, the easiest thing, you could say.

For Yoonmi, leaving Korea meant also leaving behind a professional project drawn in correspondence to social meanings that were in force there, but not in Argentina: "I wanted to be a teacher. But here a teacher receives a terrible treatment so it was not an option. . . . Besides, a Korean being a teacher, that was a no no." What was an option for her back in her native country is perceived as inaccessible now, simply due to her ethnicity. This shows how external conditions act on individuals by setting cultural, imaginary limits to possible courses of action. Again, migrant experience acquires the meaning of a shrinking of life horizons, by narrowing the range of available life projects.

> In reality I did not want to be a Pharmacist, but a Psychologist or Educational Psychologist. . . . But when I hinted that at home, "no, if you are going to be a psychologist, leave it, just don't study." So I got to the point of asking what to do so that they would allow me to study. "Pharmacy." OK, Pharmacy . . . It still did not last, because my dad was sick. . . . Then my dad died. I continued[studying] for a short while but they decided "you cannot go on, because we cannot afford it."

After a process of negotiation where Yoonmi adjusted her projects to the conditions imposed by her parents, her family situation ended up truncating her studies. Interestingly, as she recalled these events she seemed to frame the tension between the desire to study and the need to work in a new way, explicitly interpreting it as a tension between family and self: "Actually, I was just thinking, what was my brother doing? Then they needed me and I quit but what did they do? . . . They did not support me much so I had to quit." Yoonmi took charge of the family's clothing business, managing to improve its productivity and, with it, the family situation as a whole. Her responsiveness to family plans continued well after marriage, now in relation to her in-laws. In fact, she is now working in the shop her parents-in-law gave her husband and her. How she arrived there is more the result of a combination of family needs and conveniences than her own choice.

Other stories reveal that family dynamics defining the occupational path of the 1.5ers is not limited to the clothing industry. Apart from a sense of duty and obligation moving the children to stay associated with their parents in their business, we could find an explanation in the narrow world of visions and routines allowed to them throughout their childhood, which connects to the change in roles forced upon the family group by migration.

The Liberal Profession Path: Sebastian and Liz

The findings just exposed lead us to wonder: Did those who trod the professional path do so as a result of having had another type of childhood? Did they understand their own path as one of privilege, with more options, over those who went into the garment sector?

Sebastian's family was among the first to arrive in Argentina with investment capital. But in a story that is far too common, his parents were deceived by fellow Koreans and lost a big part of what they had. Their re-starting from the ground, typical of migrant narratives, acquired a somehow magnified meaning due to these events. As a consequence, Sebastian gained an early awareness of the parents' vulnerability and a sense of responsibility and protection towards them.

As the eldest boy, Sebastian was exempted from house chores or from helping in the family's clothing shop. These were his sisters' tasks. But for him, school was a way to compensate the parents' hardships by bringing them pride and satisfaction through good academic performance. His mother had a high expectation with regards to grades and he tried not to disappoint her. It was not a difficult thing because he was a high-achieving student, appreciated both by his classmates and teachers.

Sebastian's family lived in a middle-class neighborhood of Buenos Aires with virtually no Koreans, so the three siblings were the only Asians in school. There, and also later, he made long-lasting friendships, but his closest and most durable friends were those he met in the Korean church, where he used to go with his family.

After finishing high school, Sebastian opted to go to medical school and become a doctor. Reflecting on whether his immigrant condition played a part in this decision, he says:

> It does influence your decisions. . . . I have looked for something I like as much as possible—not something that I find repugnant—but that I can use as a professional path. I had to live of that. . . . Because I would have loved to do something with history, for example. But what would I have done? If you come from a relatively well-off middle-class maybe you have a different back-up. The difference is that I felt I had no margin of error, that I could not make a mistake. It is not that you can try with a career and then change and . . . no, no. That is a luxury for others. That luxury you, as an immigrant, do not have. And in that sense yes, you felt the pressure.

If Teresa and Yoonmi saw studying as a privilege they were deprived of, Sebastian thinks migrant reality imposed heavy conditions on him, too. The drive to reach an equality of conditions with middle-class locals, working the way up through personal capacity and effort, is implicit in the choice of a professional path. But perceived conditions of initial disadvantage, the awareness of having no assets, no support and no back-up are translated into scarcity of options. This understanding corresponds well with a pattern of high self-demand and intolerance to risk and error in early professional exercise that transpires from collected data on other 1.5ers. Sebastian understood his medical career as his only life option, no less than those who saw the clothing sector as their only choice. The sense of possibility offered by pursuing a professional path was continuously accompanied by the pressure not to fail, in order to satisfy the pressing need to become productive and conquer stability.

In a similar vein, for those who could opt for studies, going to college was not necessarily felt as a privilege or as being empowered over their peers who could not do so. It could paradoxically mean lagging behind and feeling excluded. When Liz started attending University in the early 1990s, most of her friends from the Korean community did, too. But a few years later, the majority had dropped and were working in the clothing shops of their families, while she kept going ahead, all alone.

> . . . there was a moment in which I said: I'll throw all of this overboard! What the heck am I doing? Am I not stupid? Because I was the only one of all the group. . . . they went to Puerto Madero, some with amazing 0 km cars and I went by bus, walking in the subway . . . . In the end, I had my diploma in hand and there was already a big gap. I was around 27 then, so everyone had settled down, their parents almost did not come [to the shop]and those my age were handling the business, as managers in charge. Money?

They used a lot of cash, and me, a recent graduate, had a salary that was—say—half that of a shop seller's! . . . It was always "Am I not stupid?"

While Liz still socialized with coethnics, the evident differences in lifestyle became a source of uncertainty about her own choice. She was shaping her professional life—a career as an architect—according to a system with different times and parameters from theirs, so she was often confused about which to adopt as normative. Pursuing a degree had always been her undiscussed default option due to her parents' ideas and practices.

My parents always told me you have to study, because they are learned people them-selves. There were many moments in which they had the chance to enter Avellaneda [the ethnic economic enclave in Buenos Aires]. . . . My dad was "we cannot sacrifice our children. If we enter Avellaneda the children will need to work" and mom was "they can do this while doing that, let's just give it a go." There was always the same discussion but in the end we went through that time without going to Avellaneda. . . . once I cried like a fool before my mom and my dad. I made them sit in front of me and cried: "Why did we not go to Avellaneda then, like idiots! Look at us now, how many opportunities we have missed!". . . Then my mom, with a broken heart, told me: "I have heard of children turning against their parents for not having educated them, but to do this to me for having made you study . . ."

The parents play a key role in the children's occupational decisions not only by instilling ideas or strategies of action, but also indirectly, by allowing a child-hood and youth experience outside the frame of the ethnic enclave. Today Liz is a successful Architect and business woman, fully engaged with her profession and with no regrets about the decision that lead her through a lonely path in the early years of her career. But other 1.5 Koreans did regret and returned to the ethnic economic enclave, moved by the same prospects that had made Liz hesitate about her choice.

Employment in the Corporate World and the Detour: Hyunbin

Among the subjects chosen for this study, Hyunbin moved to Argentina the oldest, just a few years before reaching College age. Upon arrival he worked at the sewing machines like many others, but with his father's support, he stopped in order to focus exclusively in studies.

My dad was like this: "I don't care if you don't come to work, I'll be in charge, you just study." That is one case. One friend, ok, there is work in his house, but at least the mom wanted him to go to University, at least in the evenings. . . . There is another one: In her case, she did not care at all: "If you study or not it does not matter. There have to be 100 shirts ready every night." So he had to iron. . . . It all depends on the parents. Everyone thinks that Koreans give lots of incentives to the children—see—to study. But those who came here, they were not all like that. 50% yes, but for another 50%, it was all about work. It was about earning a living.

The children's path as limited by their parents' priorities reemerges as a narrative here. Why this interpretation is not commonly heard of outside or even inside the Korean community requires an explanation. Interview data suggests that this idea is often muffled by insufficient psychological detachment from the parents due to social seclusion during childhood, or softened by a sense of responsibility over the parents of the type described earlier. What the first statement means is that social imaginaries of a life on one's own outside of the family boundaries were available to 1.5 Koreans selectively, depending on childhood experience. This way, decisions taken by the parents that had long-term effects on the lives of the children were assumed and internalized without great difficulty. By contrast, the 1.5ers habit of shielding parental vulnerability led most of them to conceive of life trajectories on the backdrop of parental needs and expectations. Having taken part in the breadwinning activity of the parents also allowed appraisal of the hard life they were leading, contributing to the narrative of parental sacrifice. A meaningful finding is that, after the protracted coming of age signified by migration, coming of age or leaving home narratives are almost absent.

But parents are not an isolated factor. Of his group of friends, Hyunbin belonged to the few who proceeded to University in order to pursue a degree.

> The majority did not study anything; they did not want. . . . It was hard for them. . . . A person who is already quite formed, say, in language, that then has to start again from scratch. . . . Me when I arrived I did not even speak the language. To enter university and understand all the photocopies they give you is difficult. Everyone tried, each in their own way, but what happened is that more than 85% failed.

The narrowing of options that frames the 1.5ers coming of age reappears here. As with Yoonmi, it is related to the difficulty to break ground into a new system, this time due to language limitations. Falling in between two worlds because of the migration timing is a common experience among those 1.5ers who moved at an older age.

Hyunbin's own career choice was the pursuit of a dream he had had since he was 16 or 17: That of being a system analyst and working at a multinational firm. He managed to fulfill it, working for important companies for several years. Today, however, he owns a clothing business in the ethnic economic enclave.

> I did the career of analyst, graduated, then did a postgrad, worked a lot with SR, the French Bank, the bank of values, the market of values in the implementation of intranet, internet and all that. But after 30 plus, it is as if I needed more, more economic power. To reach a certain degree of income in the Argentinian society, it is very limited. Instead, I was looking into the economic activities of Koreans and they had no limits. It depends, and depending on what you do, you can make much more. So it was because of a necessity.

Hyunbin explains his move to the ethnic economy in terms of economic incentives and the limitations of the Argentinian system in that respect. His was a "renouncing status and accomplishment for material rewards" story. But when asked whether he is satisfied with the decision made, he becomes hesitant and reveals more complex factors at play.

> There was an issue, one decisive thing of my manager. He asked me "how do you want to continue your career? . . . what do you want to do later, because me, I am planning to go to the board of directors." "Me too, at the end of all this I want to be at least a system manager, a security manager too." He said, "well, wait 11 years for me. Either I go to the directing board or I retire." When he said that I thought "no, I think I don't have 11 years to wait."

Here Hyunbin adds a new meaning to the merely economic one he gave before. His opinion on structural discrimination in Argentina provides some more insight about what that meaning can be.

> There is a lot. You feel it more in the Argentinian society, in the work in my profession. . . . When I left, another one came to substitute me. I think he lasted 2 months and a half. He was fired because he did not do his job well. Then they brought a bigger fish and put him as system vice-manager but also him. . . . They could have given me that position but they didn't, you see? If he would have told me, before I left "now you are going to be this, is that ok?" Never. . . . That is also quite an important discrimination, see?

For Hyunbin, the move to the ethnic economy had the added meaning of leaving a system where rules are set by others and ethnicity might mean disadvantage, to a system where things depend on personal effort and ethnicity is a resource. This tension between a career out and self-employment in the ethnic economy is a powerful symbol of the migrant condition: While career might bring social status and personal satisfaction, it is in others' hands to give. After trying his professional options, Hyunbin let go and turned not only to a different activity and working goal, but to a whole cultural system with different life horizons, meanings and codes.

> That time, yes, it was all very nice, very good. What happens is that my dream was working in a company with cravat and suit. But now I never use cravat and suit, I don't like it, I am always with sport clothing. I already got used, this is my life, see.

Dressing style becomes a powerful metaphor of system fit. Switching to the ethnic economy, Hyunbin returned to a less fanciful but more comfortable zone.

MAKING SENSE OF MIGRANT LIFE: ETHNIC IDENTITIES IN THE BALANCE

Part of the legacy of the first generation was their perception of Argentina as a provisory destination to be left when possibility or opportunity presented itself. Koreans have left Argentina in different moments of economic crisis, but the one event that hit the adult 1.5 generation in the face was the 2001 "Corralito." Big numbers exited then, but there was imbalance across different occupations. Most of the re-migrants were actually professionals because for them the possibilities abroad were far superior to those offered to professionals in Argentina. Actually, among our study cases, only those who had careers have either attempted or considered remigration more seriously: Hyunbin tried, but failed. Sebastian and Liz discarded the option thinking of their parents' needs. Staying was not the only choice for any of them. In fact, most 1.5ers still keep the possibility of migrating as a card to play in case of need, even if with age they tend to transfer that decision to the children.

However, among the 1.5ers there is also a widespread sense of achievement and satisfaction about the lifestyle and status reached in Argentina. The dismissal of Korea or the United States as better places to live, together with statements about the ultimate equivalence of all places is quite common. Below, we will present the ways in which life in Argentina is made sense of in each of our five cases.

Delayed Reconciliation: Teresa

As mentioned before, Teresa never chose to work in clothing. She did it because it was the only alternative she had, but she dislikes the informality of the sector and the stigma it brings with it. For that reason, she made sure her daughters led their lives far away from this activity and from the ethnic enclave as such.

She reconciled with her occupation as her business started to give revenues that allowed her financial stability and the enjoyment of a good lifestyle: "I said "it's ok, this is what gives me to send my girls to a good school, it gives me a comfortable life, it gives me to travel, so that's it." Then I started to like it more."

Teresa gave her daughters the best education available in Buenos Aires. She now lives in a big flat in a wealthy neighborhood, leading a middle- to upper-class lifestyle. Above all, economic security permitted her to venture into the food sector, which is her real passion. Apart from her clothing business, Teresa now owns two eateries. She recently got a title in gastronomy and has just kicked off an initiative to spread the appreciation of Korean cuisine among Argentinians of her social circle, many of whom she met through her newly found passion for marathon running. Interestingly, many of her Argentinian friends are from the Jewish community. She feels identified with them for having a strong identity kept by blood while being fully Argentinian, and for having earned themselves a position through hard work. Starting from very low, Teresa also succeeded in finding her place in the local society.

Argentina is Teresa's real home. She has no attachment to her native country nor any interest in what is going on in there. However, her two intimate, family-like friends are both 1.5 Koreans. Her community of long-term belonging is the Korean church she frequents. Relationships there might not be intense, but "these are the persons who will accompany me until the end," she says. Besides, she is now a proud promoter of Korean cuisine. "I am Argentinian and I am Korean . . . . I feel comfortable in that place," she says.

Teresa's Korean identity is undeniable, but it lives in Argentina with her. She found her place proudly owning her ethnic heritage as a full member of the Argentinian society. In this sense, she represents a case of successful reconciliation between her national origin—which changed from being a source of stigma to being a source of pride—and her acquired Argentinianness. Koreanness is retained not as national identity, but as ethnicity.

Two Forms of Duality: Hyunbin and Yoonmi

Reconciliation, however, is not always easy. Hyunbin represents a case of attempted and given-up reconciliation between his Korean self and his Argentinian identity. His return to the ethnic sector was not smooth and he had to overcome setbacks and failures. He is now financially more stable, but admits to not having had much success in his enterprises. However, if in his 30s and early 40s life's focus was work, now, at his late 40s, his priorities have changed. Friendship and family relations have taken a new centrality. He distinguishes three stages in his social life in Argentina.

> First they[his friends] were from the youth group in the Korean church, when we were 17, 18, 19. Then I started university and I did not have time for my Korean friends. . . . My life was writing papers with my classmates. . . . Then the work colleagues, I spent a lot of time with them, end of year parties, many friendships, but I can say that it is a bit superficial. It is not deep, let's say. But there was no problem with them, I was comfortable. . . . This is the second stage of my life with my friends. After my 30's I return again to the same kids I met in church, since they are all around here.

Hyunbin and his family live next to his workplace in the ethnic enclave around Avellaneda street, in a decent but simple flat, in a building where many other Korean families live. Since most of his Korean friends also work in the area, they easily improvise last-minute gatherings, frequently also in weekdays. Their shared interests do not extend much beyond family, children and privatistic issues such as lifestyle or health, but Hyunbin feels deeply united to these friends: "It is much deeper than what I shared with Argentinians. That for sure. Because you understand much more."

Hyunbin appreciates the time he spends with family and friends, and points at this as one aspect of Argentinian lifestyle that he appreciates over the United States or Korea, where everyone is busy and families spend little time together. Another aspect he considers superior is the flexibility and eventfulness in economic activity when compared to the other two countries, where "they live like ants."

Interestingly, he considers the life of Argentinians to be very limited in that sense too: "Argentinians, poor people, they are always just there. Well, there are families of great wealth, they exist. But the majority is very, very limited. Instead, I think our kids have more possibilities to see things, the world." The life in Argentina he appreciates is not the one Argentinians lead, but the one Koreans have created for themselves, comparatively characterized by a wider horizon and a broad range of possibilities. These characteristics are connected to economic success and a transnational outlook, which Hyunbin tries to secure by keeping things indoors Korean: "I try to make in the house a life like that of Korea. . . . Inside where we live, is Argentina, but it is a bit limited. When you enter the house, is different. . ."

So what is Argentina for Hyunbin? What is the exact meaning this country has for him today? As he says, "as years pass by, I'm becoming more Korean. . . . That time[when he worked in IT] was like a nice memory, but I cannot share it with my Korean friends of now. . . . You have to think it is like another world. Like you don't see the wall, but it exists." Argentina is simply the macro context where Hyunbin now leads his life as a Korean. Micro level, intimate experiences of Argentina are in the past, now virtually absent from his daily existence. After having driven quite deeply into the local system, Hyunbin desisted of his attempt to succeed there and withdrew to his ethnic community of belonging. He avoided "falling in the middle" by decisively embracing his Korean identity. Now he makes sense of migrant life within the ethnic community, around the compensations brought along by family life, quality friendships and a relaxed lifestyle.

Yoonmi lives in a mid-upper class neighborhood, where many Korean families who reached a certain financial level moved into. Her life takes place within a narrow area of Buenos Aires which limits are marked by house, shop in the ethnic enclave and the Korean church she frequents. In this sense, her places of socialization have not changed much since she arrived to Argentina as a child. Now that she enjoys economic stability she pursues more leisure activities, but even these do not take her far away from that area, since she plays tennis with other Koreans or frequents cafes and eateries popular in the community.

As we explained before, Yoonmi gave up on very defined professional aspirations to overtake her family's clothing business. Now that she has conquered a certain stability, what is her balance of life in Argentina?

> What I could have done it's over. I am a bit lost in that sense. I don't know if I'm satisfied. I'm not satisfied, because for all the things you renounced to be where you are, it is as if what you get does not have much value. . . . But there is still time, I still have some more life left. . . . What I hope is to be someone who can support, who can give a support when my children want to do something. Not like my parents that when I wanted to do something could not . . . my goal is to be a rock . . . Like the support for someone.

The support Yoonmi is talking about has to do with financial capacity. But there is another aspect to it, related to how she perceives her position in Argentina. Yoonmi's reference group is the Korean community in Buenos Aires and, more specifically, those of her age who arrived to the country around the time she did. Beyond that group of belonging, she feels foreign to both Korea and Argentina. She finds Korean issues (politics, entertainment, TV) to be much more interesting than Argentinian ones, so she shares virtually no interests with locals. Her interactions with them are limited to transactional or formal ones. But she does not interpret this distance in terms of Korean superiority, as others do. Instead, she feels a strong sense of exclusion. In her opinion, for Argentinians, all Asians are "foreigners, visitors, tourists."

> I think they accept you, but up to a certain point. It's a bit like "you reached this far and no further. There." . . . wherever you go, "this is as far as you have come." But I think it must be much more noticeable in professional fields... That does not mean I will tell my kids "it's going to be very difficult. You won't make it," no. They will do what they

want and then they will see. If they try and cannot make it, well, I will be here. That is why I want to be someone that can become a support.

Like Hyunbin, Yoonmi lives inside the Korean ethnic system. However, she has a different idea of where she stands with respect to the Argentinian system. The local world is present as an aspirational horizon because she wanted to be part of it, so Yoonmi processes the duality between the two systems in a more painful way. Maybe that is why she made a lifetime goal that of supporting her children so they manage to settle in such an uncertain situation.

Growing Out of the Ethnic Community into the Host Society: Liz

Short after graduating, and in the midst of the financial crisis that hit Argentina in 2001, Liz set up her own architect studio with funds she had saved during working holidays in the United States. She has been working in her profession ever since, first serving the Korean community and later on expanding to other fields. Her latest project is to design an ecological, sustainable, and cheap housing prototype, that can provide with a roof to the less privileged in Salta, the province to which she partially moved a few years ago. She is also actively engaged with social and political issues in Argentina through activism and volunteering.

Liz interprets her past life as a continuing process of growth and expansion. She seems to perceive a contrast between that dynamism in her life and the immobility of those Korean friends who dropped out of university to work in the clothing sector and that "are still working in shops." But work is not the most important part of Liz's life. A dedicated mother, she has very clear childrearing principles and enjoys investing time and effort on the children. This is one of the points in which she differentiates herself from Koreans in the ethnic economy: "Let's say ok, you made money. But how much time did you dedicate to your children? How much time did you dedicate to your family? . . . They think that just spending money the children will do good studies and they will become princesses but it is not like that."

While those in the clothing sector emphasize the importance of productivity—reproducing the first generation life goals—even for the education of the kids, Liz believes that, more than expensive schools, it is good parenting and life experiences that make children happy and well rounded. A key aspect is to teach them how to socialize in diverse contexts: "I want them to keep those friendships [Korean]. But their friends from Salta also came here . . . and I love that: that they keep their essence but that they learn these codes of socialization that you don't learn in youtube or google . . . . I simply want them to interact, to learn the social codes of each culture."

What does this say about Liz's own ethnic identity and sense of belonging? Liz feels proud of Korean culture and works hard to transmit it to her children. However, she does not identify as Korean or Argentinian but as a "mutant," jokingly referring to her feeling of hybridity. She keeps her Korean roots strong but aims at blending into the local society. The interest in preparing the kids for adult life led Liz in this latter direction.

In Salta, I am much more involved because it is a middle upper class school[that her kids attend]and there are many parents who are active professionals, whereas here in ICA [the Korean kindergarten in Buenos Aires] I was with the same Korean shop owners . . . So now, having been in Salta, I say lucky me, because ICA is a dot . . . So I am super integrated, my children are super integrated, I feel super comfortable.

Growing into a Cosmopolitan Horizon: Sebastian

Talking of his career as a doctor, Sebastian recalls his initial naiveté about the assets that he counted on to earn himself a position in his professional field: "I thought that hard and transparent work would always pay back. But in this country at least, that is not enough or it altogether does not count. Moving to the province was favorable in that sense."

Early in his medical career, Sebastian suffered an episode of discrimination due to his foreigner status and his lack of connections. He brought his case to court and won, but, soon after, he moved with his family to a far-away province to work in a private hospital that needed someone of his specialization. In a highly centralized country like Argentina, that move can easily be read as giving-up on professional ambition and prestige, though frequently for better working conditions and less competition. For Sebastian, it was a way to ease the constraints imposed on an upward mobility based purely on hard work and ethical behavior.

In his present city, everyone knows and respects him. Apart from professional recognition, he gets to enjoy a relaxed and humane social life. He is also very active in social media, continuously connecting with old and new contacts, lots of them Koreans from Argentina or Argentinians residing abroad. Many of them he met online, in a discussion group of alumni of the prestigious elite school of Buenos Aires he attended.

Sebastian travels frequently to Buenos Aires and always avails of the occasion to meet both his old-times friends and his more recent social media friends. He also meets up with his contacts whenever he travels abroad, which he does quite frequently. He and his family also travel to Korea every three or four years to visit his in-laws and other relatives.

Through these exchanges and avid media literacy, Sebastian keeps updated about political, social and economic issues all around the globe, even if his focus of attention and personal involvement are Argentina and Korea. He is surprisingly knowledgeable and opinionated about issues in his native country, but he is also very positive about the virtues of his adoptive country and enjoys the life he leads, despite the sadness and frustration he frequently experiences about the local situation. He particularly appreciates quality family and social life which, based on the experience of friends living abroad, he thinks are difficult to get elsewhere. He connects this appreciation for human relations to the mental horizon acquired thanks to his migrant experience.

I think that human networks are a capital. . . . ultimately they enrich your life. . . . To travel to any country for the first time and to have the chance of visiting people as if they were relatives, even if you never met them personally before, that is capital. . . . Maybe you can have those attitudes because of the life story you had. Otherwise, it might not be that easy.

Considering the multiple worlds Sebastian seems to inhabit, we might wonder how does that affect his ethnic identity and sense of belonging.

I am proud of Argentina, I am proud of Korea, as of today I don't like to categorize myself as something, I don't feel it that way, I think I have no need to take sides between one thing and the other. . . . I consider myself a citizen of the world and I think that has to be the tendency. But of course, what you were breastfed culturally, your roots, are there . . . but I don't feel it as a weight, to the contrary, I feel it as a pride . . . that is what I am. But also for the same reasons I just mentioned, I understand those who, having a similar background, left to the US, got the citizenship shortly after and are proud of having obtained that. I think that, in that sense, those of us who have always been abroad share a similar vision. We realize that geographical limits are malleable, flexible, depending on each persons' experience, and we go about fitting in perfectly in the place where we are without having to renounce identity in order to adopt new aspects.

Sebastian seems to build his ethnic identity not upon spatial, and therefore exclusive qualifiers, but upon chronological, and therefore cumulative experiences. That is why, firmly grounded in his ethnic roots, he conceives the world he belongs to as spatially one. This is the broad cosmopolitan outlook that he aspires to transmit to his children, so that their mental horizon is not restricted to the one country they happen to live in, but extends potentially to the whole world. His migrant past acquires the meaning of a mental *departure* from a fixed, narrow place for a journey of continuously expanded horizons, which is how he seems to understand his life.

DISCUSSION AND CONCLUSION

The purpose of this chapter was to throw light on how 1.5 Koreans in Argentina make sense of migrant life, by examining their occupational choices and how these relate to identity construction and notions of good life.

Childhood migrant experience affects the interpretation of reality of the 1.5ers by creating a *habitus* of responsibility and attachment that, when connected to limited socialization, results in difficulty to adopt horizons of meaning alternative to those available within the family. In this sense, the most significant finding in this part is the crucial role parents' *habitus* play in the determination of the children's professional future and, by contrast, the non-availability of narratives that acknowledge its downsides among those that saw their options actually curtailed by parental choice. This finding converges with Portes and Rumbaut (2014)'s results, which show the weight of parental education and occupation in the educational attainment of the foreign-born in the United States. Economic reasons apart, the entry into the garment industry could be understood in this context as difficulty to detach from family and community bonds and go one's way.

The option of going into the professional field would respond to a mentality that takes, not the Korean community, but the local society as a reference group, with the corresponding prospect of social integration and status change. In Argentina, the tacit character of racialization makes racial discrimination invisible, creating the expectation that hard work and competence will pay back against the odds of having no assets to rely on (Alberto and Elena, 2016; Jelin and Grimson, 2006;Ko, 2014). However, externally imposed limits do appear. When that happens, the tendency is to adjust—maybe precisely due to the political silencing of racialization, which neutralizes any attempt to systematically combat it—moving systems into a fairer one, as strategies of remigration, self-employment or voluntary downgrading prove. An interesting finding is that the ethnic community can act here as a source of alternative paths, comparison and social pressure, providing with scripts of action unavailable among locals but that often imply a reversion into the narrower world and visions of the ethnic group. It can be hypothesized that, when the individual is less subject to this influence, the chances of exploring the possibilities offered by the local system are higher.

The different "worlds" or frames of reference each individual manages become more explicit in relation to their professional trajectories. We have identified a cosmopolitan frame (Sebastian), an Argentinian frame (Liz and Teresa), a diasporic frame (Hyunbin) and an ethnic community frame (Yoonmi). Within each of these mental universes, life is given sense with different breadths. While those who chose the professional path (Sebastian and Liz) or embraced their professional interests later (Teresa) clearly include a professional or social dimension—albeit of varying reach—to their sense of self-realization, those who stayed in the ethnic economy (Yoonmi) or reverted to it (Hyunbin) seem more enclosed in a privatistic world of family and friends that recreates an uprooted Korean world. Yoonmi's universe has a similar reach to that of Hyunbin but, in her case, the aspiration and failure to belong to the wider society account for a suffered sort of in-betweenness, bolder in acknowledging the dissatisfaction it brings with it. In Argentina, the incipiency of multicultural discourses when compared to North America makes the emergence of hybrid identities more challenging. The Korean identification shared by all our study subjects acts in the first as the root for an expanded biographical identity, be it cosmopolitan or Argentinian. The tension between competing identifications has been overcome by going beyond binary distinctions. In the latter, time reinforces the exclusive character of ethnic identification and social networks. The tension is resolved by renouncing it, embracing the Korean identity over the Argentinian one and returning thus to a comfort zone of contention.

In conclusion, this research has revealed the centrality of cultural frames of reference or *mental worlds* in shaping the occupational paths of 1.5 Koreans in Argentina, thus complementing external and merely economic interpretations of the choices of this generation. It has also shown how these mental worlds are shaped during formative years, by an interplay of factors such as parental attitude, social interactions, age of arrival and personal capacity to adjust, and how they continue to evolve in dependence of the occupational itinerary—where each individual's agency is implied—and the social relations that accompany it. Finally, the cases examined have illustrated how every individual makes sense of migrant life within the limits set by that frame. What this implies is that the measure in which ethnic and local references form part of the *world* of the Koreans in Argentina might have a significant impact on the future of this community.

NOTE

1. This work was supported by the Ministry of Education of the Republic of Korea and the National Research Foundation of Korea (NRF-2019S1A5B5A07086744).

REFERENCES

Alberto, P., & Eduardo, E. (2016). *Rethinking Race in Modern Argentina*. Cambridge: Cambridge University Press.

Bae, J. S. (2014). New York Koreans from Latin America: Education, family and class mobility. *Journal of British and American Studies, 30*, 395–416.

Bialogorski, M. (2004). La Presencia Coreana en la Argentina: La Construcción Simbólica de una Experiencia Immigratoria. PhD Dissertation. University of Buenos Aires. Filosofía y Letras.

Chae-a han-in-hoe (2016). A-lŭ-hen-t'i-nahan-in i-min 50nyŏn-sa (50 years of Korean migration in Argentina). Seoul: Tae-yang-mun-hwa-in-swae-sa. (Civil Association of Koreans in Argentina.)

Danico, M. Y. (2004). *The 1.5 Generation: Becoming Korean in Hawai'i*. Honolulu: University of Hawai'i Press.

DeWind, J., Kim, E. M., Skeldon, R., & Yoon, I. (2012). Korean development and migration. *Journal of Ethnic and Migration Studies, 38*(3), 371–388. doi: 10.1080/1369183X.2012.658543

Hurh, W. M. (1998). *The Korean Americans*. Westport: Greenwood Press.

Jelin, E. & Alejandro, G. (2006). *Migraciones regionales hacia la Argentina. Diferencia, desigualdad y derechos*. Buenos Aires: Prometeo.

Joo, J. T. (2010). Culture and ethnicity in the Korean transnational community in Brazil. *Iberoamerica, 12*(2), 323–356.

Kibria, N. (2002). *Becoming Asian-American. Second-Generation Chinese and Korean American Identities*. Baltimore and London: The John Hopkins University Press.

Kim, J. (2017). Ethnicity and opportunity: Korean entrepreneurship in the Argentine garment industry. PhD Dissertation. University of Auckland. Asian Studies.

Kim, J., & Koo, S. (2017). From father to son: 1.5 and second-generation Korean Argentines and ethnic entrepreneurship in the Argentine garment industry. *The Review of Korean Studies, 20*(2), 175–201.

Kim, Y. (2016). A study on re-emigration and settlement of Argentine Korean 1.5 generations." *Journal of Koreanology, 60*, 83–111 (in Korean).

Ko, C. T. (2014). From whiteness to diversity: Crossing the racial threshold in bicentennial Argentina. *Ethnic and Racial Studies, 37*(14), 2529–2546.

Lamont, M. (2000). Meaning-making in cultural sociology: broadening our agenda. *Contemporary Sociology, 29*(4), 602–607.

Lamont, M., Beljean, S., & Clair, M. (2014). What is missing? Cultural processes and causal pathways to inequality. *Socio-Economic Review*, 1–36.

Mera, C. (1998). *La inmigración coreana en buenos aires: multiculturalismo en el espacio urbano.* Buenos Aires: Eudeba.

Mera, C. (2010). The 1.5 generation of the Korean diaspora in South America: Rethinking transnational interactions. *Comparative Korean Studies, 18*(3), 7–39.

Min, P. G. (2006). *Asian-Americans: Contemporary Trends and Issues.* Thousand Oaks: Pine Forge Press.

Min, P. G. (2012). Twice migrant Koreans in the United States: Their origins, socioeconomic characteristics, and ethnic attachment. *Journal of Diaspora Studies, 6*(1), 155–178.

Paik, Y. (1999). Imagining Asian American identities: An anthropological study of race and ethnicity through growing-up, coming of age, dating, and marriage among Chinese and Korean Americans. PhD Dissertation. Yale University. Cultural Anthropology.

Park, C. (2006). Han-min-chok ne-t'ŭ-wŏ-k'ŭ-wachae a-lŭ-hen-t'i-na tong-p'o" (The Overseas Koreans' Network and the Koreans of Argentina). *Studies of Koreans Abroad, 16*, 145–192.

Portes, A., & Rumbaut, R. (2014). *Immigrant America: A Portrait.* Berkeley and Los Angeles: University of California Press. EBSCohost eBook Collection.

Rumbaut, R. G. (2004). Ages, life stages, and generational cohorts: Decomposing the immigrant first and second generations in the United States. *The International Migration Review, 38*(3), 1160–1205.

Shinn, J. (1996). An ethnographic study on the ethnic identity of Korean American adolescents. *The Journal of Educational Research, 34*(5), 429–444.

Suh, S. (2005). La-t'in-a-me-li-k'a-wahan-kuk-in i-min: a-lŭ-hen-t'i-nahan-in-sa-hoe-wahyŏn -chi-chŏk-ŭng (Latin America and Korean migration: The Korean community of Argentina and its adjustment). *Korean Journal of Latinamerican Studies, 18*(3), 155–186.

Yoon, I. (1996). Chae-mi han-in-ŭi min-chokchŏng-ch'e-sŏng-kwaae-ch'ak-ŭi se-tae-kanch'a-i" (Generational differences in ethnic identity and attachment among Korean-Americans). *Studies of Koreans Abroad, 6*, 66–95.

Yoon, I., & Chang K. L. (2008). Chae-mi-han-in ch'a-se-tae-ŭi in-ku-hak-chŏkt'ŭk-sŏng-k wasa-hoe-kyŏng-che-chŏk chi-wisŏng-ch'wi: se-tae-pyŏlmich' min-chok-chip-tan-pyŏl pi-kyo" (Demographic characteristics and socioeconomic status attainment of the future generation of Korean Americans: Inter-generation and inter-group comparisons). *The Korean Journal of Area Studies, 26*, 409–438.

Yoon, I., Choi, W., Seong, D., Sim, H., & Lim Y. (2011). *Chae-oe-han-in-yŏn-ku-ŭi tong-hyang-kwakwa-che* (Trends and future tasks of studies of Koreans abroad). Seoul: Book Korea.

Zhou, M. (2009). How neighborhoods matter for immigrant children: The formation of educational resources in Chinatown, Koreatown, and Pico Union, Los Angeles. *Journal of Ethnic and Migration Studies, 35*, 1153–1179.

3

Experiences of Religious Marginalization and Identity Development among Non-Christian Korean Americans

Jane Yeonjae Lee

INTRODUCTION

Christianity is a critical element in the study of Korean Americans. It is estimated that over 70 percent of all Korean Americans are affiliated with Korean Christian churches (Hurh and Kim, 1990).[1] There are over 3,000 ethnic Korean Christian churches in the United States, and 54 Korean Protestant churches in the Massachusetts area alone (Kupel, 2010). Much of the existing literature illustrates that these churches provide essential resources and networks for both newly arrived and long-term, first- and second-generation Korean immigrants (Min, 2013; Kim, 1996), and they serve as important social mechanisms, consolidating Korean Americans' sense of identity and belonging (Chong, 1998). While these statistics illustrate that Korean Americans are highly religious, the statistics may "tend to perpetuate the myth and stereotype that all Korean Americans are Christian" (Suh, 2004:3). Indeed, 40 percent of Christian Korean Americans surveyed converted to Christianity upon immigration to the United States (Hurh and Kim, 1990). Studies of those who do not belong to ethnic religious communities or who are non-Christian, who comprise the "religiously marginalized" have been largely ignored within the study of religion in certain ethnic communities, including Korean Americans.

The tendency to focus on religious institutions is understandable, given evidence of the link between these institutions and a sense of belonging, community, and identity. Most of the studies on ethnic communities and religion to date illustrate the importance of churches in providing networks of ethnic minority groups, especially for the first-generation immigrants who live in a marginalized status with their limited social and language abilities (Chai, 2001; Kwon, 2004; Min, 2013). For example, a study about Portuguese immigrants in Canada explains that Portuguese churches in Toronto are open day and night to help immigrants find employment, file paperwork, and get married (Brettell, 2003). The church is more than a religious institution; it is what the study's author calls "a rallying point for the formation of ethnic interests" (Brettell, 2003:121). A study about Korean Canadian churches also illustrates that ethnic churches provide counseling services for immigrants who are stressed about changing family roles and searching for jobs while settling in their new homeland (Ley, 2008). A study about first-generation Korean women immigrants in the United States also shows that churches play a significant role as they struggle to adjust to their new society (Kim, 1996). These social/religious activities within the church enable a sense of belonging and create stronger bonds within the immigrant community (De Leeuw, 2007).

The study of religion and ethnic minorities also suggests a strong relationship between ethnic churches and immigrant identity formation, especially among the children of the first-generation immigrants. In an ethnographic account of the second-generation Korean American Christians in Chicago, Chong (1998) argues that "when an ethnic group is faced with a strong sense of social marginalization believed to arise from its racial status, the ethnic church can play a dominant role in the group's quest for identity and sense of belonging" (259). This view is shared by numerous other scholars who illustrate that Christian churches provide a sense of community, and, therefore, a higher social status within the host community, and a stronger sense of belonging through ethnic identity (Min, 1992, 2013; Kwon et al., 2001; Ecklund, 2005; Suh, 2004). For second-generation Korean Americans, the role of the Korean church may be stronger because it is the only access to Korean culture for the group (Lee, 2007). Another study about the 1.5 generation Korean immigrants in New Zealand illustrates that Korean ethnic churches provide numerous cultural and social events and group activities throughout the year, which provides an important social gathering during their adolescent years to maintain their Korean identity and heritage (Lee, 2015). Min (2013) argues that Korean Protestant churches play an important role in providing language and cultural teaching for Korean cultural retention, comparably more than what Korean Catholic churches or Buddhist temples provide.

The strong and much-studied link between religion and belonging raises questions about identity formation among those ethnic minorities who do not belong to ethnic religious communities. What happens to immigrants and ethnic minorities if they do not belong to certain religious groups? Do they end up converting to the ethnically dominant religion (Hurh and Kim, 1990; Yang, 1998)? Or do they find other mechanisms to deal with integration and their ethnic minority identities?

This study responds to the need to investigate the lives of secular migrants where religious marginalization may play a significant role in their everyday lives. Through a qualitative approach, this exploratory study examines the experiences of secular and religiously marginalized Korean Americans in relation to their predominantly

Christian communities. In particular, the study focuses on the unique experiences of those aged between 25 and 35 living in the greater Boston area. The study participants are well-educated and fall into either 1.5 or second-generation immigrant categories—groups that have been well neglected in the previous literature on Korean American religious communities. The study compiles vivid narratives of non-Christian Korean American experiences within a dominant Christian ethnic community, focusing on their religious and non-religious performances. This chapter attempts to emphasize the different types of experiences and diversities among the churchgoers and non-churchgoers within Korean American communities, as there might be some drawbacks of going to a church (Min, 1992), and there are different types of churchgoers (Park, 1997).

KOREAN AMERICANS IN THE UNITED STATES AND MASSACHUSETTS

In 2010, Koreans were the fifth-largest Asian American ethnic group after Chinese, Asian Indians, Filipinos, and Vietnamese. Much like other Asian groups, Korean immigrants are one of the many ethnic groups who entered the United States in large numbers after the 1965 Immigration Act. However, Korean immigrants did not make a smooth transition into U.S. mainstream society because of cultural and language barriers, and they experienced various conflicts in order to culturally and economically adjust to their new life in the United States. The first-generation Korean immigrants relied heavily on self-employment and operated small businesses such as convenience stores, hair salons, restaurants, and dry cleaners (Min and Kim, 2013). The 1.5 and second-generation Korean Americans have adjusted better, and many have entered the private and public sectors of the mainstream economy. Perhaps more than other Asian immigrants, for Korean Americans, religion is an important component in sustaining the sense of belonging. Importantly, Christianity exists as a strong anchor of Korean American identity.

According to the 1970 U.S. Census, there were 70,598 Koreans in the United States. By 1980, that number had increased to 357,393, with Korean Americans accounting for 10.3 percent of all Asian Americans. The 1990 census counted 798,849 Korean Americans, and the 2000 census counted 1,072,682, or 10.7 percent of Asian Americans. The most recent data of the 2010 census indicates that there are 1,423,784 Korean Americans in the United States. Korean American is the fifth-largest Asian American group and accounts for 0.6 percent of the entire U.S. population.

Korean Americans are spatially distributed across the country in an uneven manner—they are concentrated in certain cities and counties and sparse in other places. According to the 2010 U.S. Census, 43.7 percent of Korean Americans reside on the West Coast, 32.3 percent in the South, 9.7 percent in the Northeast, and 9.1 percent in the Midwest. At the state level, there are 451,892 Korean Americans in California, 140,994 in New York, and 93,679 in New Jersey, which accounts for 48 percent of Korean Americans in the United States. The states with the lowest Korean population are Wyoming (508) and North Dakota (609).

There are 28,904 Koreans living in Massachusetts. This population includes numerous students living in Boston and Cambridge and residents concentrated in Brookline, Newton, and Lexington. The existing Korean communities in the state are relatively small and are dominated by religious groups. There are an estimated fifty-four Protestant Korean churches in Massachusetts alone, three Catholic churches, and three Buddhist temples. Korean churches provide a strong network and sense of belonging for Koreans living in the Boston area (Kupel, 2010; Chai, 2001).

THE RESEARCH

Between December 2013 and March 2014, I conducted interviews with nineteen Korean Americans living in the Korean community who are either non-religious or have a non-Christian religious affiliation. Two individuals who identify as Catholic were also included in the study, since they experienced a sense of marginalization from the dominant Protestant mainstream as well. The aim of the interviews was to understand the complexities of individuals' experiences. As Bennett (2002:151) affirms, the key to interviewing is more or less to "expose differences, contradictions and, in short, the complexity of unique experiences." Along with such a methodological aim, I also took a life history approach (Wallace, 1994) in order to collect information from childhood to the present day in order to gain a holistic understanding.

More specifically, this study examines the life histories of 1.5 generation Korean Americans who are not churchgoers. There is not a universal definition of who is considered to be a member of the 1.5 generation. The term is mostly used to differentiate those who immigrated as children of their first-generation parents, but who were still born overseas. The 1.5 generation's migration and settlement experiences are different from their parents as well as from second- and third-generation immigrants who are born in the destination country. It is also argued that the 1.5 generation's adaptation strategies are distinct from those of earlier migrants (Bartley and Spoonley, 2008).

This research focused on a group of younger adults aged 25 to 35, as this demographic is likely to have graduated from tertiary education and be looking for employment and perhaps a future spouse. Therefore, in this stage of entering adulthood, this group is more likely to be seeking out social networks and forming stronger (or less strong) ethnic identities (Erikson, 1997). The recruitment of interview participants was done through a snowball sampling method. There were eight male and thirteen female participants. Out of twenty-one participants, thirteen were born in the United States, and eight were born in Korea and are considered to be 1.5 generation immigrants. All of the study participants spent their early childhood to teenage years in the United States and have lived in Boston for more than eight years in the recent past. Seventeen participants identified themselves as being either atheist or agnostic; two are Catholic, and two are Buddhists. Occupations included graduate student, lawyer, medical practitioner, accountant, and educator. All of them were highly educated and had completed their tertiary education in Boston. Fictional names have been used for all study participants in this chapter in order to keep the study participants' identities anonymous.

REASONS FOR NOT GOING TO A KOREAN CHURCH

The study participants are non-churchgoers generally because were brought up in a non-Christian family and/or simply because they do not hold Christian beliefs. However, in many cases, their beliefs evolved over the years, and they often experienced complex emotions about attending church. Some of the study participants used to attend a Korean church, have agnostic views, or have Christian faith to a certain degree. Yet, they all shared some form of negative experiences with their local Korean churches (either their own experiences or gleaned from witnessing others), which created certain barriers to joining the community. Indeed, growing up in a Korean community in America, they had many opportunities and aspirations to join a Korean church in order to be part of a Korean community and to find a sense of belonging. For many of the study participants, a Korean church was the only access they had to a Korean community within their neighborhoods or, indeed, the entire city:

> In my childhood, we went to a Korean church for many years. I think it was important, more for my parents than me and my brothers, to go to a Korean church—having cultural and language affinity. I didn't have friends, really, but I think it was one of the few spaces where I saw lots of Koreans in one space, since our suburb and school was mostly white. (Laura Lim, F, 29)

For Laura, who grew up in a rural area where there was a small Korean population, attending a Korean church was the only way to access a Korean community. As she affirms, it was considered more important from her parents' perspective because they wanted to teach their children the Korean language and culture, and church was the most accessible way of attaining both. Laura further stated that she did not enjoy going to the church because she had many personal conflicts with the preaching, and it was hard for her to make friends with other Korean kids. However, it was her parents who made the decision to stop going to the church:

> When I was maybe in middle or high school, we stopped, and started going to an American church closer to home; the Korean church was about an hour away in Baltimore—we lived in the suburbs. I think my dad had a bad experience with politics and leadership drama at the church. I was too young to totally understand.

Although Laura still does not fully understand what kind of "leadership drama" her father experienced in their local Korean church, she knew it was not a pleasant experience for her and her parents. Laura stopped going to church after attending college as she formed a stronger sense of her own religious beliefs and knew that Christianity was not suitable for her.

Similar to Laura, many of the study participants had childhood or teenage experiences of going to a Korean church. Stephen Paek (M, 35) also grew up in a small town in the Midwest. His family used to drive two hours each Sunday to attend a Korean church. The first time Stephen went to a Korean church, at the age of ten, he saw Korean people for the first time other than his family. He used to enjoy going to the church, as he made Korean friends and was able to enjoy good Korean food and cultural activities. Church was something he looked forward to every Sunday, until he had the following experience:

> Yeah, it was all good and fun in the beginning. I was very drawn into the Korean community, and back then, I think I was almost 100% Christian. I totally believed in the Bible and enjoyed listening to the priest. Then, there was the scandal. It was so huge that the church was eventually closed. Well, basically, the priest had a number of affairs with the Korean ladies who attended the church and had some money issues. Back then, I was so shocked when I first heard the news and did not want to go back to the church ever again. After all that teaching, the priest was a total joke!

The incident put Stephen off the Korean community, and he never returned to a Korean church. Although he had opportunities to join other churches throughout his life, he decided that he did not have to attend a church and follow the rituals in order to have faith in God.

Other study participants were reluctant to attend Korean churches for other social and personal reasons. Many thought Korean churches were "too tight," and they were put off by the closeness, gossiping, and being closed in a "Korean bubble:"

> I did belong to the Korean church that my parents attended. I did not agree with what the church preached as I got older and was able to make my own decisions about my religious beliefs. After I started college, I was very turned off by Korean churches and did not want to join any. I felt that a lot of people who attended Korean churches only went to socialize and gossip about other Korean people. There was so much jealousy and competition between people. I did not want to be part of the community. (Stella Kim, F, 28)

> I did have many friends at school who went to Korean church, so I used to follow them. It was a lot of peer pressure for me. Now, I don't go to church at all because I have a stronger sense of what I want. Over the past experiences, I think I did gain some kind of prejudice against Korean churches. They seem like a huge industry to me; you don't really get a sense of community, you know. There are so many Korean churches, and people attend the church just to meet other people, to make connections. . . . I keep hearing from my friends who go to church that this or that church is not their 'type', so they switch their church to go to the ones where they can find people that they like. I find it all very arbitrary. It's more of a social group than anything religious. I don't really like that. I don't like being in that circle of people and living in a Korean bubble. (Michelle Lim, F, 30)

Despite all the positive elements of having a close ethnic church within a host society, such as social support and retention of original identity (Min, 1992), the "closeness" of these ethnic communities may also have important downsides. By being too close to one another, one's social network can become limited and may create the feeling of being in a "Korean bubble." Both Stella and Michelle emphasized that the gossip, dislike, jealousy, and competition within the Korean community were some of the main features they did not like about Korean ethnic churches. Michelle further noted that she wanted to make friends from all ethnic backgrounds, blend into the wider society, and not limit herself to a solely Korean community. Although one can be part of a Korean American community and, at the same time, be part of the wider society, Michelle especially felt that she was limiting herself from enjoying other opportunities if she went to a Korean church.

The contrasting costs and benefits of having a closed ethnic community was also a theme in other study participants' narratives. Anne Kwon (F, 30), a second-generation Korean American, was encouraged by her parents to attend a Korean church when she was in high school:

> My mom sent me to a Korean church when I was at school to learn the Korean language and make Korean friends. First, I didn't really fit in at the church because the Korean girls didn't like me. After a few months, I started making some church friends and started hanging out with them more. We went to Korea-town and went to No-rae-bang2and hung out all the time. And then my mum didn't like that because she thought I was hanging out with the 'bad kids' as I didn't study much, but spent too much time with my Korean friends. So she ended up stopping me from going to the church.

Anne's story illustrates typical Korean parental behavior that prioritizes children's educational discipline over interaction with their peers. This particular account echoes the notion that there can be pros and cons of attending an ethnic church. Anne's mother felt that while the church provided her daughter with access to her own culture, she did not want her daughter to fall into "bad" behaviors. Anne still does not go to church because she was never a Christian, and she did not enjoy her teenage experience of being in and out of the Korean church community.

So far, I have illustrated various reasons why the study participants have kept their distance from ethnic Korean Protestant communities. Their narratives illustrate that they hold some hostility toward the Korean church, either coming from their personal experience or through the influence of those around them. For others, it was a simple matter of not wanting to attend because they do not believe in Christianity. No matter what their reasons for not being member of a Korean church, their desire to belong to a wider Korean community and the experiences and emotions behind their decisions are still important. In the next section, I move to the narratives of the study participants' relationships (or lack of relationship) with the Korean community and how they experienced such "distance" between themselves and the wider Korean community.

DOMINANCE OF KOREAN
PROTESTANT COMMUNITIES

Sometimes when I meet a new Korean person, I worry about what they are going to think of me. (Michelle Lim, F, 31)

As mentioned in the introduction, over 70 percent of Korean Americans are affiliated with Korean Christian churches (Hurh and Kim, 1990). Aside from the Christian group, 6 percent are Buddhists, and 23 percent are unaffiliated (Pew Research Center, 2012). Such disparity between the number of Christian churches and other religious groups is common in other regions where there is a significant Korean American population. In this section, I examine whether secular and non-Christian Korean Americans identify themselves as being part of a wider Korean community despite their non-affiliation with dominant Protestant churches. In doing so, I attempt to understand their sense of belonging and experiences of being religiously (and socially) marginalized.

The narratives indicated that the study participants recalled their teenage and college lives as being somewhat difficult due to their religious minority status. Most expressed a feeling of "not fitting in" and not being able to blend in with their peers due to their non-affiliation with the mainstream Korean American community. The teenage period is considered to be the most formative and sensitive phase of one's life course in terms of identity construction (Kroger, 2007), which was reflected in the narratives of the study participants' memories of their school life. The participants were never explicitly left out, but they felt isolated because they could not take part in the "fun" church activities their peers enjoyed:

> There were times when I went to school, I really wanted to be part of the Korean church, mainly because of the fun camps that they go to. My friends would go to a ski camp and summer camps with their church people, and they looked really fun. That's where my friends made new friends or made girlfriends. For me, I always had to search for my own. . . (Raymond Kim, M, 29)

> On many weekends when all my (Korean) friends went to a camp or a church picnic or something, I used to just sit alone in my room, wishing that I could join. I didn't want to go along with them just for the sake of it. I didn't want to go and pray and all that, but I did feel a little anxious and felt left out that I didn't get to hang out with all my friends. (James Lee, M, 30)

Both Raymond and James recalled their teenage years and stated that they felt isolated at times when their friends went to church gatherings. They did not want to go to church because they were not Christian, but still felt they were "missing out" on many things such as making new friends, forming romantic relationships, going to camps and picnics, and being connected to the Korean American community. It is important to note that most of the Korean American study participants hold strong ethnic ties and identities and are discouraged from interethnic marriage. Hence, finding a potential Korean spouse is important, and this was often seen as an advantage of going to a Korean church. As Raymond's and James' narratives illustrate, the non-churchgoers had to find Korean social connections through different means.

For some participants, being disconnected from the Korean church community and holding onto their non-Christian identity made their teenage and early college years somewhat more difficult. Anne Kwon (F, 28) became non-religious when she entered college. She decided that Christianity was no longer her belief and stopped attending her local Korean church. While this was not an easy decision for her, its difficulty was compounded by the changed way that her friends behaved around her:

> When I stopped attending the Korean church in my first year in college, that's when my friendship with my girl group ended. We just stopped hanging out for no reason. It just ended. They gradually stopped inviting me to hang out, and I didn't want to ask them to invite me. (Anne Kwon, F, 28)

Anne further explained that she was initially very happy with her group of Korean friends at college. They all went to the same church every Sunday and spent all their time together during the first few months of college. However, as soon as Anne stopped attending their local church, she was isolated from her Korean peers. Anne has since started making non-Korean friends. Feeling isolated does not necessarily come from being explicitly bullied and excluded. Many of the participants stated that they felt like outsiders on some occasions due to their "religiously marginalized" position. Often, a subtle feeling of inferiority was inflicted by the people they were close to, as exemplified through Anne's story. As a result, the feeling of exclusion was more severe and distracting.

The sense of being inferior can be a product of the mainstream's ignorance of one's culture and/or subtle gestures that constantly remind the minorities that they are "different." Helen Park (F, 29) shares a similar, yet different story from Anne's. Helen is a Buddhist Korean American, and there were many occasions during her teenage and college years when she had to defend or hide her non-Christian identity:

> I started becoming more and more insecure with being a Buddhist as I entered my teenage years. Some Korean kids at school would kind of tease me that I would go to hell if I don't go to church. They would say it in a kind of joking manner, but it was not that funny for me. So I learned to hide my religious identity as I grew older. At college, I never really talked about my religion with my friends; I would just tell them that I don't really practice any religion. Even on Facebook, I don't post anything that's to do with my Buddhist temple because I am scared about what they are going to think of me. You just always have to be quiet.

Helen further noted that it was difficult for her to share her everyday life with her Korean friends because they could not understand the Buddhist rituals. There are certain rituals that Koreans traditionally practice, such as "Jae-Sa." "Jae-Sa" is a Korean ceremony for ancestors. Koreans prepare certain food and drink for their deceased family members and ancestors and bow to them in front of the prepared foods arranged along with pictures or written names of their ancestors. Helen was afraid that if she shared this ritual, her friends would think of her as someone who was too "traditional" and part of an older generation. Helen also stated that this feeling of insecurity was more severe during her teenage years, and she is still learning to be comfortable with her religious identity:

> I think being a Buddhist, I am a minority in America, but as I grow older, I am becoming comfortable with it. I think I am still learning to be comfortable with who I am, but I am getting better. In Korea, I don't think I ever thought that being Buddhist is bad or different. And I am sure I would have met more people of my age at temples if I was in Korea.

As can be seen in this narrative, Helen makes an important point about her religious status being a "placed" experience (Cresswell, 1998). As a Buddhist, Helen has always felt "out of place" in America because Buddhism is not the mainstream in Korean American society. However, in Korea, Buddhism is the largest religious group, with 22.8 percent of the population practicing. Only 18.3 percent are Protestants in Korea. Koreans in Korea generally understand the teachings and rituals of Buddhism, and Helen would have felt much more comfortable in this sense had she been living in Korea. Helen realized this when visiting Korea on holiday trips and staying in various temples in Korea. She was able to freely express her religious identity with the people she met in Korea. She also found that there were more people of her own age in Buddhist temples in Korea, which was something she missed in her local Buddhist temple in America.

Having trouble expressing their non-Christian identity in front of other Korean Americans was a shared experience among study participants:

> One time, I went on a blind date with this guy. We both felt that we really connected and we had a great time chatting. Then towards the end of the date, he suddenly asked me if I went to church. When I said no, that's when the silence came, and we both knew that we weren't going to meet again. Well, I mean, I wouldn't mind dating him, but I had a sense that he wouldn't want to meet me because I am not that good church girl, you know. (Janet Park, F, 26)

As the narrative illustrates, Janet was aware of the general perception held by Protestant Korean Americans that non-religious people are not "good people;" hence, she used to feel that she needed to be extra careful in displaying her identity. Janet did not want to be judged based on her non-religious identity. Having to negotiate such stereotypes was mentioned by a few other study participants. As children, they were told by their peers at school that they could not be friends anymore because the parents of their peers had told them not to hang out with kids who do not go to church because "they will influence you in bad ways." Having had such childhood experiences, as well as understanding general taboos against atheism, Janet was hesitant to tell others that she was non-Christian, especially on a blind date with a Korean American. As soon as the silence came, Janet knew she would not be seeing the man again.

Similar to the case above, many of the study participants' everyday experiences were filled with either being forced to admit that they do not go to a Korean church or consciously hiding the fact. Almost all of the study participants agreed that when

they meet a new Korean American, they are always asked about church affiliation. For Korean Americans, church affiliation becomes "a point of connection (or
disconnection):"

> I do kind of 'feel a person out' when I meet a new Korean American. Inevitably the
> religion question comes up, mostly like 'Do you go to church?' I don't ask that question,
> but I often find that other Korean Americans, especially churchgoers, ask that question.
> And if it doesn't come up at first, it'll come up later. So it's a point of connection or
> disconnection sometimes. (Alicia Choi, F, 33)

> People definitely treat me differently after finding out I'm not Christian. Hmm . . . well,
> it's like they assume I am like them, like I go to church. Then when they find out I don't
> go to church, they don't really know how to follow up. Like suddenly they can't relate.
> There have been a few instances where some people seem to lose interest in me. Almost all
> Koreans go to church, so if you don't go, you are almost automatically excluded from the
> community. (Laura Lim, F, 30)

The above quotations strongly represent the everyday negotiations and challenges
that non-Christian Korean Americans have to go through. Throughout this research,
I constantly asked myself, "Are the terms marginalization, prejudice, religious discrimination too strong?" The study participants have never been explicitly or publicly excluded or marginalized from their own ethnic group based on their religious
status. However, the secular Korean Americans did feel limited and excluded at
times because the Korean American population is overwhelmingly Christian, and
on many occasions, non-Christian Korean Americans were instantly seen as the
"Other." Such exclusions (although not made explicitly), through everyday conversations, behaviors, and structural constraints, are hard to pin down as instances of
discrimination. Yet, these are small acts of discrimination that exist clearly in the
feelings and memories of those who experienced them.

FINDING "ALTERNATIVE" GROUPS
AND STRONGER SELVES

So far, I have illustrated various narratives of those Korean Americans who experienced difficulties and a sense of marginalization due to their religious status. In
this section, I explore how much their sense of "religious marginality" affects their
Korean American identities and how these identities change and mature. My analysis
of the study participants' narratives showed that the most difficult period of religious
marginalization was during their high school and college years. As the study participants entered adulthood and found stable positions through their jobs and other
institutions, they were able to form their own groups and communities and gain
stronger religious (and ethnic) identities.

I use the term "alternative" group because some of the study participants wished
to belong to the ethnic Korean community, yet it was hard for them to find a Korean
community that was not religious:

I do sometimes wish there were more Korean Americans that I could hang out with. I feel like there's a common understanding of culture and ethnicity with other Korean Americans. Some of my closest friends are Korean Americans, and from things like being able to say some key Korean words that are not translatable to just understanding family dynamics that are unique to being Korean, I feel a connection to other Korean Americans that isn't quite there with other Asian Americans or non-Asian Americans. (Tara Hong, F, 27)

Some of the study participants stated that they were able to find an alternative Korean community by actively engaging in cultural activities and gathering people with similar interests. For instance, Michelle Lim (F, 30) stated that she currently runs a small "food club" for Korean Americans, which she started while she was in college:

During college, I was so lonely at first because I was never part of a community. Back then, I had just come back from my one-year stay in Korea. I was an exchange student at a Korean university, and I loved spending time with Korean people and sharing the Korean culture. I knew that I felt mostly true to myself when I am surrounded by Korean people. But I didn't want to go to a Korean church just to meet people because I was never religious. So one day, I started this Korean group called 'food club'. It was started with a group of three or four friends. We would meet once every month and go and try new restaurants and just eat good food. The group became bigger, and at one point, we had more than ten people who were active members. When I had a larger group of Korean friends, that's when I felt like I was part of something.

Michelle stated that it was easy to gather Korean people and run this group because there were always new students in college, and she always invited the newcomers. She still runs the club, and she is satisfied with her own group of Korean friends and how she can express her Korean identity through the group. She believes that she can always find her own community and sense of belonging and will not be untrue to herself and attend a Korean church "just to meet people." Like Michelle, Helen Park (F, 28) also finds that being part of a Korean American community is integral to sustaining her Korean identity. Helen, who is a Buddhist, found it difficult when she was younger, yet she went on to find a community of tolerance to practice her religion and identity:

It is very important for me to be a part of the Korean community. I'm like the perfect medium between Korean and American. I can be very American sometimes, and at the same time, I am very Korean. So I think it's really important for me to be part of the Korean American community. It did take me a very long time to get to this point. At college, I didn't really know, but it really took a long time to make that balance because I couldn't show my religious identity in front of my Korean American friends. I think I finally felt comfortable with myself during college.

Now that Helen feels more comfortable with her religious identity, she practices Buddhism more freely in front of her peers and is actively involved in the Korean American Buddhist community, which was not as accessible to her during her teenage years.

While it was important for most of the study participants to be part of a Korean American group, some others felt more comfortable being part of the Asian American community:

> In college, I was on the board of the Asian American Student Union (AASU) for three years. It was a very big part of my college experience, and I met a lot of wonderful friends through it. As a part of the student organization, we collaborated with the Korean Student Association a few times for social events and cultural shows. My last year of AASU, we hosted a large conference for all of the Midwest schools to attend. We had many keynote speakers, workshops, and a large banquet dinner. These conferences touched on many topics, including Asian identity, professions that Asian families frown upon, Asians in the media, pop culture, Asian LGBT awareness, etc. I really felt like it made a difference in many lives. I really enjoyed being a part of AASU in college and wish I had more time to be involved with something like that again. However, I do not want to limit myself to just a Korean organization itself. (Stella Kim, F, 29)

Stella noted that she felt more comfortable around her Asian American friends than her Korean American friends. Although this does not necessarily affect her Korean American identity, she finds a stronger sense of belonging in the wider Asian American community. The narratives below run parallel to Stella's feelings about her identity and her sense of belonging:

> I was involved with the Korean club at my college. Haven't been involved in Korean organizations at any other time. I kind of wish there were a Korean American association that I could be part of, but the ones that exist don't really speak to me. I've felt more comfortable in Pan-Asian American organizations. (Alicia Choi, F, 35)

> I relate to Chinese Americans the most and other Korean Americans who are atypical. (Laura Lim, F, 30)

Both Alicia and Laura noted that they would have been involved in Korean American communities if they were not all Christian groups. As Alicia states, the already-existing Korean American organizations did not seem fitting for her. Both participants felt more stable being part of the wider Asian American community and practicing their Asian American identities rather than trying to fit into the Korean American community.

There are three major forms of interacting elements that formulate one's sense of identity: biological, physiological, and social/cultural (Erikson, 1968). The social element of one's identity is mostly formulated from adolescence to adulthood (Erikson, 1968) and also changes throughout one's life course as social circumstances change over time. Kroger (2007:8) explains further, "Optimal identity development involves finding social roles and niches within the larger community that provide a good "fit" for one's biological and psychological capacities and interests." Indeed, many of the study participants stated that as adults, they find their current community to be fulfilling. As they grew older, they found identification and association through interests and work:

I don't feel an urgency to socialize with Korean people only. I enjoy hanging out with people who have the same interests that I do. Because I am not in college anymore, I don't have the time to go to many social events and gatherings outside of work to meet other Korean people. If I happen to meet some cool Koreans, then I would definitely continue to hang out with them, but I would not actively search for Korean friends. I currently have a few Korean American friends and see them every so often, but I am mostly hanging out with the people that I meet at work. We know each other the best because we spend the entire day together, and they are pretty awesome. I love being part of this community. (Amy Woo, F, 32)

Amy felt excluded by her Korean American friends at times during high school due to her religious marginality. Now that she has entered the workforce and is working as a medical practitioner, she feels that she has found her "good fit" in both a psychological and social sense. She still feels strongly Korean American when she is around her family and close friends, but she does not desire to be part of a Korean American community. She is fully satisfied with her work community, where she feels well-placed and that she is being true to her identity. Jerrod Han (M, 30), a second-generation Korean American, illustrated a similar narrative:

I feel very comfortable as a Korean American. But I am also equally American, since I have lived in the United States my whole life. I am not involved in any Korean organizations at the moment. I socialize with my medical school classmates and co-workers/patients at the hospital where I work. I am very comfortable in my working and academic environments.

Jerrod stated that he never really felt a sense of marginalization from the Korean American community as a teenager. He tried going to a Korean American church as well, but he eventually attended an American church because that is where he felt more comfortable. He feels that one should not limit one's identity to being just Korean American and be closed in that circle:

Not being part of your ethnic community can be isolating at times. But we have to realize that we are in the United States and that while it is perfectly fine to attend a Korean church, it is also important that if someone is a U.S. citizen and votes in the United States, that they integrate themselves in America. This does not mean cultural compromise but rather sharing one's culture in the melting pot that is America.

CONCLUSION

While previous studies have examined the important role of ethnic Christian churches in creating a sense of belonging and community for Korean Americans, in this study, I wanted to understand the experiences of those who are not affiliated with the dominant Protestant Korean American community. In the first result section, I illustrated that not all of the study participants were non-churchgoers simply because they were non-Christians. Some participants had experiences or involvement in Korean churches in the past as children or teenagers. Most of those experiences involved negative feelings and incidents that caused them to stop attending the Korean church. While religious communities can create spaces of peace and belonging for immigrants, they also create hierarchies and exclusions based on different religious views. The study participants had mixed feelings about not being part of the Korean church community. At certain points in their lives, especially during their teenage and college years, they felt marginalized because they were not part of the dominant Korean American group. They could not "fit in" and take part in certain cultural activities that were organized by churches; hence, they felt isolated from their peers. The study participants were definitely aware of the dominance of Korean churches, and it often shaped their everyday lives. The secular Korean Americans felt limited and excluded at times due to the fact that Korean Americans are predominantly Christians and, on many occasions, the study participants were instantly seen as the "Other." I have argued in this study that these are small acts of discrimination.

However, the study participants also indicated that they now prefer to be part of wider American society and not limit themselves to a closed "Korean bubble." Also, there were strong narratives suggesting that they would not convert to Christianity in order to be socially included in the Korean American community. In other words, they were still satisfied with their current religious status and social positions.

The study participants' experiences with the Korean church changed over their life phases and, as they entered adulthood, they gained a stronger and more stable sense of self. Although there was a "price to be paid" for not taking part in the Korean American community, they felt much more confident and true to themselves by finding "alternative" communities and groups with similar interests. I have illustrated that not taking part in the Korean church did not have a strong impact on sustaining the participants' Korean American identities. They still held onto their Korean culture through family and close friends (and by having connections to Korean food and media). Having a connection to a Korean church was not necessary to sustaining their "Koreanness." This was especially the case for the 1.5 generation study participants who still held many connections to their Korean culture and did not have to rely on churches to learn the Korean language, for instance.

There were a number of limitations to this research. The study examined a specific group of young professionals living in the Boston area and those who grew up in the United States. If the study participants were first-generation immigrants (who would presumably be culturally and linguistically less adapted to U.S. society), or from a lower-income and less-educated background, the findings could have been rather different. Due to the limited time available and the snowball sampling method used, the study was unable to find a wider range of participants but had to limit its focus to a group of young professionals. The study has not been able to delve into other themes such as intergenerational differences, regional differences, gender, class, family, and power. These themes and interlinking ideas would be excellent domains for future research.

This research was not intended to discourage participation in or criticize ethnic religious communities. Rather, it emphasized the fact that while it is good to have those communities, they can also be limiting. The fact that the Korean American community is predominantly Protestant Christian makes it difficult for those who are not religious or who practice other denominations and faiths to be part of the wider Korean American community. The research calls attention to these issues and argues that there is a need for civic organizations that are inclusive of people from the same ethnic group regardless of their religion (or gender, class, and body).

NOTES

1. This chapter is largely based on "Living as a non-Christian in a Christian community: experiences of religious marginalisation amongst young Korean Americans," published by Taylor & Francis Group in *Journal of Ethnic and Racial Studies* on 22/01/2019, available online: https://www.tandfonline.com/doi/abs/10.1080/1369183X.2018.1427565
2. Noraebang refers to Karaoke, a singing room in Korean.

REFERENCES

Bartley, A., & Spoonley, P. (2008). Intergenerational transnationalism: 1.5 generation Asian migrants in New Zealand. *International Migration*, 46(4), 63–84.

Bennett, K. (2002). Interviews and focus groups. In P. Shurmer-Smith (ed.), *Doing Cultural Geography*(pp. 151–164). London: Sage Publication.

Brettell, C. (2003). *Anthropology and Migration: Essays on Transnationalism, Ethnicity, and Identity*. Lanham: Rowman & Littlefield.

Chai, K. (2001). Intra-ethnic religious diversity: Korean Buddhists and Protestants in greater Boston. In Kwon, H., Kim, K. and Warner, R. (eds.), *Korean Americans and Their Religions: Pilgrims and Missionaries from a Different Shore* (pp. 273–294). University Park: The Pennsylvania State University Press.

Chong, K. (1998). What it means to be Christian: The role of religion in the construction of ethnic identity and boundary among second-generation Korean Americans. *Sociology of Religion*, 59(3), 259–279.

Cresswell, T. (1998). *In Place and Out of Place: Geography, Ideology, and Transgression*. Minneapolis: University of Minnesota Press.

De Leeuw, K. (2007). Faith and community: The significance of the ethnic church for Chinese and Korean migrants in Auckland. Unpublished Master's Thesis. Auckland: University of Auckland.

Ecklund, H. (2005). 'Us' and 'Them': The role of religion in mediating and challenging the 'model minority' and other civic boundaries. *Ethnic and Racial Studies*, 28(1), 132–150.

Erikson, E. H. (1968). *Identity: Youth and Crisis*. New York: Norton.

Erikson, E. H. (1997). *The Life Cycle Completed*. New York: Norton.

Hall, S. (1996). Who needs 'Identity'? In S. Hall & P. du Gay (eds.), *Questions of Cultural Identity* (pp. 1–17). London: Sage Publication.

Hurh, W., & Kim, K. (1990). Religious participation of Korean immigrants in the United States. *Journal for the Scientific Study of Religion*, 29(1), 19–34.

Kim, A. (1996). *Women Struggling for a New Life: On the Role of Religion in the Cultural Passage from Korea to America*. Albany: State University of New York Press.

Kim, D. (2006). Stepping-stone to intergenerational mobility? The springboard, safety net, or mobility trap functions of Korean immigrant entrepreneurship for the second generation. *International Migration Review*, 40(4), 927–962.

Kim, I. (ed). (2004). *Korean Americans: Past, Present, and Future*. Elizabeth: Hollym International Corp.

Kroger, J. (2007). *Identity Development: Adolescence through Adulthood*. Thousand Oaks: Sage.

Kupel, N. J. B. (2010). *Korean Americans in Massachusetts: Profiles of Asian American Subgroups in Massachusetts*. Boston: Institute for Asian Americans Studies.

Kwon, H., Kim, K. & Warner, R. (eds). (2001). *Korean Americans and Their Religions: Pilgrims and Missionaries from a Different Shore*. University Park: The Pennsylvania State University Press.

Kwon, O. (2004). The role of religious congregations in formation of the Korean community of the Washington, DC area. In Kim, I. (ed.), *Korean Americans: Past, Present, and Future* (pp. 239–272). Elizabeth: Hollym International Corp.

Lee, H. (2007). Diverging identities: Ethnic and religious identities among second-generation Korean Americans. In Zhou, M. and Gatewood, J. (eds.), *Contemporary Asian America: A Multidisciplinary Reader*, 2nd edition (pp. 360–380). New York: New York University Press.

Lee, J. Y. (2015). Returning diasporas: Korean New Zealander returnees' journeys of searching 'home' and identity. In Christou, A. and Mavroudi, E. (eds.), *Dismantling Diasporas: Rethinking the Geographies of Diasporic Identity, Connection and Development* (pp. 161–174). London: Ashgate.

Ley, D. (2008). The immigrant church as an urban service hub. *Urban Studies*, 45 (10), 2057–2074.

Livingstone, D. (1998). Geography and the natural theology imperative. In Aay, H. and Griffioen, S. (eds.), *Geography and Worldview: A Christian Reconnaissance* (pp. 1–17). Lanham: University Press of America.

Min, P. (1992). The structure and social functions of Korean immigrant churches in the United States. *International Migration Review*, 26 (4), 1370–1394.

Min, P. (2013). A comparison of Korean protestant, Catholic, and Buddhist religious institutions in New York. In Min, P. (ed.), *Koreans in North America: Their Experiences in the Twenty-First Century* (pp. 75–102). Lanham: Lexington Books.

Min, P., & Kim, C. (2013). Growth and settlement patterns of Korean Americans. In Min, P. (ed.), *Koreans in North America: Their Experiences in the Twenty-First Century* (pp. 35–56). Lanham: Lexington Books.

Park, K. (1997). *The Korean American Dream: Immigrants and Small Business in New York City*. Ithaca and London: Cornell University Press.

Park, K. (1999). "I really do feel I'm 1.5!": The construction of self and community by young Korean Americans. *Amerasia Journal*, 25(1), 139–163.

Pew Research Center. (2012). *Asian Americans: A Mosaic of Faiths*. http://www.pewforum.org/2012/07/19/asian-americans-a-mosaic-of-faiths-overview/ (Accessed July 15, 2014).

Sopher, D. (1981). Geography and religions. *Progress in Human Geography*, 5, 510–524.

Suh, S. A. (2004). *Being Buddhist in a Christian World: Gender and Community in a Korean American Temple*. Seattle: The University of Washington Press.

Wallace, J. B. (1994). Life stories. In Gubrium, J. F. and Sankar, A. (eds.), *Qualitative Methods in Aging Research* (pp. 137–154). Thousand Oaks: Sage.

Yang, F. (1998). Chinese conversion to evangelical Christianity: The importance of social and cultural contexts. *Sociology of Religion*, 59(3), 237–244.

Yang, F., & Tamney, J. (2006). Exploring mass conversion to Christianity among the Chinese: An introduction. *Sociology of Religion*, 67(2), 125–129.

4

Ritual and Visibility

The Plays of Ins Choi

Alicia Corts

INTRODUCTION

In the late 2000s, Ins Choi was ready to give up the theater (Schultz, 2012). Unable to get Canadians to see him in any roles except stereotypical Asian parts and struggling to find roles by Korean playwrights, the actor turned playwright began to wonder if he should continue in the profession. Instead, he began to write a story of his own experience as a 1.5 immigrant in his new Canadian homeland, a work that eventually brought him the visibility he was seeking as an artist.

Born in South Korea, Ins Choi joined thousands of Generation 1.5 immigrants arriving in Canada. Just like his counterparts, his life and talents were put under the stress of living in two separate communities with widely different social norms and expectations for communication. Choi uses embodied performance to explore these two communities from the 1.5 perspective, specifically through live theatrical events. These stories give both Choi and other 1.5 immigrants the means to ritually negotiate a place between two worlds and return them to a visible position both within their cultural communities and with their adopted Canadian homeland. I argue in this chapter that Choi uses the audience as the priest of a ritual conversation around the 1.5 immigrant's place within society. Choi's plays suggest that children who arrived in Canada as immigrants must ask permission of both their Korean and adopted nation's communities before entering into a true sense of identity.

Rumbaugh and Ima would label Choi as a member of the 1.5 generation, a group caught between the memory and community of their parents and that of their adopted land:

> They are neither part of the "first" generation of their parents, the responsible adults who were formed in the homeland, who made the fateful decision to leave it and to flee as

refugees to an uncertain exile in the United States, and who are thus defined by the consequences of that decision and by the need to justify it; nor are these youths part of the
"second" generation of children who are born in the [the adopted homeland], and for
whom the "homeland" mainly exists as a representation consisting of parental memories
and memorabilia, even though their ethnicity may remain well defined. (1988, p. 1)

This liminality between the two generations implies that Generation 1.5 is asked
to perform in two ways, code-switching between the two groups they sit between.
This code-switching does not indicate a deficit in their day-to-day lives, but the "in-
between" quality of their identities demonstrates the extra work they must do to fit
in with their community. They must remain the keepers of parental memories, giving them a connection to their ancestral home. They must also be able to negotiate
an identity that allows them the ability to perform the memories of their adopted
homeland. In everyday life, this necessity causes a split in how they are called to
behave: with family, they must perform in a manner that indicates an understanding of the past with an understanding of the future. With friends and the community outside of their immigrant home, they must perform the values and customs
required in their new land. When these values clash, it creates the need for what
Victor Turner calls a social drama, a performance that remediates the crisis moment
when an individual or small group within a society finds themselves outside of the
values and norms of that community. These performances allow others to see the
difficulties in their society—in the case of Choi, the difficulties faced by 1.5 Korean
Canadian immigrant—and give them a means to negotiate a new identity that mediates the conflicts they face.

Generation 1.5 is caught straddling between two worlds, neither one nor the
other. They are in a type of limbo that requires society to recover them and their
story. Rituals are designed to bring such conflicts to a close. They are a means of
guiding the member caught between two worlds toward a better sense of identity.
Arnab Banerji posits that these social dramas provide a "blueprint for . . . identity
intended to bind" the performer to society (2019, p. 2). Choi's plays become social
dramas because of the audience who participate in and provide feedback for the
performance. As the lights go down and the story begins, a ritual occurs between
the performers and the audience, and if the stories are successful, the audience and
performers leave with a transformed vision of the place of Generation 1.5.

The Plays

In 2011, Ins Choi broke into the world of Canadian theater with his spectacular hit,
Kim's Convenience. The play tells the story of a Korean immigrant family living in
Toronto whose lives revolve around their convenience store. While a colorful group
of neighborhood characters pass through the doors of the shop, the true heart of
the story is the relationship of Appa and Umma, the parents, with Jung and Janet,
the two children. Appa is the old-school patriarch of the family, and he has firm
opinions on everything from Japanese cars (evil) to Korean energy drinks (good).
Although quite happy running the family store, a new superstore is set to open

nearby, and a wealthy developer offers Appa a great deal of money to sell the store, retire, and walk away from the business. This narrative development causes Appa to consider the future of the store—should one of his children take over the store or should he sell?

Janet, the thirty-year-old unmarried daughter born in Canada, is a photographer, much to the chagrin of her father. In one scene, Appa asks Janet to take over the store. She rejects the offer, firmly explaining to him that she is a photographer and focused on that career.

> Don't you want me to succeed in life? Look, Appa, you did what you had to do, right? And I appreciate that. I do. But didn't you do what you had to do so I wouldn't have to do what I had to do but could choose what I wanted to do? (Choi 2012, p.26)

These two characters represent the first- and second-generation Korean Canadians. Appa is firmly focused on providing for his family no matter the cost: as a successful teacher in Korea, he gave up his dreams to provide for his family in Canada. As Rumbaugh and Ima noted, Appa accepts the responsibility for the decision to leave and has taken on a different career as a result. Janet, on the other hand, rejects the life offered by Appa, preferring instead to pursue her artistic goals. She does not remember the homeland at all, but she sees Appa and Umma's quaint ways as a throwback to the place that she comes from. She corrects their English, chastises Appa for his racist comments, and talks about dating non-Koreans. Her "Koreanness" exists as a side note to what she sees as her regular life.

One theater critic diminished this relationship as too reductive, complaining the relationship between Appa and Janet is "a rather selfish concept and serves to distinguish first and second-generation arrivals" (Roberts 2017). Choi, on the other hand, describes Appa as unapologetically "old-school" with a pride in the way he's worked hard for his children, and he writes Janet as a proud Canadian making her way in the greater world. The clear delineation between first- and second-generation characters serves to show that Appa "doesn't see her [Janet's] choices as being viable options" (q on cbc 2016, 11:06).

While theater critics might point to the simplicity of the characters' portrayals, Appa and Janet must be strongly associated with the first and second generations distinctly to serve as the backdrop for the story of Jung, the oldest child, only son, and 1.5 immigrant in the tale. Choi states that Jung's relationship with Appa is the crux of the story, and the resolution of the story gives Jung a position in the world that accepts the straddling he has done between Korea and Canadian cultures (Palmater, 2015). Jung's story becomes a modern-day prodigal son story. Earlier in the family's history, Jung and Appa argued over Appa's treatment of Umma, resulting in Appa beating Jung and sending him to the hospital for several days. Not long after, Jung stole the money from the store's safe and ran away from home. Other people tell these stories onstage, leaving Jung invisible to the audience until much later in the piece. What this back story tells the audience is that Jung not only does not fit into his family relationships but has also broken the laws of his adopted homeland. While he does have positive experiences with these two communities, as in the way he felt at home at his Korean church with his family or with his Canadian schoolmates, his code-switching between first and second-generation identities has led him to a position where he does not feel heard or known by either group. Choi paints Jung as stuck in a kind of limbo between these two groups while simultaneously implying that Jung's negative position is a direct result of the stress 1.5 immigrants feel.

Choi paints Jung's experience as negative on purpose to highlight the need for the position of the 1.5 immigrant to be better understood. Clearly, not every 1.5 immigrant ends up being a convicted criminal incapable of caring for a family. The 1.5 immigrant, however, does experience a level of acculturation stress due to the trauma of immigration (Arbona et al., 2010; Harker, 2001; Kim, Brenner, Liang, and Asay, 2003; Roberge, 2002), and specifically in the Korean diasporic community, the 1.5 immigrant has the added role of bridge builder between the first- and second-generation immigrants (Park, 1999). What Choi does through Jung's character is highlight the stresses on the 1.5 immigrant by turning the character into the prodigal son of the story, as a character who has been unable to fit into either the Korean or Canadian roles. Choi's own experience in this position was not always negative, but he did feel a sense of being an outsider. Jung's character allows him to speak to the stresses of the 1.5 immigrant and their need for an identity and voice that is their own.

To accomplish this task, Choi purposefully paints Jung as someone who can deftly accomplish the code-switching between his Korean and Canadian identities, but who never quite fits in completely in either identity. When he first appears onstage, Jung slips into church to talk to Umma, telling her about Sonam, his infant son, and the crisis he has reached after realizing all his high school football team friends are more successful in the eyes of Canadian culture.

> I was their captain. I was their captain, Umma. I was smarter than all of them, faster, stronger. I didn't dream I'd end up renting cars to people. Nine to five. Checking for dents and scratches. Living in a shithole in Parkdale. Apartment's a constant mess. Fight all the time, his mom and me. She thinks I'm a loser—I don't even know why I'm with her anymore. And all he ever does is cry and cry and cry and cry and cry. Just wanna leave, y'know? Just go. Start over. Somewhere else. Calgary, Vancouver—doesn't matter where. It'd be so easy too. Bay and Dundas, hop on a bus and leave. I rent cars to people, then take the streetcar home. What is that? That's a joke. (Choi, 2012, p. 78)

Jung is isolated from both the Korean and Canadian identities he interacts with. His Canadian friends hunt for him through social media and connections with the Kim family, and Janet points out that Appa looks out the window of the store every day as if to see him coming down the street. Yet just as he remains offstage until late in the play, these people cannot see Jung and the trials of being between the two groups. He is, in essence, invisible, held in the margins between two groups.

It is only when he returns to the store to present his broken attempt at living fully in Canadian culture that he finds a place. Jung walks in the store at closing time. An awkward conversation ensues. Attempting to break the ice, Appa offers Jung a Korean energy drink, and Jung notices he's been selling the beverage for $1.50.

Much earlier in the play, a scene entitled "Steal No Steal" reveals Appa explaining to Janet how to tell if someone is shoplifting. His description shows a propensity for targeting racial, ethnic, and queer customers. While there isn't outright hatred in his method for catching shoplifters, there is a strong sense that Appa is attempting to understand the different groups that live outside his store. Jung in this later scene suggests higher prices, mirroring the same racialized profiling Appa shows at the beginning of the play but with a better knowledge of how much different Canadian groups will be willing to pay for the drink. It's a small suggestion, but it demonstrates to Appa that Jung not only understands his Korean heritage—the importance of the store—but can navigate the outside Canadian world as well. Appa, faced with the news that he is now a *halabujee* as well as finally seeing the worth of Jung's position in society, offers his son the store, freely and with no conditions. This acceptance, however, is not without a complicated symbolism: it is only after Jung is able to produce the next generation, the normalized non-immigrant child, that he is once again seen and accepted.

The theme of invisibility extends to Choi's second play, *Subway Stations of the Cross*. A one-man show, Choi uses the performance as a means of dramatizing an encounter he had with a homeless man in Toronto, an identity that Choi connects with through the performance (Robins 2014). The man rambled through a variety of subjects, though Choi believed his various subjects pointed toward a religious epiphany. When pressed if there's a message to the show, he said: "Maybe the message has something to do with seeing, seeing past me, seeing past seeing, past receiving, past what's perceived as believing, i.e. relieved to just be living rather than justly living" (Ibid.) Choi dresses himself as the homeless man, standing on a square of cardboard. The evening mirrors the stations of the cross, a particularly Catholic ritual remembering the death of Christ along the Via Dolorosa. Choi's version uses references to Toronto subway stations (and references to whatever city the show is playing in) to ground the work in the particular locale in Canada as well as indicating the suffering of those invisible to society, despite the wisdom they have to offer.

This character, like Jung, is the overlooked, the unseen. In this show, however, Choi is suggesting that we overlook these people to our peril. The songs and spoken word poems tackle topics from wine to dancing to stream of consciousness ruminations on the nature of God. In the script of the show, Guno Park adds illustrations of subway passengers, and Choi says these images look "like lost travelers on a holy pilgrimage who, after many years, forgot where they were going and why; like keepers of an ancient secret veiled in a performance of apathy and sleep" (Choi, 2015). The focus on the lost and invisible mirrors the experience of Generation 1.5, the group of people whose own stories and songs are forgotten and unheard because there isn't an audience for people to hear them, since they fall outside the stories of the first and second-generation stories normally told.

Subway Stations of the Cross, therefore, is the more abstract telling of the prodigal son started in *Kim's Convenience*. The narrator is very clearly part of an invisible segment of society: the homeless. The costume and rantings mirror Choi's own experience with the homeless man who gave him the inspiration for the show. While he first believed the man to be mentally ill, he gradually came to believe his ramblings to be more divine than mad (Choi, 2014). In other words, rather than passing by the mentally ill homeless man, Choi is challenging us to consider such encounters as evidence of the invisible stories we cannot pass by. He is setting the audience up to understand that these stories have value with the added component that they, the audience members, must listen and accept the stories for them to have true value. He is setting up the ritual where the audience must, through their acceptance of the story, look on the invisible with new eyes.

It is important to note the fact that Choi himself plays the lone role in *Subway Stations of the Cross*. Rather than making the homeless character one that anyone can play, Choi first steps onstage as himself, telling of his encounter with a homeless sage. He puts on the costume and makeup in front of the audience, gradually turning himself into the outcast. The symbolism here mirrors Jung's position in *Kim's Convenience*. The solo performer is outside of society, just as Jung is rejected from the world of wealth and social standing. An important distinction between *Kim's Convenience* and *Subway Stations of the Cross* is which societal group is being interrogated. *Kim'sConvenience* is set in the domain of the first-generation immigrant, a location ultimately by rejected the second-generation and reclaimed by the 1.5 generation. *Subway Stations of the Cross* is set in the world of the adopted Canadian nation, where the society around him has rejected his existence. Much like Jung can't relate to the world of wealth and privilege that his classmates have found, the lone, dirty ragged character in Subway rejects the world of:

Compare
Laissez-faire
Up in the air
On a whim and a prayer
Neither here nor there
Neither hide nor hair
Multi-million dollar home five car garage private jet plane mega-billionaire
MDiv PhD summa cum laud professor director member fellow published
textbook nicky picky air tight I'm right doctrinaire ye the way of the Lord

Unfair
Who gives a care
Despair
Solitaire ye the way of the Lord

Beware
Beware
Beware ye the way of the Lord (Choi, 2015)

In the case of both characters, the despair mentioned in this section of *Subway Stations of the Cross* shows what happens when society doesn't see the lives of the 1.5 immigrant. Jung cannot lean on his family, yet Canadian society has rejected him and pushed him to the margins. Similarly, the homeless man can preach and proclaim to unwilling ears, despite his prescient outlook on society. The distance both characters have from society indicates that there must be a mending of relationships for the character to be reintroduced to both Canadian and Korean communities. Ritual performance offers a way for those outside the bounds of society to negotiate a place, and both *Kim's Convenience* and *Subway Stations of the Cross* provide a way for the 1.5 immigrant's story to be told, considered by both societies, and accepted as a valid identity. Most importantly, the plays provide a story that society can reference as a shared memory of the 1.5 immigrant experience.

Collective Memory

The key to a successful ritual for the 1.5 immigrant is the collective memory of both the Korean and Canadian communities in which they live. Any social group has a set of memories, a collection of stories and performances that are rehearsed and recounted to bring the past into the present (Bergson, 1996). These shared memories give people a means to share their common identity and transfer the meaning of objects and activities to new community members as they enter the group (Nicholson, 2009).

Paul Connerton suggests that a community's social order is given its legitimacy through the shared and collective memory of that group (1989, p. 3). The 1.5 immigrant experiences a disconnect both from the culture of their ancestral land as well as their adopted country because of a lack of communal memory with both groups, caught between two social orders with two different sets of memory. Each of these immigrants must therefore navigate between the communities by assuming memories that may be in contradiction to each other or give different perspectives on the same event. In Toronto, for example, the Korean Canadian enters a community with a communal memory of multiculturalism as an "idealist dream" that some have claimed is more of a way of "managing (containing and controlling) diversity" (Knowles, 2009: 49). The cultural memory in Canada, therefore, attempts to usurp the place of communal memory of the home community under the name of multiculturalism, and this action plays out in the embodied performance of the 1.5 immigrant. It is up to the 1.5 immigrant to navigate the path toward a common memory more in line with one of the two communities, yet this struggle places them into conflict with each community they are attempting to join.

In Ins Choi's own life, we can see an instance of this memory transference and pressure to assume the adopted country's social norms. Choi's full first name is Insurp, a name he describes as difficult to pronounce and easy to make fun of (Canadian Life Changers). Even the spelling indicates the tension between the two cultures: with no "r" sound present in Korean, the immigration official responsible for Choi's papers translated the "ㄹ" sound, which falls somewhere between an "r" and "l," into Insurp when a better Anglicized spelling would be Insub (Bell, 2018). In fact, Choi felt burdened by the name, calling it "weird" and a strange hybrid that "wasn't Canadian or Korean" (Ibid.).

When he entered high school, he actively began telling people that his name was Danny, a name he chose after seeing the movie *Grease*. That film is a part of the collective memory of the westernized country where he was living, and his choice to take the lead character's name indicates a desire to fit into the collective memory of the social order of Canada. Sarah Benesch suggests that this desire to rename oneself according to the social mores of the adopted land comes from colonial pressures inside the school system to assimilate (2008). This urge comes from the way that the 1.5 immigrant is seen as both Self and Other, a concept that parallels the notion that their collective memory is seen as both native (first-generation) and assimilated (second-generation) (Ibid.). Choi uses the story of his discomfort with his name at the start of *Subway Stations of the Cross*. As he transforms himself into the homeless man, he talks about the expectations put on him from family and friends, using his name as a way of explaining his own Otherness (Nichols, 2015). Once he puts on the costume and makeup of the homeless man, he begins to tell the secrets the character has to offer, but only after showing the audience that he understands what it's like to be invisible from another perspective. As Choi notes in an interview, his struggle for normality between two cultures drove his search for a name: he was "trying to try to be more normal. Trying to be more what the images of what is Canadian. Then you kind of learn to love your culture and love the differences that it has made in your life and then I think kind of reclaim it. And reclaim both. Being Canadian and Korean. That's who I am" (Canadian Life Changers, 2017, 5:18). Note that this 1.5 immigrant found a need not just to fit within Canadian society but within the Korean community as well. This in-betweenness is the liminality that pulls the 1.5 immigrant and leaves him without a singular society.

While Choi's desire to rename himself illustrates the pull between two cultures, his subsequent return to his given name demonstrates the back-and-forth negotiation undertaken by the 1.5 immigrant. On his first day at York University, he impulsively returned to Insurp because he "fell in love with the name again," an indication of a desire for the community who gave it to him (Bell, 2018). This seemingly simple act of changing names demonstrates the quandary of the 1.5 immigrant as they attempt to find their place between the two communities: whether to move to the Anglicized world or remain in the unpronounceable native language. Choi has come to rest in the name Ins, a shortening of his given Korean name that remains easily pronounced in Canada. It is the compromise that allows him to live in between the two cultures.

Kim's Convenience uses this issue with names in the names of the children, Jung and Janet. From the play, it's implied that the family moved to Canada for more opportunities for Jung, suggesting he was born in South Korea before emigrating. Given Appa's dedication to Korea, Janet would have been given a Korean name, yet she has an Anglicized name, symbolizing her birth in the new nation. Janet has no issue with fitting into her education and career, yet Jung, the one attempting to enter Canadian society, feels the lack of success keenly. As Bensch notes, he sees his Self as competent and willing to work within both Korean and Canadian societies, yet he is viewed as Other by his father, his friends, and a society that has marginalized him.

Kim's Convenience uses names in a way that goes beyond the simply autobiographical and moves into a means of transferring information to the audience as a means of collective memory. Janet and Jung's Canadian and Korean names demonstrate two different memories despite coming from the same household. Jung, as the Korean-born son, is the one that Appa and Umma discuss in scene that flashes back to just before they came to Canada. As they talk about what to name their store, Jung's parents place requirements on him even before he's born and before his move to Canada. He holds the promise of the immigrant (first-generation) while simultaneously being launched into his new society (second-generation).

Choi's suggestion that Jung is a prodigal son extends to the unnamed homeless man at the center of *Subway Stations of the Cross*. His far-reaching ruminations on everything from wine to politics to the subway indicate a wide range of experiences, a demonstration of his ability to see and understand the culture and important collective memory of society. He remains nameless, however, a distant Other whose dirt and grime keeps him separated from society. He doesn't name himself, preferring to stay distant from his audience. While Jung longs to be the welcomed home prodigal, the homeless man in *Subway Stations of the Cross* remains aloof. He doesn't want to be integrated into the collective memory: he demonstrates through his song and poetry that he understands and sees what society values. The homeless man wants his authentic Self, not his representation, to be included in that memory. Jung longs to be integrated into either world, but the homeless man insists on society remembering him as he is, unassimilated.

Paul Sun-Hyung Lee, the actor who has played Appa since the earliest performances of *Kim's Convenience* and himself a 1.5 immigrant, describes the play as "my story, my family's story . . . . You don't realize that you . . . don't hear your stories or see your stories up on stage or on the screen. You don't realize the effect it really has on you until you see something that truly represents you" (Palmater, 2015, 12:02). While he was anxious to see his own cultural heritage onstage, he also struggled with the role's requirement of Korean-accented English: "Growing up, I wanted to assimilate and be so Canadian that subconsciously I just put the way that my Korean heritage and my Korean accent would sound like I was Russian. [I] couldn't do it." (Ibid.). Lee's perception once again notes the difference between the Self and Other in the collective memory. He recognizes the need for Korean representation, yet when asked to perform within that collective memory, he struggles with authenticity and becomes an Other, lesser version of the memory being shared.

These plays, however, go beyond simply offering representation and negotiation of collective memory. The plays offer an alternative ending to the struggles represented by Paul Sun-Hyung Lee's Korean accent, Ins Choi's search for a name, and the struggles of the prodigal characters to be remembered in the way they choose. Choi's works offer a ritual as a means to take the in-betweenness of the 1.5 generation and reintegrate their experience into the collective memory of both their immigrant and adopted homeland societies so that the 1.5 immigrant has a social standing in each community.

Ritual Performance

When people find themselves marginalized from society, it can create a breach between those in control and those at the margins. These breaks between groups are crises that require remediation in order for the two groups to be brought back together. Clifford Geertz in his exploration of social science and theater described the theater as having the potential to be communion and temple, rhetoric and persuasion (1980, p. 172). In other words, when a ritual is needed to bring society back into order, theater is a way of approaching that goal. Theater has its roots in ritual (Jennings, 2018; Schechner, 1973; Shepherd and Wallis, 2004), but it goes beyond just the basis of theater to being interwoven with theater, influencing theater and performance as well as becoming a part of theater (Schechner, 2003). In the case of Choi's plays, theater acts as a redress to a social dilemma requiring a ritual.

Victor Turner asserts that theater is the most culturally "active" means of creating a dialogue within a society (1980, p. 104). Indeed, in Turner's estimation, the story of the 1.5 immigrant is a social crisis that needs a ritual to bring society back into order. Critics certainly recognize that something is happening in Choi's works: the invisible is brought into view (Li, 2018; Baccari, 2012). Most critics, however, ignore the position of the 1.5 immigrant in Choi's work; one critic, for example, describes *Kim's Convenience* as a "complicated social dance between immigrant parents and their Canadian-born children" (BWW News Desk, 2018). This estimation ignores the distinction between Jung, the Korean-born older son, and Janet, the Canadian-born daughter. Janet is not invisible in the play. She has a career path, Canadian friends, and a direction in life that seems driven by the Canadian culture. She rejects Appa's offer to take over the store, and as she does so, Janet asserts her comfort with being a second-generation immigrant accepted into Canadian society.

The social crises in the two plays come from Jung and the homeless man's uncertainty of place. Turner describes the start of every social drama as a breach in which "regular, norm-governed social life is interrupted" by the presence of a person, relationship, symbol, or other object which goes against the rules of society (1982, p. 83). Jung, the homeless man, and the 1.5 immigrant transgress the norms of both the first-generation immigrant, who remains attached to the culture of their homeland, and the second-generation immigrant, who is expected to be integrated into the adopted culture. The 1.5 immigrant breaks that established pattern. They are "betwixt and between," a liminal performance that lies outside of the two groups to which he belongs (Turner 1979, p. 466). Arnold van Gennep describes these liminal states in terms of travel centuries ago (2013, p. 66). When a traveler moved across territory before the establishment of countries and borders, their journey was punctuated with "formalities" in each locale designed to bring them into an understanding of the local customs and beliefs. As society has modernized, the barriers to travel have disappeared, but the rites of passage remain.

In Van Gennep's conception, there are three rites to any passage: preliminal, liminal, and postliminal (2013, p. 71). In each of these steps, the traveler through the three rites to arrive safely at their destination. I propose that the 1.5 immigrant has not arrived at the final destination of being accepted into society because they must continually travel between the origin society and that of the new homeland, essentially never ending in the resting, postliminal state of being. Consider the hypothetical journey of the first-generation immigrant. The preliminal ritual consists of saying goodbye to their homeland, perhaps through final goodbyes and special family moments. The liminal rite is during the journey to the new country and the settling into the new life, when the first-generation immigrant feels neither at home in the adopted country and no longer within the society of their homeland. This stage could be exemplified by not knowing how to use public transportation, stumbling on the new language, or making a social faux pas. Finally, as the first-generation immigrant makes connections with the diasporic community and the world around them, they move from being outsiders to knowing how they fit into the new society. This rite can be noted by things such as giving directions to a stranger, having longer conversations in the new language, or pointing out the faux pas of someone else in the new society.

The 1.5 immigrant, on the other hand, goes through the same passage as the first-generation but with distinctly different results. As a child, the 1.5 immigrant says the same goodbye as the first-generation immigrant, but without a full sense of the gravity of the situation. Saying goodbye to relatives when you're a child is much different than departing from family for what could be the last time. While the first-generation immigrant might struggle with the new language and culture, the 1.5 immigrant is more quickly integrated through mandatory school attendance (Park, 1999). The first-generation Korean immigrant finds solace in the diasporic community (Noh and Avison, 1996), but for the 1.5 immigrant, that community can feel foreign and raise the stress of adapting to the new culture (Kim, Brenner, Liang, and Asay, 2003). At the same time, they are labeled as immigrants at school and in the wider community because they have gone through the liminal stage where they made the trip from the country of origin to the adopted nation. The second-generation immigrant doesn't need the liminal rite of passage. Rather, they are understood to be a part of the culture of the adopted homeland from their birth; their mannerisms, language, and ability to navigate the social norms of the adopted homeland. The difference, therefore, between the first-generation, second-generation, and 1.5 immigrant in ritual terms is the problem of the 1.5 immigrant not ever leaving the liminal phase. They remain in between cultures. Their rites of passage have never been completed, yet no ritual exists for them to be assimilated into the culture at large.

One way to look at the experience of the 1.5 immigrant is to think of them as tourists in their own hometown. Tourists perform with varying degrees of authenticity, and locals see those performances as something that is outside of their everyday set of social norms (Zhu, 2012: 1496). To use van Gennep's language, the tourist's performance indicates that they are just "passing through" and don't need the rites of passage someone requesting permanent status. Ning Wang posits that authenticity is determined by those viewing the performance (Wang, 1999, p. 790), and if we view the everyday performance of the 1.5 immigrant as something outside of both Korean and Canadian norms, these bodies represent a different kind of authentic.

The collective memories of the two cultures shape these judgments of authenticity, and without common ground in either group, the 1.5 immigrant runs the risk of being judged as a false imitation of either Korean or Canadian at any given moment.

Society at large is constantly viewing and judging performance according to the norms of that culture. Authenticity flows from that judgment, which occurs when "authentic" bodies perform in a way outside of what is expected. Yu Wang uses the example of two Naxi women approached by two Western tourists; after taking a photograph of them, the Naxi women demanded money, which caused the tourists to question whether they were "real" Naxi (2017). I propose that the 1.5 immigrant performs "inauthentically" on a regular basis because of the straddling between two cultures that they are forced to perform. To translate that to the performance of the 1.5 immigrant, consider the hypothetical situation of a 1.5 immigrant taking selfies. For Korean Canadians, the customs and apps used in Korea would color whether or not the immigrant community would approve of the selfie. Since *aegyo,* the Korean concept of cuteness, is often used in *selcies,* stickers, specific poses, and wide-eyed facial expressions are the norm (Dugnoille, 2016). At the same time, a selfie that used Korean conventions would be deemed unacceptable in the Canadian community. The 1.5 immigrant must perform between the two. The first-generation immigrant can take selfies according to Korean tradition, and the immigrant community and the Canadian homeland would see an authentic performance. The second-generation immigrant can adhere to the Canadian homeland's traditions and still be deemed authentic. The 1.5 immigrant, however, has the expectation of a performance that both matches the immigrant community and the adopted homeland, and while they might be able to find a way for such a dexterous performance in taking selfies, the 1.5 immigrant cannot maintain an identity that it constantly traversing between the two societies. In addition, being deemed inauthentic means that the 1.5 immigrant's performance in everyday life is an exhausting jumping between expectations that continually results in failure to be having an authentic identity.

The 1.5 immigrant is viewed, therefore, as an inauthentic performer by both the immigrant community and that of the adopted homeland. Just as the tourists judge whether or not the performers in local performances are authentic, the 1.5 immigrant does not conform to the expectations of authenticity for either community. A tourist would walk past a performance they deemed inauthentic, rendering it invisible; in the same way, the 1.5 immigrant is rendered invisible. To be seen as authentic, the 1.5 immigrant's unique perspective—their authentic self—must be negotiated with both groups. Paul Sun-Hyung Lee's comment that his Korean accent sounded more Russian would deem him inauthentic, a pretender as an immigrant. As we know, however, he is a 1.5 immigrant and performing authentically, though without an accent that Canadians and Korean Canadians would deem "authentic." Lee tells of his struggle as a comedic episode, but in fact, his hesitancy to use a Korean accent despite growing up in a household with strong, native Korean accents demonstrates the constantly shifting ground of performance for the 1.5 immigrant.

The exhaustion of performing inauthentically—as a tourist in two societies— opens up a societal schism between the immigrant community, the 1.5 immigrant community, and the adopted society. In Ins Choi's situation, he speaks of being viewed suspiciously when he went into theater instead of a more acceptable profession; his mother wanted him to follow in his father's footsteps and be a pastor (SIPO Foundation). While Canada views theater as a valid career path, the only accepted way of accomplishing that profession as he started his career was to be a bit player in the background. In terms of his career, he couldn't return to the world of Korean entertainment in his home country, yet he was not accepted in Canada. He could not authentically fit into either world.

Choi's characters experience the same issues with authenticity. Jung feels that he neither fits with the Korean family he came from nor the Canadian world he grew up in. The lone performer in *Subway Stations of the Cross* is similarly stuck in a performance that questions authenticity. The homeless man appears on the surface to have the characteristics of the homeless: raggedy, dirty appearance that seems to indicate a rough life. The performance, however, waivers between authenticity and performance. The homeless man speaks in wise poetry and song, outside of the expectation for the homeless, but if that same performance is viewed as a preacher or sage, the ragged clothes make it seem inauthentic. Accepting the homeless man as a sage straddles the same kind of gulf that Jung battles against in Kim's Convenience.

The theater, however, is a place where stories like Choi's can not only be told but validated by the community. In the case of both of his plays, the audience is not just at the theater to see the shows but to act as the priest of a ritual designed to give acceptance to the 1.5 immigrant. The story they see is a performance of the 1.5 immigrant, and if they accept the tale as authentic, the audience validates the experience of that identity.

Social dramas begin with a social schism, a problem that needs redressing (Turner, 1982). The 1.5 immigrant is the product of this schism, the child who is required to perform as the first generation with the weight of the decision to leave the homeland but who only remembers as the second generation where the requirements for authentic performance are vastly different. These requirements parallel Choi's own life. When he arrived in Toronto, he lived with his family above a convenience store; he uses his own memory of counting money in the store (Vue story), but then was a skater boy in high school (Leadlay, 2017). Jung works in the store with his father, but longs for the days when he was the football captain of his school. What we see in these two figures are people stretched between, not fitting into either group. This separation/breach begins the social drama.

In *Subway Stations of the Cross*, the costume and Choi's appearance represents the separation of the character from society. He wears layers of dirty clothing representing the slow, painful process of moving from functional citizen to person on the street. His costume is outside of the regular, ordered behavior expected from Canadian society, which Turner identifies as a breach with that society's norms (1985, p. 196). While the homeless man in *Subway* visibly doesn't fit with society's norms, societal expectations cause the breach in *Kim's Convenience*, since Jung neither has succeeded as a first or second-generation immigrant. These breaches cause the characters in these works to fall out of favor: the homeless man into invisible poverty,

Jung to a life of a mediocre job with no prospects. J. Lowell Lewis describes such performances as the alternatives to everyday life not usually considered by society, and when these performances result in negative consequences, they bring the usually hidden performances into view (2008: 43).

The 1.5 immigrant is caught in liminality, neither first-generation immigrant nor second generation, and because of the persistence of the performance, the idea that they are inauthentic or just passing through like tourists does not allow them to build an identity acceptable within societal norms. This situation causes a crisis for these individuals, resulting in lives like Jung's and the homeless man. As Jung confesses to Umma, "I don't like my life" (Choi, 76), and while his confession could just be the moaning of an underemployed Canadian, his story is wrapped up in the narratives he lives between. The homeless man from *Subway Stations of the Cross* lives outside of society yet with much to offer it. In each case the character is without a way to establish identity in their new nation, living in a state of crisis, traveling between the socially acceptable positions available to them because those performances do not match their authentic selves.

In social dramas, there is an attempt to redress the crisis, and these two plays offer a means for Jung and the homeless man to tell their stories. Most importantly, the plays are offered in a way that allows both Korean and Canadian audiences the chance to legitimize the stories on display and accept the performances. Both plays have a specific moment when the marginalized character has an opportunity to express their story and their experience, and in each case, the audience is given a chance to validate the story through their applause and acceptance. Jung talks through his situation with Appa, the first authentic communication between the two men since the young man ran away. Moved by his son's struggle, Appa gives him the store and watches as his son picks up a pricing gun to change the price of his cherished Korean energy drinks. Jung's crisis is redressed by reintegrating on his own terms into his family's store.

The homeless man of *Subway Stations of the Cross* also finds a moment of acceptance, though differently than Jung in *Kim's Convenience*. Without a name and invisible to society, his redress comes in the form of an evening where he gets to speak. As his humor and wisdom ebb and flow, the audience begins to recognize the value of the person in front of them, the marginalized 1.5 immigrant body that has something to offer society. Critic Glenn Sumi notes that the audience leaves the theater more aware of the busker or the artist on the street (2015), and while I argue that visibility extends to Choi's own experience as a 1.5 immigrant, that recognition of the homeless man's visibility is the redress of the play.

Choi was purposeful in the way he sought out both Korean and Canadian audiences for *Kim's Convenience*, the first play. He alerted Korean churches and community centers of *Kim's* premiere at the Toronto Fringe Festival, and the play's move to Soulpepper Theatre following the festival exposed it to a larger Canadian audience. In both cases, the audience was enraptured by Jung's story. Choi tells that on opening night he sat in silence as the lights descended on the show, wondering in the silence if anyone had enjoyed the play. The theater then erupted in applause, validating Choi's work just before the bows. Albert Schultz, the artistic director of Soulpepper Theatre, writes that the applause continued in its subsequent run in a way that made *Kim's Convenience* a "story about our family in our community" (Michel, 2012).

Reintegration is the final phase of the social drama, and here is where Choi's fame following the premiere of *Kim's Convenience* and *Subway Stations of the Cross* becomes important. *Kim's* was made into a hit television series, extending the story of Jung and making it available for a wider audience. *Subway Stations of the Cross* has played across Canada and the United States. As these plays garner fame and new fans, the stories continue to be legitimized, retold, and remembered by both Korean and Canadian societies, effectively reintegrating Ins Choi as a native son. No longer marginalized, Choi is praised across both societies.

CONCLUSION

Choi's plays serve as a ritual that serves as a way for the cultural memory of the 1.5 immigrant to be transmitted to a mixed audience, remixed within the ritual space, and a new identity retrieved at its finish. It is a way to discontinue straddling the world of Korea and the world of Canada and begin writing their own story which is stored in the collective memory of both societies. It establishes their aura and authenticity that separates them from first and second-generation social actors.

The theater is a place where stories are told to entertain, inform, challenge, and authenticate lives previously unseen. Ins Choi has found the sacred ability to use the theater as a ritual space where the audience can see the story of the 1.5 immigrant played out in real time, adding to their collective memory the stories of hundreds of other immigrants. While the crisis may need to be revisited in subsequent years as further stories need to be told, *Kim's Convenience* and *Subway Stations of the Cross* serve their purpose: to ritually legitimize the stories of Korean Canadian immigrants who came to Canada as children.

REFERENCES

Baccari, A. (2012). As store or play, Kim's convenience is Canonically Canadian. *The Toronoto Review of Books* (blog). Retrieved from https://www.torontoreviewofbooks.com/2012/02/as -store-or-play-kims-convenience-is-canonically-canadian/.

Banerji, A. (2019). The social drama of durga puja: Performing Bengali identity in the diaspora. *Ecumenica, 12*(1), 1–13. Retrieved June 15, 2020, from www.jstor.org/stable/10.5 325/ecumenica.12.1.0001

Bell, D. (2008). Kim's convenience co-creator on anglicization, role models, and comedy as a unifying force. *CBC News*. Retrieved from https://www.cbc.ca/news/canada/calgary/ins-ch oi-kims-convenience-1.4889951.

Benesch, S. (2008). Generation 1.5 and its discourses of partiality: A critical analysis. *Journal of Language, Identity, and Education, 7*(3–4), 294–311.

Bergson, H. (1996). *Of the Survival of Images: Memory and Mind*. Trans. Nancy Margaret Paul and W. Scott Palmer. New York: New York Books.

BWW News Desk. (2018). Pacific Theatre Presents Ins Choi's Kim's Convenience. *Broadway World Vancouver* (blog). Retrieved from https://www.broadwayworld.com/vancouver/artic le/Pacific-Theatre-Presents-Ins-Chois-KIMS-CONVENIENCE-20180731.

Canadian Life Changers. (2017). Ins Choi/CANADIAN LIFE CHANGERS PT. 1. 100 Huntley, posted May 10, 2017, YouTube video, 5:54, Retrieved from https://www.you tube.com/watch?v=Wj1CY5uFaF0.

Choi, I. (2012). *Kim's Convenience*. Toronto: House of Anansi.

Choi, I. (2014). Ins Choi's Subway Stations of the Cross. *Soul Pepper Blog* (blog). Retrieved from https://blog.soulpepper.ca/2014/04/10/ins-chois-subway-stations-of-the-cross/.

Choi, I. (2015). *Subway Stations of the Cross*. Toronto: House of Anansi.

Connerton, P. (1989). *How Societies Remember*. Cambridge University Press.

Dugnoille, J. (2016). Digitalising the Korean cosmos: Representing human–nonhuman continuity and filiality through digital photography in contemporary South Korea. *Visual Studies, 31*(4), 324–334.

Geertz, C. (1980). Blurred genres: The refiguration of social thought. *The American Scholar, 29*(2), 165–179.

Jennings, S. (2018). *Theatre, Ritual and Transformation: The Senoi Temiars*. Routledge.

Kim, B. S., Brenner, B. R., Liang, C. T., & Asay, P. A. (2003). A qualitative study of adaptation experiences of 1.5 generation Asian Americans. *Cultural diversity and Ethnic Minority Psychology, 9*(2), 156–170. doi:10.1037/1099-9809.9.2.156.

Knowles, R. (2009). Performing intercultural memory in the diasporic present: The case of Toronto. In *Signatures of the Past: Cultural Memory in Contemporary Anglophone North American Drama*, edited by Marc Maufort and Caroling de Wagter. New York: Peter Lang, pp. 16–40.

Leadlay, C. (2017). 15 Things You Didn't Know About Playwright Ins Choi. *The Hill Times*. Retrieved from https://www.hilltimes.com/2017/02/08/15-things-didnt-know-playwright -ins-choi/95352.

Lewis, J. L. (2008). Toward a unified theory of cultural performance: A reconstructive introduction to Victor Turner. *Victor Turner and contemporary Cultural Performance*, 41–58.

Li. (2018). "Kim's Convenience." *Mediaversity* (blog). Retrieved from https://www.mediaver sityreviews.com/tv-reviews/2017/10/29/kims-convenience.

Michel, J. P. (2012). How a Korean Prodigal Son Landed on Toronto's Stage. *Christianity Today* (blog). Retrieved from https://www.christianitytoday.com/thisisourcity/7thcity/ how-korean-prodigal-son-landed-on-torontos-stage.html?start=2.

Nichols, L. (2015). Fringe Review: Subway Stations of the Cross. *Edmonton Journal*. Retrieved from https://edmontonjournal.com/entertainment/festivals/fringe-review-subw ay-stations-of-the-cross.

Nicholson, H. (2009). Re-locating memory: Performance, reminiscence, and communities of diaspora. In *The Applied Theatre Reader*, edited by Tim Prentki and Sheila Preston. New York: Routledge, pp. 268–275.

Palmater, C. (2016). Ins Choi & Paul Sun-Hyung Lee on Kim's Convenience. *Q on CBC*, posted. YouTube video, 19:43, Retrieved from https://www.youtube.com/watch?v=hOg ygDO5YkE.

Park, K. (1999). "I really do feel I'm 1.5!": The construction of self and community by young Korean Americans. *Amerasia Journal, 25*(1), 139–163.

Roberts, D. (2017). Off-Broadway Review: "Kim's Convenience." *Onstage* (blog). Retrieved from https://www.onstageblog.com/reviews/2017/7/7/off-broadway-review-kims-conve nience.

Robins, M. (2014). Subway Stations of the Cross can be an Equal Opportunity Offender. *Vancouver Presents*. Retrieved from http://www.vancouverpresents.com/theatre/subway-st ations-cross-can-equal-opportunity-offender/.

Rumbaut, R., & Kenji, I. (1988). *The Adaptation of Southeast Asian Refugee Youth: A Com-parative Study*. Washington, DC: US Department of Health and Human Services, Family Support Administration, Office of Refugee Resettlement.

Schechner, R. (1973). Drama, script, theatre, and performance. *The Drama Review: TDR, 17*(3), 5–36.

Schechner, R. (2003). *Performance Theory*. Routledge,

Schultz, A. (2012). *Foreword to Kim's Convenience*, 3–5. Toronto: House of Anansi.

Shepherd, S., & Wallis, M. (2004). *Drama/theatre/performance*. Routledge.

SIPO Foundation (2016). Ins Choi – SIPO foundation Conference 2013. SIPO foundation, posted YouTube video, 13:43, Retrieved from https://www.youtube.com/watch?v=KV1 GNzB29Fw.

Sumi, F. (2015). Review: Subway Stations of the Cross. *Now* (blog). Retrieved from https:// nowtoronto.com/stage/theatre/review-subway-stations-of-the-cross/.

Turner, V. W. (1982). *From Ritual to Theatre: The Human Seriousness of Play*. New York: Paj Publications.

Turner, V. (1979). Frame, flow and reflection: Ritual and drama as public liminality. *Japanese Journal of Religious Studies*, 465–499.

Turner, V. (1980). Social dramas and stories about them. *Critical Inquiry, 7*(1), 141–168.

Van Gennep, A. (2013). *The Rites of Passage*. Routledge.

Wang, N. (1999). Rethinking authenticity in tourism experience. *Annals of Tourism Research, 26*(2), 349–370.

Wang, Y. (2007). Customized authenticity begins at home. *Annals of Tourism Research, 34*(3), 789–804.

Zhu, Y. (2012). Performing heritage: Rethinking authenticity in tourism. *Annals of Tourism Research, 39*(3), 1495–1513.

II

FAMILY AND GENDER

5

Bridging Loves

How Korean American Mothers and Daughters Trouble—"Tradition and Modernity" through Love

Su C. Choe

INTRODUCTION

As a woman of twenty-nine years old, I have been sternly told that I have one more year left of being single. "Make sure you don't turn over thirty unmarried." "I had you and your sister when I was your age." "Your child is going to be weak if you are pregnant over thirty." "Among my friends, I am the only one who is not a grand-mother yet." These are tiresome lines that I repeatedly hear every time I try to have a good dinner conversation with my mom. Thankfully, I don't lose my appetite easily since I am so well-trained in listening to what she's saying from one ear and dispos-ing it through the other one. But still, I am anxious because she makes me anxious.

Seemingly, love was a negligible factor in my mom's decision about marriage. Her husband was chosen by her parents, and the timing was just right. She was a young and beautiful college graduate, and he was the perfect match for her: his job, family background, and the fortunate age gap based on a Korean superstition that a four-year age difference between spouses is the best. They married three months after they had first met. When I was younger, I asked my mom if she loved my dad so much that she decided to marry him soon. She said she did not have enough time to know and love him since they had met only a handful of times before marriage: "it was like that back then." However, it is not like that now. I will not marry someone whom I do not love, and I cannot marry just because I am getting older.

One time, I told my mom that *bihon* ("not married" based on the notion that marriage is a choice) is a current social phenomenon in Korea today. Many young people in Korea, predominantly Korean women in my age group, shun marriage in favor of career and single life and due to the economic burden and the unequal division of labor in marriage. I tried to convince my mom that my life with marriage

79

could be more difficult if I am not mentally, emotionally, and, most importantly, financially prepared. However, my shrewd mom instantly made me speechless. She replied: "You are not in Korea."

This chapter explores mother and daughter generations of Korean American women and their stories regarding love and marriage. However, this study is neither a cross-generational study between "traditional" and "modern" nor a comparison of Korean culture and American culture. Rather, the study focuses on how these two generations of Korean American women negotiate traditional values and new concepts of love and marriage in the context of modernization, immigration, and transnationalism and how their love narratives in these specific social and cultural circumstances appear to challenge the tradition and modernity dichotomy. I argue that under the processes of modernization and immigration, both generations of Korean American women nostalgize the past and traditions and characterize and enact what it means to be modern subjects in their own senses. This cross-generational study does not anticipate the transformation from the traditional values to the modern ideals but suggests the flexible interaction between tradition and modernity in the discourse of Korean American women's love.

Modern Love

A theoretical framework that is relevant to this research is Anthony Giddens' investigation on the self and intimate relationships in the course of modernity. Giddens (1991) asserts that modernity changes our social life and personal experience (p. 1), and the mechanisms of self-identity are shaped by, yet also shape, the institutions of modernity (p. 2). According to Giddens, modernity is a post-traditional order, which facilitates the transformation of time and space and propels social life away from pre-established practices. Thus, modernity fosters reflexivity: "modernity's reflexivity refers to the susceptibility of most aspects of social activity, and material relations with nature, to chronic revision in the light of new information or knowledge" (p. 20). In this context, the self becomes a reflexive project (p. 32); moreover, the body becomes part of the reflexivity of modernity. The self becomes responsible for the design of his or her own body (p. 102), attributing subjectivity to the self.

Giddens also argues that modernity and self-reflexivity lead to the "transformation of intimacy," producing the "pure relationship" (p. 6). The pure relationship, a relationship of sexual and emotional equality, exists merely for the value of trust and mutual disclosure and commitment, thus may release one from kinship, social duty, or traditional obligation (Giddens, 1991, 1992). Thus, romantic love, the model of modern kinship shaped by pure relationship, is a narrative of modernity and a product of modern transformations. Furthermore, romantic love is essentially feminized love (Giddens, 1992, p. 40). Romantic love, together with other social changes, is deeply involved with momentous transitions affecting marriage as well as other contexts of personal life (p. 44). Romantic love presumes some degree of self-interrogation; questioning "how I feel about the relationship" subsequently places a woman in an active role. Thus, she actively produces love (p. 46). Romantic love also affects the changing relationship between parents and children. In modern society, emotional warmth between parents and children is considered to be significant, and the center of the family moved from patriarchal authority to maternal affection (p. 42).

To sum up, Giddens suggests that modernity creates the modern self and modern love based on individuals' freedom and gender equality. This is so in a general way, but in order to understand what drives modernity, the self, and love, we must look at the development of modern institutions led by different scales of social, cultural, and economic changes in different places and time. The global forces and social changes in different places shape people's perceptions of the self, which eventually change the local meanings of love and intimacy. Industrialization places increased demands on the workforce for both men and women, and the spread of global capitalism facilitates people's practices in material consumption. Such processes of modernization and globalization change people's lifestyle and family structures and subsequently shift the values and expectations of love. Furthermore, modernizing forces such as increased demand in the workforce, access to education, economic opportunities and material consumptive practices of global capitalism have allowed women to be aware of their own subjectivities. In this case, women become reflexive selves by articulating and reconciling their desire to be good modern subjects in the middle of their everyday experiences and global influences. One of the desires women express is their aspiration for intimacy and agency in love relationships.

Using this theoretical framework, this chapter aims to understand how social changes affect women's meanings of love, or more precisely, how processes of modernization and immigration shape Korean American women's experiences in love and expectations of marriage cross-generationally and how the complexity between traditional values and modern ideals of intimacy travels between two generations. I explore the stories of first-generation and 1.5 generation Korean American women in Duluth, Georgia to analyze how their different sociocultural experiences before and within immigration construct the women's understandings of love, marriage, and most importantly, the creation of the self and family and the systems of gender and sexuality in the failed dichotomy between tradition and modernity. Their generational differences shaped by different social and cultural contexts do not always conform to our expectation that the mothers are traditional, and the daughters are more modern. The mothers can be seen as modern subjects who experienced shifting gender roles in the context of Korea's modernization; in the context of immigration, they are still challenging traditional roles on behalf of their cosmopolitan daughters. Meanwhile, the daughters' experiences as cultural in-betweeners and with immigrant parents make them fit models of the modern individual less well than might be expected; rather, they are more family oriented. Circumstances that are distinctive to immigrant families strengthen the daughters' willingness to take on traditional familial obligations.

Methods

For this research, I recruited three pairs of Korean American mothers and daughters in the Korean community in Duluth, Georgia: first-generation Korean

American mothers and 1.5 generation Korean American daughters. The first-generation Korean Americans are defined as immigrants who emigrated from South Korea to the United States of their own free will, without following their parents, and the 1.5 generation Korean American refers to those Korean immigrants who had to immigrate to the United States together with their parents because they were minors. In this research, the qualified informants are the first-generation Korean American mothers who married in the 1980s in Korea, whose marriages were arranged by matchmaking, and immigrated to the United States in the early 2000s with their husbands and children. The informants of the 1.5 generation Korean American daughters are younger Korean women who were born in the 1980s and the 1990s in Korea and moved to the United States with their parents in their teenage years, so they were educated in both Korea and the United States and familiar with both cultures. The daughter informants, single Korean women in their late twenties and early thirties, have experiences in romantic relationships and expect their marriages to be based on their own decisions to choose their husbands.

Nearly half of the Korean American population in Georgia resides around the Korean community in Duluth; according to the U.S. Census Bureau's 2014 American Community Survey, 22,001 of the 52,431 Korean Americans that call Georgia home are living in Gwinnett County (including the city of Duluth) (Yeonams, 2016). The qualified informants in this study are categorized explicitly as mother and daughter pairs and the first- and the 1.5 generation Korean American women of specific age groups with similar lengths of immigrant experiences. Therefore, I conducted respondent-driven sampling to avoid randomly selecting informants and to meet the criteria from a large number of people.

One strict qualification I intended for the mother informants was their practice of arranged marriage. Korea's modern arranged marriage appointed by matchmakers was not only common but also encouraged for young Koreans during the 1980s, but then it became less influential as romantic relationships and love marriage without the formal interventions of parents and matchmakers have become the norm in contemporary Korea. Juxtaposing the mothers' experience in an arranged marriage with the daughters' expectation for love marriage enabled me to observe how the core feelings in marriage are produced and changed between the two generations. I expected examining the two generations' distinct types of marriage could provide a conventional generational study between traditional and modern. However, this would later be challenged by my findings and argument for the failed dichotomy in the case of Korean American women specificity.

This chapter is based upon qualitative ethnographic research, which requires in-depth interviews of the informants. The strict qualifications of the informants resulted in small sample size, three mothers and three daughters. The sample size used in qualitative research is often small, and its methods work to gather an in-depth understanding of a phenomenon and focus on meaning, "which are often centered on the how and why of a particular issue, process, situation, subculture, scene or set of social interactions" (Dworkin, 2012, p. 1319). Because this chapter is an abridged version of my thesis, the chapter may not include ethnographic accounts such as participant observations, informal conversations, and field notes. However, I note that this research was conducted ethnographically, the researcher worked as a participant-observer in this particular Korean American community in many years and attained comprehensive understanding while conducting different field studies of these two generations separately. The interviews were semi-structured with open-ended questions, which allowed the informants to focus on the detailed accounts of their life and experiences in dating and marriage. The questions helped to examine how various social changes and practices before and during immigration on both generations have shaped their expectations of love and marriage differently and similarly. Furthermore, it illuminated their changing and unchanging values about the self and the family.

The Mothers: Korean Women of 7080 *sede*

"Only *nalnari* were dating. Like players. Ordinary students were not interested in it."

Mrs. Kim said that dating was inappropriate to young Koreans back then. In fact, all of my other mother informants would have agreed with her. Mrs. Park shared her memories from high school:

> Some students were dating just like you guys today. I knew few from my neighborhood. But they were different. They were *noneunehdeul*. You know, those students who altered their school uniform skirts short and put makeups on. They liked hanging out with boys, sitting back in the boys' motorbikes. (Mrs. Park)

Mrs. Lee had the same impression about dating when she shared the story about her housekeeper when she was in high school. Mrs. Lee was from a rich family, and her family hired two female housekeepers who were only two or three years older than her. Mrs. Lee remembered one of the housekeepers as *ggajida*, who smoked cigarettes secretly every day in the back of the kitchen and ended up quitting the job when she got pregnant by her boyfriend.

Nalnari, noneunehdeul, and *ggajida*are different words but used in the same context: when describing someone who tends not to behave by instructed ways, often with the implication of one's impurity. All of my mother informants are *7080 sede* (generation), referring to Koreans who lived their eventful twenties and thirties amidst Korea's growing urbanization, industrialization, and democratization in the 1970s and 1980s. According to the mothers, dating between a man and a woman in this period was not common. They considered dating as a social taboo and described people who were dating as disobeyers. Much of this perception relates to how Korea's traditional notion of gender has been disciplined and practiced since the Confucian transformation of Korea.

The spread of Confucianism in the Joseon Dynasty (1392–1897) Korea strengthened a patriarchal-based society that considered men to be stronger position in society and the family. The rigid Confucian gender roles restricted men's sphere to matters outside of the house, and conversely, women to internal family matters

(Han, 2004, p. 115). The Confucian moral of ideal women represented that a "virtuous woman" should preserve her chastity before marriage, be a good daughter-in-law and a wife, and obey only one husband (p. 117). Moreover, the stringent sex segregation during the Joseon Dynasty attempted to embed the notion of chastity on women's bodies (p. 115) and separate women from men's sphere, which indicated the restriction on Korean women's lifestyles and the oppression of their sexuality under the Confucian influences.

Institutionalized sex segregation in Korea was implemented in the school system. Under the Confucian ideology, education was only for men, while women belonged in the home, where they were taught and "educated" to be virtuous wives and mothers: "Reading and learning are the domains for men. For a woman it is enough if she knows the Confucian virtues of diligence, frugality, and chastity. If a woman disobeys these virtues, she will bring disgrace to the family" (Kim, 1976, p. 154). During colonial modernity in Korea (1910–1945), educational institutions were established for Korean women by western missionaries; however, still, male and female students were strictly segregated. In 1984, Banpo high school in Seoul initiated Korea's first public co-education, and many single-sex schools have transformed into co-educational schools since the co-education policy under Kim DaeJoong administration (1998–2003) for gender equality in education. In this administration, the Presidential Commission was upgraded to the Ministry of Gender Equality, and the primary goal of the Ministry was to build a democratic nation based on gender equality and the concept of gender mainstreaming for women's competency development and women's social participation in international society (Kang et al., 2017, p. 87).

The mother informants attended high school in the late 1970s, and all of them went to women's schools. Although they did not have many chances to hang out with male students, it did not mean that they never had male friends. The young students of *7080 sede* Korea still found their ways to meet each other.

Meeting (a pseudo-English Korean word; a group blind date) in the 1970s and the 1980s Korea is probably young Koreans' claiming themselves as modern subjects. *Meeting* was an initial stage for the young Koreans' forming intimate relationships between men and women. The young Koreans in this period enjoyed the modern culture. They met at a *dabang* (a coffee house with a disc jockey), had cups of coffee, and listened to the Beatles' songs. Then, they went to the cinema to watch a movie and had dinner at a *gyeongyangsik jib* (a light-western food restaurant), rolling spaghetti using forks and spoons. The rise of consumer society since the 1980s in Korea provided a new vision of subjectivity that was transformed by Korea's economic success and young Koreans related experiences of a global culture united by capitalism (Cho, 2002, p. 168). This modern era's idealization of modern and urban cultural models allowed *7080 sede*'s new lifestyles and practices in intimacy. Challenging the old notions of gender relationship and the practice of sex segregation, the young Koreans found *meeting* as a path to express their desires for love and intimacy, ultimately, their modern subjectivity.

However, in the discussion of the desires for love and subjectivity, the young Korean women performed passive roles in their intimate relationships. Mrs. Kim also shared her story with the boy she met at the church when she was in college. She admitted that she had few dates with this boy. However, when I asked her whether he was her boyfriend, she said, "We were just friends, but special." Mrs. Kim noted that she never introduced him to anyone as her boyfriend because she was afraid of people might misunderstand her:

> Korean culture and society were very harsh to women. If a woman was dating one man and another, people easily assumed that she was cheap and not pure. So, it was better not to have a boyfriend unless she was going to marry him. But for men, it was okay. (Mrs. Kim)

The preconceptions about the traditional concept of gender and sexuality were embedded in Korean women of *7080 sede*. When discussing women's subjectivity in romantic relationships and agency in dating, the mother informants denied that they were proactive in participating in *meeting* and hesitated to profess that they actually had boyfriends before marriage. Because what the mothers had seen and taught from their families and society was to be chaste, passive women and subordinate wives, the mothers internalized and condoned the traditional norms about gender. In the early stage of modernization in Korea in the 1970s and 1980s, the traditional gender relationship was still relevant. Despite young Koreans' attempts to discover their desires for love and intimacy during the 1970s and the 1980s with the culture of modernization, Korean women's journey to the realization of the self and the agency in love was slower than Korean men's.

Korea's rapid industrialization and modernization since the 1960s led to a critical shift on women in Korean society in the areas of culture, education, movements, and law and politics, as well as in the realm of daily lives including socioeconomic participation, the family, and sexual relations. Many women became better educated and were more able to participate in socioeconomic activities due to modernization. However, due to continued gender discrimination, most women continued to suffer from inequality in the workplace, in the family, and in their sexual relations. Although women's participation in economic activities increased dramatically during this modernization period, the employment structure for women remained underdeveloped in many aspects. By occupation, men heavily dominated well-paying, senior-level public administration and professional management. On the other hand, women performed mainly auxiliary duties in these occupations and were mostly confined to "women's work," such as textile-making, sewing, electronics assembly, and food processing (Shim, 2002).

Under Korea's patriarchal social system, marital ideology was reinforced by the prevalence of gender-related division of work. Upon marriage, a majority of men and women naturally formed nuclear families, and women assumed responsibility for housekeeping and child-rearing. In other words, the separation of public and private realms and the division of work by gender became institutionalized. Despite Korean women's growing participation in economic activities, this division of labor by gender was indispensable upon marriage. Married men continued to spend time outside the family as Korean society and employers expected men to toil arduously in the course of industrialization and modernization, while married women were obliged to take exclusive charge of family affairs like housekeeping, child-rearing, and maintaining relations with their parents-in-law.

All of my mother informants were very conventional examples of the women of *7080 sede*. They were educated college graduates. Mrs. Park was a nurse. She studied nursing in college and worked as a nurse for seven years until she was married. I asked her if she had ever wanted to pursue her career, and she said, "It was impossible because I would have children after marriage. And children need mothers all the time. As a nurse, I took care of patients, and as a mother, I took care of my children. So basically, I did the same job."

Joongmeh Gyulhon (**arranged marriage**): **Marry Before Love**

Rapid industrialization and modernization in Korea in the 1960s and the emergence of a prosperous consumer culture in the 1980s marked transformations in Korean society. Many young Koreans moved to the urban areas, and both Korean men and women increasingly participated in work forces and higher education. The modern notions of individualism and the new forms of love marriage appeared in this period.

Kendall (1996), in her ethnographic accounts with young urban Korean men and women in Seoul in the 1980s, explores modern courtship and marriage in the changing circumstances of gender relations during the twentieth-century capitalism in Korea. One of the phenomena Kendall observed is the rise of arranged meetings and love marriage. During this period, many young intellectuals advocated marriage by personal choice and mutual understanding in the name of individualism and free will, but the "personal choice" was perceived differently by men and women. Korean young men's personal choice reflected their choosing of own wives, rather than arranged by their parents, and they preferred beautiful and educated women whom they believed to be "beloved wives" and "wise mothers" (p. 101). For Korean young women, their personal choice entailed being chosen by "good groom material" (p. 111). To achieve the demand for "rational" marriage (p. 89), the market for arranged meetings, *masson*, hiked during this time, and the goal of this market and matchmaking practices was to bring "love marriage." This new ideal of love marriage in modern Korea, however, was still embedded within the patriarchal standards of gender.

> From time to time, my mom brought me the dates and locations for *masson*. Mostly, it happened in hotel cafes in Seoul. On the *masson* days, I dressed up really nicely and visited a salon in the morning. I just needed to say it was for a *masson* day to a hairdresser, and she took care of me. At the meetings, I remember I was just sitting there quietly and listened to what men were saying. I never had any thoughts about those men. I did not do anything. I guess the follow up meetings were made between parents. Esther's father was the only one who asked me for the second date. After three months, we were engaged, and then another three months after, we married. (Mrs. Lee)

Similar *masson* stories were shared by two other mother informants, Mrs. Kim and Mrs. Park. However, unlike Mrs. Lee, they only had one *masson* that led to their marriage.

In Korea, *masson*, the arranged meeting, aims to blend "traditional wisdom (marriage is too important to be left to the young) and progressive ideals (marriage should be a matter of individual choice made on the basis of mutual attraction) (Kendall, 1996, p. 89). Based on the mother informants' personal experiences, *masson* was an essential step to achieve marriage, and the mutual attraction was secondary to this achievement. The mutual attraction between the candidates was supposed since their match was rational and carefully scrutinized and approved by their parents' lived experience and wisdom. Rational marriage in Korea's traditional arranged marriage and modern *masson* marriage shared commonalities. Their rationality was based on the interest of two families' unification and a husband's economic and social stability (a successful husband) and a wife's beauty and domestic ability to serve in both families (a beloved wife and a wise mother).

In the discussion of love, the mothers tended to place more emphasis on the love of family than the love between men and women, and their definition of love was based on respect and responsibility as parents rather than romantic and passionate attraction between men and women. The mothers' experience in love heavily relied on the institution of marriage and was tied to duty and obligation as wives and mothers. For the Korean women of *7080 sede*, love came after marriage.

The Daughters: *1.5-se* Korean American Women

> *Su:* What do you think love is?
> *Grace:* I knew you were going to ask that! Can I skip this question? (laugh) hmm . . . it's hard.
> *Su:* The question is?
> *Grace:* No, love is.

Grace moved to the United States when she was thirteen with her family. "When we were coming here, my parents never told me that we were actually immigrating. I thought we were just traveling. I never got to say good-bye to my friends in Korea." She went to middle school and high school in Duluth, Georgia. After graduating high school, she went to Manhattan to study fine art. However, after two years, she had to come back to Georgia because of financial and legal status issues. After a few years of working in the local area, she now attends an art school based in Atlanta and is living with her parents.

At my second interview with Grace, she finally revealed her love stories. I asked how her love life was going, and she said, "still recovering from a recent breakup." Grace continued sharing her very recent experience in *sogeting* (a combined Korean word *soge* (introduction) and *ting* derived from the English word *meeting*; a one-on-one blind date set up by friends) in the previous week:

> I am not a big fan of *sogeting* because it is artificial . . . I met him last week. I have seen him only one time, but he seems nice and calm, and he is also funny. He seems like he

can understand my craziness (laugh). But he is not so attractive. He is not bad-looking, but his looks are not my type. See, this is what I was saying before. I like his personality, and he has U.S. citizenship! He has things I need, but not what I want. (Grace)

Today's modern and cosmopolitan young women are the actors in their love relationships and seek for self-realization through love (Hirsh, 2007; Faier, 2007; and Rofel, 2007). Unlike the women of older generations, who internalized and were restricted to the old notions of gender and sexual morality, the women of younger generations under the institutions of modernity challenge pre-established practices and orders (Giddens, 1991, p. 2), and the constant interrogation of "how I feel about the relationship" subsequently places the woman in active roles in intimate relationships (Giddens, 1992, p. 46).

The daughter informants are *1.5-se*. They moved to the United States in their teenage years and attended middle school and high school in Gwinnett and Fulton counties, where the most Korean immigrant families reside. All of my daughter informants shared their cultural shock when they first came to the United States. Interestingly, they all mentioned the teacher and student relationship. To them, how American students expressed their thoughts and opinion to teachers was quite new because it was very different from how they were taught in school back in Korea. "Good students were those who listened to teachers and waited for break time to use a bathroom," said Esther. Moving from the culture where passivity is respected to one where expressiveness is valued, the daughters are stuck in-between these two distinct cultures.

The bicultural identity of the *1.5-se* daughters allows them to travel between Korean and American cultures freely, while assimilating to neither culture. The daughters recognize cultural differences between Koreans in Korea and Koreans in the United States, differentiating them from typical Koreans from Korea. According to Grace, she is more "open" and understanding to racial, cultural, and sexual diversity issues than typical Koreans are. While being able to integrate culturally and participate socially in American society with language proficiency, education, and a secure job, Esther is not interested in becoming American. Esther said she is proud of her ethnicity and cultural identity and comfortable with her social circle around Korean immigrant communities. Instead of staying in one or moving on to the other, the *1.5-se* daughters have formed and lived with this in-between character as their unique generational identity.

YeonehGyulhon (Love Marriage): Marry Whom I Love

In the course of the interview, the daughter informants emphasized that they were "not really Koreans and not Americans" on the topic of ethnic identity, and this identification became more comprehensible when they shared their experiences in intimacy and discussed expectations for marriage. The daughters' experiences in intimate and love relationship directly reflected the *1.5-se* identity in the United States. The particular social change called immigration has placed immigrant children in dual cultural context. In the private sphere like home, the *1.5-se* preserved the traditional cultural values by maintaining the traditional familial structure and custom and the continuous communication with their parents. In the public sphere, school and workplace, the *1.5-se* learned and adapted new cultural values and became cultural mediators between the two cultures. Due to this distinct and unique identity as "in-betweener," the *1.5-se* daughter informants expressed their preference for 1.5-*se* Korean men yet claimed that it is more challenging tofind the right person to marry because of the limited numbers of *1.5-se* Korean men in the community.

Among my daughter informants, Sarah is the only one who is in a relationship. She met her boyfriend from the church community, who is a *1.5-se* like her. Grace and Esther are single and in their early thirties. In the discussion of love and marriage, Esther stressed her delayed marriage as she was reaching mid-thirties, while Grace was more concerned about not finding a man with U.S. citizenship. Grace was a DACA (Deferred Action for Childhood Arrivals) recipient under the Obama administration. Although Grace refused to talk more about her and her family's current legal status in the United States, she expressed her concern regarding the Trump administration's rigid deportation policy for undocumented immigrants and mentioned, "The safest and the fastest way is to marry a U.S. citizen."

The daughter informants' expectations for love and marriage were much complicated and entangled with both idealistic desires and realistic matters. Ideally, the daughters prioritize love. They seek for someone whom they can love and who can love them. The mutual attraction is significant in initiating their intimate relationships. At first, mutual attraction is sparked between men and women for their attractive physical appearances, then it is maintained through mutual conversation and shared interests. However, realistic matters interrupt. The matters of anticipated age for marriage and legal status for the *1.5-se* daughters make love less powerful, and marriage becomes a more practical, survival issue for aging *1.5-se* daughters in the United States. Thus, they are caught in the dynamics of modern subjectivity, traditional gender values in marriage, and secure status in the United States.

ChinguGateun (Friend-like) Mothers and Daughters

Giddens (1992) argues that the power of romantic love gives women rights in the family, and the nuclear family centered on the "invention of motherhood" becomes an ideal. Patriarchal power in the domestic milieu becomes weakened with the division of labor in the modern family structure, and women's control over child-rearing grows as families become smaller and as children are in need of long-term emotional training (Giddens, 1992, p. 42). With the division of spheres in the family, the separation of the home and the workplace, the fostering of love becomes predominantly the task of women. Although this idea about romantic love indicates women's confinement to home and relative separation from the outside world, the development of such idea, conversely, expresses women's power at home, allowing motherhood as a new domain of intimacy (p. 43). Using Giddens' idea about romantic love and the invention of motherhood in the modern family structure, I argue that Korea's modern matrifocal family identity shapes an intimate relationship between mothers and children as the mothers' control over domestic responsibilities and emotional support for their children become stronger. Here, I am developing Giddens' invention of motherhood in the context of transnationalism and immigration. The experiences of immigration change the division of labor not only between husbands and wives but also between parents and children.

When I asked my daughter informants about their relationships with their mothers, they emphasized they were "very close" and "*chingugateun.*" The daughters often planned ladies' days out with their mothers, and the mothers said that with their daughters, they could enjoy things that they had never experienced themselves as young girls. Sarah, Mrs. Park's daughter said:

> Sometimes I feel sympathy for my mom. She likes to enjoy good things too. But most immigrant mothers are busy with life and just do not know what and how to enjoy. They are restricted to many opportunities because of the language mostly. So, I think it's my job to have her experience more. Like taking her to musicals and foreign cuisines. Without me, she can never leave the Korean town in Duluth.

It was not only the daughters who felt sympathy for their mothers, but the mothers also expressed deep caring for their daughters. Mrs. Kim, the mother of two daughters and two sons, cared for her daughters more than her sons: "To be honest, men are better off in any society. That's why I never took deep care of my sons. But for my daughters, because I have been experienced that [inequality], I poured more attention to my daughters and wanted them to be different from me." Besides, Mrs. Lee said she was still sorry to Esther for not being able to help her when she was in high school: "Like us, the language was a big challenge for Esther too. Even though I knew she was struggling with her school work, all I could do was to tell her to do her best."

The shifting gender roles brought by the change in family structure have created an emotional relationship between mothers and children, and the experiences of immigrant mothers and children have shaped the relationship to be even more affectionate. From my informants' accounts, social and cultural changes upon immigration have shifted immigrant parents' and children's roles in the family. In Korea's traditional family structure, patriarchal authority caused the parent and child relationship to be highly hierarchical. Under this family model, a father was the ultimate decision-maker and was expected to exhibit dominance and guidance towards his children in return for filial piety, respect and obedience. In the modern nuclear family structure, both father and mother now share a disciplinary power over their children, but the hierarchical relationship between parents and children still perpetuates (Evason, 2016). In the shifting familial roles of immigrant families, the parents are no longer in the position where they teach and supervise their children. The children, who are more adapted to the new culture and language, take adult roles and responsibilities in the family, for instance, completing and translating family paperwork and bills, and they feel more obligated to care for their parents who are less privileged in social and cultural integration in the event of immigration. The experiences of immigration change the parent and child relationship, and the hierarchy that existed between them becomes less visible. Thus, immigrant parents and children tend to become more *chingugateun*.

Yeoneh (Romantic Love) and *Gyulhon* (Marriage)

Cho (2002) examines the surveillance of Korean mothers over daughters in con-fronting the patriarchal standards of gender during the modernization era in Korea. Cho's daughter informants are at the same generation of my mother informants. Cho defines this daughter generation (my mother generation) as the generation caught between her mother's desire and her own self-realization and argues that this generation has adapted to the existing patriarchal system rather than resisting it, as their mothers' teaching of self-realization never attempted to challenge but to affirm the existing patriarchal norms of gender roles (p. 181).

From this interpretation, we may analyze that there exists an ongoing attempt for inculcation of values and ideals from mothers to daughters. In the mother and daughter relationship between Mrs. Park and Sarah, I have examined that Mrs. Park continuously attempts to instill her desire and expectation for dating and marriage to Sarah. Mrs. Park does not like Sarah's boyfriend and hopes Sarah to find a more suitable and faithful partner who can help to achieve Mrs. Park's dream for Sarah: to become a missionary. However, Sarah, who self-realized her subjectivity through her actual experience in *yeoneh*, does not give up her ideal love and marriage for her mother's desire. When the *chingugateun* mother and daughter relationship erases the hierarchy between mothers and daughters, the mothers' words are less of absolute truth, and both mothers and daughters are inclined to share and express their ideas and feelings. Mrs. Lee emphasized chastity must be retained before marriage and added that too many *yeoneh* experiences are not appropriate to women. However, Mrs. Lee also said she did not stress her thoughts to her daughter, Esther, saying "I don't think she will listen to me."

In today's modern and cosmopolitan world, conservative views on love and sex seem less appealing. Although the mother informants still are aligned with the Confucian-based traditional gender roles and morality, they do not express and inculcate their ideals, or they know that these ideals are less influential to their daughters because they know that the traditional ideals are less desirable in today's society. While *yeoneh* enables the daughters to transcend the "traditional culture" and to assert a new self and desire, the daughters' *yeoneh* helps the mothers to acknowledge "desiring subjects" embedded in their daughters, the individuals who operate through sexual, material, and affective self-interests (Rofel, 2007, p. 3). The experiences of the daughters' *yeoneh* allows self-realization for both generations in the ways in which the daughters express their desire and agency through romantic relationship, and the mothers acknowledge their daughters' modern forms of the self through romantic love.

Furthermore, the *chingugateun* relationship between mothers and daughters makes their positions shift. In the immigrant family structure, not only the hierarchy between parents and children becomes invisible as parent and child roles change, but also this changing power dynamics grant the children more power since the children are benefited from higher levels of cultural and social integration in immigration. Thus, in the discussion of *yeoneh* between Korean American mothers and daughters, the recognition of the mothers' undesirable traditional values and the daughters' desirable modern ideals emerges due to the shifted power dynamics in the *chinguga-teun* mother and daughter relationship.

Although the mothers were educated professionals before marriage, their socio-economic statuses were changed upon marriage based on those of their husbands. After marriage and before immigration, all my mother informants were full-time housewives. The families relied solely on their husbands' income, and the primary role of the mothers was the housekeeping jobs including assisting the husbands and nurturing children. In the discussion of the daughters' marriage expectations, the mothers expressed concern that marriage would be an obstacle for the continuation of the daughters' career. They hoped their daughters to marry good men but said marriage would change women's life. To the mothers, marriage comes with practical issues like reproducing children and managing their own and in-law's family, and these familial duties are solely on women's shoulder. Because the mothers' marriage was based on a distinct division of labor—husbands in the workplace and wives in the house—they do not expect women's concomitant fulfilment of work and family roles.

The mothers of *7080 sede* experienced change in their socioeconomic statuses with immigration. With immigration, the mothers again experienced change in their socioeconomic statuses by becoming ethnic minorities and working-class immigrants in the United States, but their decreased statuses offered the mothers new opportunities to enter the workforce and provide substantial economic contributions to their families. Interestingly, the downgraded immigrant families' socioeconomic statuses upon immigration result in immigrant mothers' upward status, granting the mothers economic power. The mothers believed America is the land of opportunity and freedom, which provides new vision for women. From their experiences and their daughters' integration in American society, the mothers find that women's roles are not restricted to home and that women can also be self-sufficient. Thus, the mothers are proud of their daughters being active members in society and discover the daughters' possibility for social mobility without depending on men. The daughter's self-sufficiency becomes the mothers' new desire. The mothers instill this desire to their daughters, hoping the daughters do not give up their potency with the entrance to marriage. To the mothers, marriage is a private sphere that perpetuates gender inequality, where wives' sacrifice follows.

However, the daughters' expectation for marriage is fairly different from their mothers' experience in marriage. *Yeoneh* (romantic love) produces the ideal of "pure relationship" between men and women (Giddens, 1991, p. 6; Giddens, 1992, p. 2), and women's increased social and economic participation has shifted marriage expectation from economic security to emotional fulfillment (Hirsch and Wardlow, 2006, p. 8; Padilla et al., 2007, p. 101). The daughters believe that husbands and wives take equal contribution and responsibility at home and work. Men can be stay-home dads, and women are working moms, in which these roles depend on the individuals' ability and inclination. Therefore, the gendered division of labor and the patriarchal system are inconspicuous in the marriage institution of the daughter generation. For the daughters, marriage is the domain for individuals' psychological and emotional stability, rather than the reproduction of structural inequality of gender. As the beneficiaries of *yeoneh*, the daughters believe marriage built on love and mutual attraction is an ideal image of marriage. However, the daughters' experiences of immigration cause the traditional familial obligation of filial piety grows stronger. Although modern intimacy declares "pure relationship" between men and women and modern marriage stresses a union of two individuals, when it comes to the experiences of immigrant families, the daughters' ideal relationship for marriage becomes less "pure" and less individual. Knowing their mothers' loneliness and sacrifice in keeping the families in the midst of immigration, the daughters find one way to reciprocate their mothers' love and support is by committing filial obligations, marrying men whom their mothers would like and taking care of their aging mothers.

CONCLUSIONS

Korean American women's experiences of love and marriage reveal how they organize social life and intimate relationship and how they create family and selfhood. The women's experiences of love and marriage differ cross-generationally and shift amidst various social changes. For Korean American mothers and daughters, the differences in meanings and values of love and marriage are evident, and their differences illuminate the women's distinct sociocultural experiences with the processes of modernization and immigration. Their different generational experiences of love and marriage under different forces and phases of social changes define who they are. Moreover, bridging these differences reflects how certain social changes affect the meaning of love and marriage and transform the self and the family cross-generationally. This cross-generational study not only displays the generations' different values of love but bridges the differences, so that it can provide deeper understandings between mothers and daughters.

We look at the experiences of older and younger generations and their negotiating traditional values and modern ideals of love and marriage. However, the shift from traditional to modern in this study does not attempt to illustrate the mothers' traditional values as something "old" and "worn" that needs to be replaced by the daughters' modern, "new" or "better" ideals. It is valid to say that modernity is a tool for particular kinds of self-realization and associated with claiming women's subjectivity, but it may be wrong to presume that tradition restrains, and modernity liberates women's subjectivity entirely. This flexible interaction between tradition and modernity is observed by the Korean mothers' and daughters' experiences of intimacy in the discourses of specific Korean culture in modernization and immigration of Korean Americans. While the mothers, working with traditional Korean notions and values of intimacy, did not prioritize nor achieve individualistic choice in their intimate relationships and marriage decisions, these values contributed to create the mothers' sense of caring and compassionate love for their husbands. Ultimately, the mothers have become emotional and intimate subjects in familial relationships and accomplished it through their negotiation and recognition of both traditional values and modern ideals of intimacy. On the other hand, the modern daughters, who are supposedly "free" in their choice of partners and "pure" in their intimate relationships, encounter constraints in this modern intimacy due to the complexities in immigration experiences. The daughters' longing for the similarity with their partners, secure legal status, and filial obligations in repaying their parents' sacrifice makes their marriages more like traditional ones, where material and practical needs and familial responsibilities overpower one's emotional satisfaction and individualistic desire.

The mothers and daughters create and define their own distinctive identities and it is crucial to study these in the context of their own generational, cultural, and social experiences, most importantly the mother and daughter relationship. The mothers' and daughters' shifting values and ideals of love and marriage provide a useful site to observe how ideas about intimacy change generationally as well as a significant domain to address how the love between mothers and daughters is delivered and received. In these ways, women's experiences of love and marriage construct the basis of womanhood.

Stories about love and desire are personal, but these personal stories are created by one's interaction with various factors and processes of social change. In the field of love, where the forces of social and cultural change and people's lived experiences and feelings are equally important, the methods and perspectives of anthropological research provide powerful insights to organize people's emotional experiences and analyze the socioeconomic and cultural processes affecting such experiences. Therefore, the anthropology of love draws together personal desires with the structures that shape them. In this sense, it addresses some of anthropology's most essential questions about humanity.

REFERENCES

Cho, H. (2002). *Living with Conflicting Subjectivities: Mother, Motherly Wife, and Sexy Woman in the Transition from Colonial-Modern to Postmodern Korea.* Honolulu: University of Hawaii Press.

Dworkin, S. (2012). "Sample Size Policy for Qualitative Studies Using In-depth Interviews." *Archives of Sexual Behavior* 41: 1319–1320.

Espiritu, Y. (2008). *Asian American Women and Men: Labor, Laws, and Love.* Lanham: Rowman & Littlefield.

Evason, Nina. 2016. "South Korean Culture." *Cultural Atlas.* https://culturalatlas.sbs.com.au/south-korean-culture/south-korean-culture-family#south-korean-culture-family

Faier, L. (2007). "Filipina Migrants in Rural Japan and Their Professions of Love." *American Ethnologist* 34(1): 148–162.

Giddens, A. (1991). *Modernity and Self-Identity: Self and Society in the Late Modern Age.* Stanford: Stanford University Press.

Giddens, A. (1992). *The Transformation of Intimacy: Sexuality, Love, and Eroticism in Modern Societies*. Stanford: Stanford University Press.

Han, H. S. (2004). "Women's Life during Choson Dynasty." *International Journal of Korean History* 6: 113–159.

Hirsh, J. (2007). "Love Makes a Family: Globalization, Companionate Marriage, and the Modernization of Gender Inequality." In *Love and Globalization: Transformations of Intimacy in the Contemporary World*, edited by Mark B. Padilla et al., pp. 93–106. Nashville: Vanderbilt University Press.

Hirsch, J. and Holly W. (2006). *Modern Loves: The Anthropology of Romantic Courtship and Companionate Marriage*. Ann Arbor: University of Michigan Press.

Kang, H., Hong, I. and Ko, H. (2017). "Policies and Legislation for Women in Korea from the 1990s to the Present." In *Korean Women in Leadership*, edited by Yonjoo Cho and Gary N. McLean, pp. 81–98. London: Palgrave Macmillan.

Kendall, L. (1996). *Getting Married in Korea: Of Gender, Morality, and Modernity*. Berkeley: University of California Press.

Kim, Y. C. (1976). *Women of Korea: A History from Ancient Times to 1945*. Seoul: Ewha Womans University Press.

Padilla, M., Hirsch, J. S., Munoz-Laboy, M., Sember, R. E. and Parker, R. G. (2007). *Love and Globalization: Transformations of Intimacy in the Contemporary World*. Nashville: Vanderbilt University Press.

Rofel, L. (2007). *Desiring China: Experiments in Neoliberalism, Sexuality, and Public Culture*. Durham and London: Duke University Press.

Shim, Y. H. (2002). "Sexuality Policy in Korea in the 1990s: Changes and Factors." *Korea Journal* 42(2): 136–159.

Yeonams, C. (2016). "Gwinnett a Large Draw for Koreans in Georgia." *Gwinnett Daily Post*. https://www.gwinnettdailypost.com/local/gwinnett-a-large-draw-for-koreans-in-georgia/article_02338702-b0a7-56af-9dbd-355df0fd17ac.html

6

Negotiating Cultural Tension

Parenthood and 1.5 Generation
Korean New Zealanders

Hyeeun Kim

This chapter explores how 1.5 generation Korean New Zealanders (colloquially known as "Kowis") as parents navigate cultural tensions in New Zealand. It provides a brief profile and discussion of the "in-betweenness" (Bartley & Spoonley, 2008, p. 68) of this group, before introducing a parenting model that was developed from qualitative research into Kowi parenting. The research involved interviews with 1.5 generation Korean New Zealanders who migrated with their parents as children, and were now bringing up their own children (Kim, 2014).[1]

KOREAN MIGRANTS IN NEW ZEALAND

The Korean population is the fourth largest Asian group in New Zealand. They currently represent over 0.7 percent of the total New Zealand population (4,242,048) and 6.5 percent of the Asian population (471,708), having grown from 930 in 1991 to 30,171 in 2013. (Statistics New Zealand, 2002, 2014)

Each wave of Korean migration was driven by different historical factors in Korea, and the motivations and characteristics of Korean immigrants in each country differ from one another. In the case of Korean New Zealanders, the majority have emigrated under the influence of the globalization policy, *Sagyewha*,[2] established by President Kim Young-Sam in 1992 (Yoon, 2005, 2006). After the financial crisis and the subsequent International Monetary Fund (IMF) bailout in 1997, Korea opened its doors widely to foreign investors, and more Koreans began emigrating overseas for better economic opportunities. The Confucian emphasis on education and the pursuit of status also led more families to look for migration opportunities for their children's education overseas (Shim et al., 2008).

Korean migration to New Zealand has been similarly motivated. Future family prospects, especially better opportunities for children's education in English, have been cited as the major factor behind the migration decision (Chang et al., 2006). Other reasons included an escape from the competitive and stressful education system, work regimes and gendered family roles in Korea; hope for a more relaxed lifestyle in an uncrowded and natural environment; as well as access to an alternative destination with lower exchange rates and immigration policies that cater for family reunification and related chain migration (Chang et al., 2006).

The changes in the 1990s in Korea coincided with a significant change in New Zealand immigration policy. When the Immigration Amendment Act 1991 took effect, potential migrants were ranked according to a "points system" in which they were assessed on factors such as education, age, occupation and wealth (Beaglehole, 2006; Phillips, 2006). The new policy began attracting skilled Asian immigrants with the ability to invest capital in New Zealand (Ho et al., 2003). People from Korea were able to migrate to New Zealand easily, and the number of Korean New Zealanders increased dramatically. However, the number of arrivals from Korea dropped after 1995, when the New Zealand government introduced an English language test as a condition for immigration. In 2002, growth slowed still further when the English language requirements for entry were raised to the same level as those of students entering university (Beaglehole, 2006).

The parents of the 1.5 generation Kowis in this study arrived before 2002, prior to the introduction of the more stringent English language requirements. Due to New Zealand immigration criteria, Kowis' parents have normally been highly skilled and/ or wealthy entrepreneurs. It means that they have had adequate ability to support their children financially and they have ensured that their children were introduced to wide-ranging opportunities to experience and adapt to New Zealand culture. However, they may have struggled with language and cultural barriers. They were assessed for migration on factors such as education, age, occupation and wealth but, as indicated above, they did not have to pass the English language requirements as a condition for migration.

1.5 Generation: "Stuck *in-between* Worlds' VS 'Living *in* Two Worlds"

The migration process of parents of the 1.5 generation suggests connections between the 1.5 generation children's development and the first-generation parents' degree of adaptation in New Zealand. Due to language and cultural barriers experienced by their parents, the 1.5 generation Kowi children had responsibilities as mediators between them and the host society, like the Korean migrant children of working-class families in the United States (Danico, 2004). Migrant children are often reported to have developed a "double consciousnesses" and they are frequently considered "bridge builders" (Park, 1999, p. 158) between their parents and the local community. Kowi (or Korean-Kiwi[3]), the casual term of Korean New Zealanders, also speaks to the meaning of "in-betweenness" experiences. It is used to indicate the unique identity shaped by the dual cultural heritage of Korean and Kiwi, an aspect of the in-betweenness of two very different cultures.

The term "in-betweenness" is used to convey "the sense of displacement and difficulties of cultural adjustment common to all migrants" (Bartley & Spoonley, 2008, p. 68). The 1.5 generation often face ambiguity and confusion as they are usually perceived by the first generation as the second generation, but they are seen as the first generation by the second generation and are identified as "just Koreans" by non-Koreans and locals (Danico, 2004). The 1.5 generation Kowis reported their struggle with ambiguity and confusion about their identity as children, and found "Where are you from?" one of the most confronting questions that they have lived with. This question highlights their ambiguous sense of place "in the middle" (Kim & Age, 2019, pp. 40–41). Moreover, they do not all feel exactly 1.5 in their cultural identities either and rate these differently, ranging from 1.1 (being closer to the first generation) to 1.9 (being closer to the second generation), depending on their experiences in different aspects of their lives such as preferred food, language fluency, cultural adaptation, workplace, friendship circles and religious ethnic communities (Kim, 2014).

Bartley and Spoonley (2008) identified three layers of "in-betweenness" experienced by the 1.5 generation Asian migrants in New Zealand: in-between origin and destination societies, in-between childhood and adulthood, and in-between the majority and other minority and indigenous cultures in the host country. It was noted in their research that the 1.5 generation young people struggled with disruption of normal roles, routines and structures of power within the family. This may be due to the fact that changes in the natural and complex dynamics between parents and children as they grow up overlap with the challenges of family migration (Orellana et al., 2001).

It was reported in Bartley and Spoonley's (2008) New Zealand study that "in-betweenness" also facilitates young people's development of some advanced life skills at a young age, while supporting their parents in matters of daily living due to the language difficulties parents experience in their settlement processes. The 1.5 generation Kowis also identified similar strengths that they acquired while growing up as 1.5 generation migrants: language ability, cultural competency, broad perspectives and diverse life experiences (Kim, 2013). According to Danico (2004), young Korean Americans have also carried an added sense of responsibility to the family, which helped them to maintain their Korean language abilities and hold onto some traditional Korean family values.

It is important to note that 1.5 generation Kowis have grown up in a world of globalization and belong to a technologically advanced generation. Globalization has enabled increased communication possibilities, and has resulted in increasing awareness of the world beyond immediate national boundaries (Block & Buckingham, 2007). Falicov (2003) observed that today's migrants are likely to live *in* two worlds rather than being stuck in-between two worlds. In fact, the influences of family, peers, and the larger social forces of both countries are multiple and complex for each individual migrant nowadays (Black & Buckingham, 2007). Researchers have documented evidence of such phenomena when investigating "transnational migration" (Falicov, 2003; Janes, 2004; Kong, 1999; Lee et al., 2009; Orellana et al., 2001; Zhou, 1997).

Kowis have benefitted from new means of cyber communication such as emails, internet chatting, Skype, Instagram, and Facebook, and cyber technology has provided them with easier access to friends and families, as well as news about Korea and other parts of the world. Adult Kowis have grown up with strong financial support from their parents, and have had more opportunities than their predecessors to have close contact with Korean culture by visiting families and relatives in Korea on a regular basis. The experiences enabled by globalization and new technology may have helped them to maintain their Korean language ability, and continue embracing traditional Korean family values. It may also have given them broadened perspectives and life experiences, developing their cultural competency to access different cultures. The *Kowi Parenting Model* (see next section) shows how the 1.5 generation Kowis live *in* two worlds while "taking the best of both worlds to raise the next generation" (Kim, 2013, p. 78).

Cultural Negotiation: *"Kowi Parenting Model"*

Experiences of growing up as migrant children have shaped the perspectives of the 1.5 generation Kowis on family dynamics, parent–child relationships with their own children, their couple relationships, and their ways of integrating different parenting styles while navigating multiple cultures (Kim, 2014). This qualitative research was conducted using grounded theory to understand participants' perceptions of their world as migrant children who were now parents, and their identification and understanding of factors that influenced their parenting experiences, from their perspectives. Eighteen 1.5 generation Kowi adults who were married with their own children were interviewed for up to two hours. They had migrated with their parents to New Zealand prior to 2002 when they were between the ages of five and 17 years. Interviewing was selected as it is an appropriate tool for exploring personal and sensitive issues (Rubin & Rubin, 2012) as it provides the potential to elicit both depth and breadth of data (Fontana & Frey, 2008). Participants explored their experiences broadly in their preferred language—Korean and/ or English.

A constructivist grounded theory approach provided a framework for the analysis and interpretation of the participant narratives in this research, as it acknowledged the inevitability of the researcher's position in relation to the enquiry (Charmaz, 2006; Strauss & Corbin, 1994). The author shared a common ethnic relationship with the participants and had an insider's understanding of the data as a migrant and professional counselor with on-going relationships with the Korean community. In insider research, "the investigator studies herself, those like her, her family or her community" (Wilkinson & Kitzinger, 2013, p. 252). Hence, it was acknowledged that this research gave special attention to the position of the researcher as a co-author of participants' stories and partner of the participants, consequently bringing

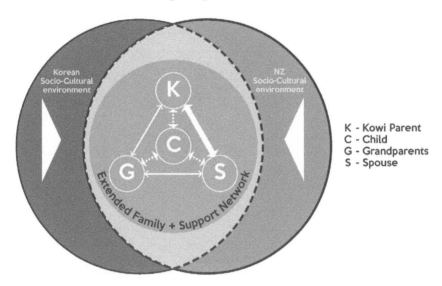

Figure 6.1   Kowi Parenting Model.

a strong participants' presence throughout, enriching the meaning and interpretation of the data (Charmaz, 2000; Mills et al., 2006, 2008).

Findings from the interviews indicated that there were multiple aspects of the 1.5 generation Kowis' perceptions that influenced, resourced and challenged their parenting. These included: Kowis' own perceptions and worldviews, as well as their experiences in the Korean and New Zealand sociocultural environments; their first-generation parents[4] or parents-in-law (grandparents)[5] and their cultural views; their spouses and the spouse's cultural background and worldviews; and multiple support networks and resources around them as challenges and resources. These aspects revealed a systematic interaction of dynamics that interlinked in the life of Kowis. Reflecting these influences, the *Kowi Parenting Model* (figure 6.1) was developed from the findings.

There are three different types of arrows that are used in the *Kowi Parenting Model*, showing the patterns of interaction[6] in the family, although it needs to be noted that the arrows do not indicate a quantitative measure of each interaction.

- The primary arrow (⬤➤) indicates very frequent interaction.
- The secondary arrow (◄──►) indicates frequent interaction.
- The tertiary arrow (◄┈┈┈►) indicates minimal, limited, or invisible interaction.

In this model, four main parties have been identified and placed at the core: the child, Kowi parent, grandparents, and spouse. Each component is not isolated from the others in the world of Kowis' parenting; rather, they are interlinked, constantly present, and part of the world of the Kowis that they have interacted with as children and as parents. The position of the extended family was embedded in the

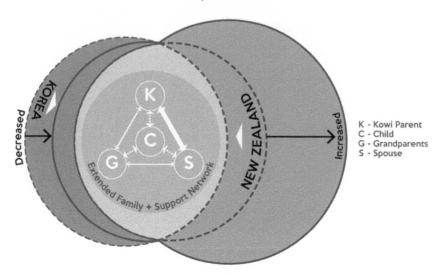

Figure 6.2   Changes in Cultural Forces.

social networks that were surrounded by a larger circle representing the sociocultural environment.

The degree of influence of both Korean and New Zealand cultures decreased or increased over time in Kowis' lives after migration (for instance, Korean influence lessened due to physical distance) and again when they became parents (for instance, exposed more to New Zealand medical/social services for children, or the start of schooling) (see figure 6.2 below). Each component of the *Kowi Parenting Model* is explained briefly in this section[7].

The Child

"The child" represents a second-generation child and the children of the Kowis. They are at the center of the diagram because they are the focus of the Kowis' parenting. Tertiary arrows connect the child with three other parties in this model, indicating the less visible interactions with them due to the way the research was conducted. Because the parent-child relationship was not the focus of the research, participants were not specifically asked for details of their interactions with their children, yet their children are centrally important to Kowi parents. The majority of second-generation children were under five and parental interactions with them would focus on age-appropriate day-to-day care instead of meaningful conversation about their relationship with each other. Each Kowi's spouse and their parents—the children's grandparents—also have their own relationships with the second-generation child. Their relationships and interactions with the child, as well as their involvement in the child's life, influence, resource and challenge the Kowis' parenting.

The arrows from and to the child will change as s/he grows up and has more interactions with the other parties over time. For instance, Pitt spoke about his wish for more frequent interactions in the future with his son who was an infant at the time of the study:

> I really want to be like a friend to my children. A lot of dialogue! Eating out together often, really spending time to play together, [and] kicking the balls together. When they become adults, I would still like to go out with them for a drink, a beer! Really hope they can talk to me about anything like to a friend, without any hesitation. I really want to be a friend to them. That is my goal. (Pitt)

The Spouse

A primary arrow connects the spouse and the Kowi parent, indicating the strength and close nature of their relationships. In terms of parenting decisions, the Kowis make their own decisions more independently of the grandparents (their own parents) in comparison to their counterparts in Korea. Kowis distance themselves from the grandparents due to cultural clashes in parenting values, even though they still show more respect towards the grandparents and their opinions in comparison with their counterparts in New Zealand. See Amy's decision-making process with her spouse, independently from her own parents and professionals.

> I mix both Kiwi and Korean [ways of parenting] after I listened to my mum, the Plunket[8] nurses and make my own decision for what is right for me. I didn't particularly choose something because it is the Korean or Kiwi [way]. We [Amy and her spouse] just decided what is right for us. (Amy)

Like Amy, participants often made parenting decisions with their spouse. The Kowis realized that in their unique circumstance as Kowis bringing up the second-generation, they would have to consider what was right for their families. Hence, the bonding between spouses is strong, and developing their capacity to make decisions for themselves may be understood as part of their developmental process as young parents.

The Korean grandparents also acknowledged the position of Kowis as parents in their own right, and showed respect for their adult children's decisions when they became parents. As grandparents aged, they also relaxed and became less strict, as John and Peter's comments illustrate:

> My father now acknowledges me as a father and head of my own family. (John)

> My father is a lot, a lot more relaxed, a lot mellower now. A whole lot more changed now, because the relationship has changed [as we aged]. (Peter)

The primary arrow also highlights the degree of influence that the identity and worldview of the spouse have in a Kowi's parenting relationship. Each spouse brought a different understanding of cultural values to parenting, depending on their cultural background. Some were able to strengthen their parenting practice by bringing different but creative perspectives to parenting as a resource, while others were challenged by contradictory cultural values that they were faced with in the process of negotiation with their spouse.

For instance, the first generation Kowi husbands[9] had a different understanding of gender roles from their 1.5 generation Kowi spouse, based on typical Confucian values (Keum, 2000; Kim & Hoppe-Graff, 2001; Won, 2002). Unique aspects of Confucianism that are related to traditional family values include "authority of fathers, wives' obedience to husbands, children's obedience to parents, filial piety, submission of self to family and high expectations in education" (Kim et al., 2012, p. 125) in this case. Angela's husband expected the wife to be a traditional mother and serve the family.

> He thinks that he doesn't need to do any housework because he works outside (laugh). In his mind, he is entitled to go out socialising and to have own time. But he doesn't think it applies to me. It is only for himself. He doesn't have any idea that a husband and wife need to spend some time together either. (Angela)

Participants like Bryan and Ginny, who were married to 1.5 generation Kowis, commented on a lot of commonalities between them. These related to life experiences in childhood, family dynamics, migration experiences, understanding of cultures, and language use. They understood each other as 1.5 generation Kowis, enjoying support and understanding from one another which they did not often receive elsewhere.

> We understand each other well because of similar life experiences. It is the biggest strength [in our relationship]. It would have been difficult if I were married to a new migrant from Korea. (Bryan)

> There are a lot of common understandings as well as stories that we can share with each other. (Ginny)

A secondary arrow connects the spouse and the grandparents (the parents-in-law). The spouse, like John and Pitt, cannot easily discard the opinions of the parents-in-law, especially when they are the first port of call for practical and/or financial help.

> My mother and father travel often between Korea and New Zealand. So my mother-in-law helps us a lot [with child care]. (John)

> He [father] paid for our wedding and funded us when we started the family. He supported us well. It unloaded a lot of stress when we got married and started the family. (Pitt)

In comparison with their New Zealand counterparts, in-laws are engaged in more interactions and obligations with them and consequently, their influence is stronger. In Korean culture, the parent-in-law traditionally has a strong voice about, and influence on, children's parenting, especially with the daughter-in-law. *Hyo* (filial piety) (Keum, 2000; Kim, 2006; Won, 2002) applies to the relationship with the in-laws and dismissing the opinion of the parents-in-law would bring shame to the family. Such shame causes loss of face in their relationship, disrupts group harmony and brings further shame to the family and other related group units (Lee, 1999).

A Kowi daughter-in-law normally finds it difficult to deal with the traditional and cultural demands on females. A primary arrow would connect the young parents with the in-laws in Korea. However, the Kowi daughter-in-law relates to the in-laws differently, either due to the distance from Korea if the in-laws live there, or because of cultural adaptation to the New Zealand relationship style (Cribb, 2009)[10]. The 1.5 generation Kowis have strong minds of their own and would not submit to the in-laws the way they would in Korea. Suzan clashed with her parents-in-law often.

We [Suzan and her parents-in-law] have clashed a lot. They [parents-in-law] don't understand us [Suzan and her husband]. Our way of thinking is so different. My husband and I are straight forward in expressing how we feel. We like it that way. It is cultural! However, they are not. For example, they would offer us a plate to try but would not take no for an answer. You know how Koreans are like. Perhaps it is a cultural difference. However, they are beyond the typical Koreans. They get offended and cannot accept our answer. It was really hard . . . expressing [your feelings and thoughts]. (Suzan)

The Grandparents (Kowis' parents)

A secondary arrow connects "the grandparents" and "the Kowi parent." In terms of connection, if the significance of their childhood was considered, a primary arrow should connect them. However, the influence of the grandparents changed over time after the Kowi parent started his or her own family and as a result of the cultural clashes mentioned before. As the grandparents' influence decreased, the relationship has therefore been represented by a secondary arrow.

In terms of Kowis' childhood, Kowis' parents have significantly influenced their perceptions of parenting while they were growing up in Korea and New Zealand. The data indicated that the degree of similarity or difference between Kowis' style of parenting and that of their own parents depended on their current and past relationships with their parents, and their experiences of growing up at the interface of the two cultures. In general, participants were flexible and adopted aspects of parenting from both cultures.

Aspects of Korean culture were especially adopted during the first few years of their second-generation children's life. Participants chose aspects that they valued from Korean culture, illustrated by the following examples:

But it's interesting when I first had a baby, that postpartum period. I guess I kept to the Korean tradition and customs because my mum was there, helping me. She would make sure I was warm, the baby was warm. She fed me lots of seaweed soup, things like that. That was very Korean. It's quite Asian, you know. I don't know that Kiwi mums come and "stay" for weeks and help with your daughter, daughter-in-law having babies. I think that is Asian practice or custom. (Jean)

It was too hard for the baby and also for me that he slept in a separate room. Kiwis seem to manage it well when their baby cries. But I couldn't do it [leaving the baby crying alone in his room]. When I think about it, my mindset may still be Korean. It is more comfortable to have the baby in my bed. (Angela)

We actually, we do similar things [to my parents]. Probably not as strict! But we will still, I still try to teach them very similar things in terms of manners and make sure they bow and they greet. Make sure that when their grandparents had a visit and are going home, make sure they all come to the front door to say goodbye and things like that. So it's all there. (Peter)

Adapting aspects of New Zealand Pākehā[11] culture was linked to aspects of Korean culture that they did not like when they wished to parent differently from the way they were brought up. To illustrate:

Must be a Western culture [that I use]! It's more about encouragement, and I suppose, praising. (Bella)

I really would like to implement some of the local parenting approaches. To be specific, it is about respecting a child's opinion. It doesn't matter what their gender or age is. Admit that I am wrong if they are right. I think it is very important. (Suzan)

The majority tried to integrate both the Korean and New Zealand ways and to choose what worked for them. Hana and Amy spoke about integration of two different cuisines for their convenience.

I mix both because I cannot find all the right ingredients here that are in the Korean cookbook. (laugh) I didn't cook rice soup with cheese but put a piece of cheese on top of it when introduced solid. Yes, I mixed it. (Hana)

Breakfast? Sometimes we have rice, other times bread. (Amy)

The Extended Family Members and Support Networks

In the *Kowi Parenting Model*, the place of the extended family members is not so significant in terms of their influence on the Kowis' parenting when compared to the way the traditional family functions in Korea. In Kowis' childhood, the influence of extended family members had already decreased due to physical distance from Korea after migration, unless some of the extended family was already living in New Zealand. Hence in this model "the extended family" has been placed together with "support networks" in a different circle where the Kowi parent, child, spouse, and grandparents actively interact.

After migration, because of the loss of a wide range of support networks, the Kowi and their first-generation parents had to re-establish a new set of support networks that included their workplace, new friendship circles, and religious ethnic communities. These were important resources for and influences on Kowis in their childhood during the challenging period of migration and they have continued to resource and support the Kowi parents in the present, replacing their extended family. See, for example, Suzan's view on the church as support:

During my adolescence, I clashed with my parents a lot because I became my own person with a new-found ego and began to see who they were. That was the time when I turned to the church. Someone who I used to talk to [about my issues] encouraged me to explore some resolution in a spiritual dimension. So, I suddenly started attending early morning services. (Suzan)

Participants used networks such as other Korean fathers in the community, mothers at school, and other experienced mothers who had children around the same age or older. They consulted both 1.5 generation and first-generation Korean parents, and one used Facebook to consult with friends in her network. Among their friendship groups, they had both Korean and non-Korean friends. Sarah consulted both Korean and local mothers in her child's school while Jane did with Korean mothers who were her students' parents.

Some of the mums in the school as well. We are all on the same journey. We have similar problems. A couple of Kiwi, um, well, Western people, and a couple of Koreans. (Sarah)

I ask other [Korean] mothers. They are my students' parents. For instance, when I ask "My child is not well. What do I do?" Then they will say, "It is part of growing up." I ask them whatever I don't know. I also learn how other mothers discipline. (Jane)

Bella used a social media, Facebook, and Peter utilized Korean Christian fathers who he regularly spent time together.

I said, "Toilet training where do I start?" [on Facebook]. People said "just when she is ready" is the Kiwi way. The Korean way is "you just put her . . . take her nappy off and she will be fine in a few days. (Bella)

I also have a small group of Christian fathers, Korean Christian fathers. We are all 1.5 generations as well. We kind of get together . . . and all fathers, young fathers talked about being a father, and you know all those kinds of things. (Peter)

It is important to note that the Kowi parents' support networks are much wider than those established by their Korean parents after migration. Because of their language and cultural competency, Kowis are able to enter and utilize both worlds effectively.

The Sociocultural Environment

In the *Kowi Parenting Model*, there are two sociocultural environments that the Kowis are exposed to: Korean and New Zealand. They have grown up with these two sociocultural forces and are still exposed to their ambiguities and complexity today in their parenting, as seen in these examples:

I used to be criticised by other mothers for not teaching my son Korean well because he spoke more English. They also criticised me because my son sucked his thumb (laugh). "It is bad to suck the finger." I used to argue with them (laugh). My husband would intervene and ask me to ignore them. But I was so annoyed about that. Those [first generation] mothers also complained about my son not wearing socks but jandals. "He will get sick." (Erica)

I could not dismiss what my mum said, as we lived together 24/7. But I could not ignore what the Plunket nurse insisted on from her professional point of view either. (Hana)

The biggest thing [challenge] is that two cultures offer you completely different advice. (Sarah)

It is confusing. They all say differently. The midwife would say one thing, and the Plunket nurse would say something different. Different midwives would say something different again. It is a bit confusing. (Scott)

Participants also reported a form of discrimination that concerned them and that they believed got in the way of optimal parenting.

We went to one kindergarten in North Shore. They actively discouraged us from speaking in Korean to the child, [and] said that kids don't learn the language and that we have to speak to her in English. We were quite shocked. We didn't like it (laugh). We didn't particularly appreciate it. But that kindy had a really good reputation, especially among Kiwis, especially European style in mainstream society, and so on. . . . Increased pressure on the parents to somehow mould their children into, fit into mainstream society somehow, which I don't necessarily see as a positive thing. (Peter)

The sociocultural environments to which the Kowis were exposed as children depended on their parents' level of integration, their geographic locations (i.e., more exposure to Korean in Auckland than any other cities in New Zealand), and the extent to which they experienced positive interactions with the host–nationals and other Korean migrants. Their perceptions and worldviews were shaped by their exposure to each environment—Korean and New Zealand.

For example, Pitt's father was a conservative and traditional Korean man who remained an authority figure and did not spend any time with Pitt. Hence, he planned to spend a lot of time with his son when he grew up, which he identified as a New Zealand style of parenting.

I would love to have a lot of conversation with my children. I want to make sure there is no blockage in our relationships. A good flow of conversation is really important between children and parents, and husband and wife. I did not have it with my parents. I really would like to with my children. A parent like a friend! (Pitt)

Jane hated "Confucianism that is placed in Korean adults' mentality" because it brought restrictions and created excessive formality to daily life in her perception. Hence, she preferred the values of New Zealand culture that prioritized practicality over formality, structure and order.

I want to teach my children the freedom to express their opinions, express their emotions and thoughts clearly. Express them to adults or anyone, really! (Jane)

Peter did not agree with the openness of New Zealand culture in the area of premarital sex and felt strongly about keeping children away from the New Zealand's cultural influence on this matter.

Things we hear about is a 13-year-old getting pregnant and going to school counsellors. Not to dismiss counsellor. Sorry. But going to a school counsellor and getting an abortion without parents knowing, I think that kind of thing really makes me feel sick to my stomach about it. So those things that we want to make sure that we guard against or quite vigilant about. (Peter)

Some participants, when they were younger, had become independent and more mature while helping their parents in their business, as they were better equipped with language and cultural proficiency. Erica lived with added responsibilities, but it worked positively for her by boosting her self-esteem and a sense of independence. She brought the same values to her parenting with confidence.

I let him [the child] explore. I let him touch things in the kitchen, so he can learn to be careful. (laugh) But [my husband] stops him and over-protects him. I don't like his approach. I cannot accept that. (Erica)

Reflecting the movement and links between the cultures, in the *Kowi Parenting Model*, the boundaries to the two cultural circles are depicted with dotted lines (-----) which indicates accessibility, because Kowis live in the space in the middle with their language skills and cultural competency in both. The dotted lines indicate their freedom to move in and out of both cultures as strengths. For instance, Suzan pointed out her ability to "almost flawlessly come in and out of the Korean culture and Kiwi culture" and "bridge the gap between the second-generation and the first-generation." She believed that these were "the biggest strengths" of the 1.5 generation Kowis, and that facilitated the ability to "take the best of both cultures to raise the next generation." Scott and Jean also reported something similar.

If I do well, my children are likely to have no problem in integrating both Korean and Kiwi cultures. I can bridge the two. You know, what the 1.5 generation can do well! It is the greatest strength that the 1.5 generation can introduce both cultures to children. When my son faces an identity crisis in the future, I can share my own experiences and guide them through too. (Scott)

Having lived, breathed, [and] immersed myself into two cultures, understanding of two cultures, even three because of Māori culture as well. (Jean)

Kowis enjoy accessing multiple resources in both cultures. They can buy books, read magazines, watch media, and access the internet for their parenting information in both languages, from Korea as well as other parts of the world.

For instance, Jane used a growth chart from a Korean website. Abby used the internet for medical information "when her [Abby's child's] temperature suddenly dropped." Peter watched a Korean TV program on child rearing and said "part of it is learning actual skills because they teach certain techniques. These are a good source." Angela read "books printed in New Zealand, the United States and Korea." Amy, with her Kowi husband, also read books both in Korean and English. In the case of internet searches, Kowis used both Korean (i.e., *Daum*[12] and *NAVER*[13])

and English (i.e., *Google*[14]) websites. Some of them accessed parenting websites in
New Zealand and received regular emails on parenting tips. Bella used "a lot of
Google!" and "some Korean sites, some baby sites, Huggies and Plunket [parenting
sites]." Jane registered with BabyCenter[15] on the internet and received monthly
information [email newsletter], and also searched *NAVER*. In addition, internet
social sites like Facebook were also used to gather information.

The Kowi parents also accessed both Korean and New Zealand health and social
services in New Zealand, important sources of influence and resources.

> The [Korean] midwife was a really great help, culturally very sensitive as well because she
> was from our culture (laugh). That really helped my wife. My wife loves her to bits. She
> still calls her from time to time to pay her respects, to say how things are, and to thank
> her. The pregnancy and actual birth were greatly helped by having a very experienced
> and very calm Korean midwife there. (Peter)

> Plunket offers regular check-ups for babies for their development and growth. It offers
> real assurance of a baby's healthy development. It would be expensive to do the same,
> and they don't offer that kind of service in Korea. I think it is really good to have Plun-
> ket services here. (Richard)

However, the reality of globalization was both a source of confusion, with information overload, and a source of richness and creative practice in Kowis' parenting. When the Kowis were unsure of their direction in life and felt inadequate
as parents, the flood of information confused them, giving them contradictory
messages.

> There is so much information out there when you raise children nowadays. There is the
> internet, what other mothers would tell you, and you also see what other mothers do
> when you go to school. There is so much information but there is no one you can actu-
> ally consult to find out what is right for your children. I get confused. When you do it
> the Korean way, it [the schedule] is too tight for children. When you do the Kiwi way,
> it is too loose. I cannot find the middle ground. (Angela)

> There are neither answers nor instructions. You read a lot. But you still have to find
> your own answer at the end of the day, which fits with your baby the best. (Richard)

DISCUSSION

Systems theories, ecological models, and other interactional theoretical perspectives
have been developed to explain the dynamics of parenting and human development
and how these systems interact. The bioecological models of human development,
for example, addressed influences between individuals' development and their sur-
rounding environmental contexts (Bronfenbrenner & Morris, 2006). Earlier, a
process model of the determinants of parenting introduced aspects of parental func-
tioning (Belsky & Jay, 1984). Models like Bronfenbrenner's and Belsky's are generic

models and very useful to explain aspects of parenting in general. They demonstrate the interactions among systems.

However, the *Kowi Parenting Model* introduces the systematic interaction of multiple dynamics that are uniquely interwoven in the lives of Kowis and in their parenting styles. While some of the findings from the study (Kim, 2014) highlight experiences which may resonate with those of other refugee and migrant families from other parts of the world who have also settled in New Zealand, there are some areas that seem unique to the 1.5 generation Kowis. This adds to the existing systemic models and contributes information about some ethnic and cultural aspects.

The *Kowi Parenting Model* demonstrates that 1.5 generation Kowis navigate their way in-between multiple, complex and unique cultural influences on their parenting practices as migrants. To support their children, they are faced with challenges in terms of negotiating cultural tension. They are searching for a system to integrate multiple cultural heritages in their parenting, without losing sight of their own culture, and while integrating into the host culture more fully.

The *Kowi Parenting Model* confirms that there is a connection between 1.5 generation children's development and first-generation parents' degree of adaptation in New Zealand. Due to language and cultural barriers that were experienced by their parents, the 1.5 generation Kowi children have developed different sets of life skills that as adults they have applied to their parenting. Language ability, cultural competency and broad perspectives and life experiences are some of those. These attributes equip them to become the "bridge builders" between their ethnic community and the local community, and between the first-generation grandparents and second-generation grandchildren. They also provide them with confidence and freedom to negotiate between different cultures when confronted with contradictory external pressures and expectations.

The *Kowi Parenting Model* shows how Kowis, being a technologically advanced generation, have benefitted from new means of cyber communication in a world of globalization. Cyber technology has enabled them to access the world of information, as well as friends and families beyond immediate national boundaries, helping them to maintain their Korean language abilities and hold onto some traditional Korean family values, while integrating into the host culture more fully. However, the reality of globalization was both a source of confusion as well as a source of richness and creative practice. When they were unsure of direction in life and felt inadequate as parents, the flood of information confused them, giving them contradictory messages.

Contradictory messages and related confusion stood out as being one of the core struggles of the 1.5 generation Kowis: that "there is no one [who can truly understand the 1.5 generation] you can actually consult to find out what is right for your [second-generation Korean-New Zealand] children" (Angela) and "you still have to find your own answer [being the 1.5 generation]" (Richard). They searched for a culturally appropriate intervention that is unique to the 1.5 generation.

This challenge indicates the necessity of taking into account migrants and their needs in developing the framework of migration policy. The World Health

Organisation (WHO) and the International Organization for Migration (IOM), in collaboration with the Ministry of Health and Social Policy of Spain, held a Global Consultation on Migrant Health and outlined an operational framework for further action in this field (World Health Organisation, 2010). One of the key priorities suggested was migrant-sensitive health systems that deliver services in a more culturally and linguistically appropriate way. Such systems and services will be welcomed by 1.5 generation Kowis while they negotiate cultures throughout their lives.

CONCLUSION

Certainly, there is no one simple way to ensure an effective migration process and prevent migrant families from having negative experiences that would hinder optimal living including parenting. However, results from the current study offer us some clues as to where we can start. The *Kowi Parenting Model* indicates that Kowis have the potential to relate to their children's experiences in a more profoundly understanding way than is often the case when based solely on their own childhood experiences of migration and adaptation. Their potential will be nurtured and further developed if there is no "pressure on the parents to somehow mould their children into, fit into mainstream society" (Peter). Instead, they need to be supported and/or guided by professionals (e.g., school teachers, health professionals) and people in the community in a more culturally and linguistically appropriate way when navigating and negotiating contradictory values, messages and pressures.

> We [1.5 generation Kowis] can see more than one way to do things. Perhaps you can say that we have more understanding of our children . . . deeper understanding! It is not easy to have understanding parents. It is more common that your parents don't understand you. . . . These children [second generation Kowis] will have to walk on two roads, you know. (Ginny)

NOTES

1. Korean people refers to South Koreans (hereafter Korean).
2. "Sagyewha" means "globalization" in Korean.
3. Kiwi generally refers to people from New Zealand
4. The term *first generation parents* describes those adult Korean migrants who migrated to New Zealand with their 1.5 generation Kowi children.
5. The term *parents-in-law* describes the parents of 1.5 generation Kowis' spouses. They either live in New Zealand or Korea.
6. In this study, *interaction* refers to time spent together, communication frequency, the close nature of their relationships, or involvement in each other's life.
7. Some quotes from participants that appear in this chapter have been used in previously published articles by the author. The quotes were incorporated in this chapter when relevant

and appropriate in order to convey participants' unique voice. See Kim, 2013, and Kim & Agee, 2019.

8. A nationwide support services for the development, health and wellbeing of children under five in New Zealand.

9. The term *first-generation husband/spouse* refers to those who were over 18 years old at the time of migration.

10. Historically, multiple cultural influences, including Māori (indigenous population of New Zealand), Pacific Island and European cultures, have contributed to the formation of New Zealand culture. Hence, it is difficult to define the New Zealand style of relationship and culture. In this case, the New Zealand style refers to the combination of dominant culture of individualistic aspects of European culture with an egalitarian worldview.

11. The Māori word for people of European ethnicity.

12. A Korean information website: http://www.daum.net/

13. A Korean information website: http://www.naver.com/

14. An English information website: https://www.google.co.nz/

15. A website for parenting information: http://www.babycenter.com/

REFERENCES

Bartley, A., & Spoonley, P. (2008). Intergenerational transnationalism: 1.5 generation Asian migrants in New Zealand. *International Migration, 46*(4), 63–84.

Beaglehole, A. (2006). Immigration regulation. In Ministry for Culture and Heritage (ed.), *Settler and Migrant Peoples of New Zealand* (pp. 52–59). David Bateman.

Belsky, J. (1984). The determinants of parenting: A process model. *Child Development, 55*(1), 83–96.

Bronfenbrenner, U., & Morris, P. A. (2006). The bioecological model of human development. In R. M. Lerner, & W. Damon (eds.), *Handbook of Child Psychology* (pp. 793–828). John Wiley & Sons.

Buckingham, D., & de Block, L. (2007). *Global Children, Global Media: Migration, Media and Childhood*. Palgrave Macmillan.

Chang, S., Morris, C., & Vokes, R. (2006). *Korean Migrant Families in Christchurch: Expectations and Experiences*. The Families Commission.

Charmaz, K. (2000). Grounded theory: Objectivist and constructivist methods. In N. K. Denzin, & Y. S. Lincoln (eds.), *Handbook of Qualitative Research* (pp. 509–535). Sage.

Charmaz, K. (2005). Grounded theory in the 21st century: Applications for advancing social justice studies. In N. K. Denzin, & Y. S. Lincoln (eds.), *The SAGE Handbook of Qualitative Research* (3rd edition, pp. 507–535). Sage.

Charmaz, K. (2006). *Constructing Grounded Theory: A Practical Guide through Qualitative Analysis*. Sage.

Cribb, J. (2009). Focus on families: New Zealand families of yesterday, today and tomorrow. *Social Policy Journal of New Zealand, 35*, 4–16.

Danico, M. Y. (2004). *The 1.5 Generation: Becoming Korean American in Hawaii*. University of Hawaii Press.

Falicov, C. J. (2003). Immigrant family process. In F. Walsh (ed.), *Normal Family Processes: Growing Diversity and Complexity* (pp. 280–300). Guilford Press.

Fontana, A., & Frey, J. H. (2008). The interview. In N. K. Denzin, & Y. S. Lincoln (eds.), *Collecting and Interpreting Qualitative Materials* (pp. 115–159). Sage.

Ho, E., Au, S., Bedford, C., & Cooper, J. (2003). *Mental Health Issues for Asians in New Zealand: A Literature Review*. Mental Health Commission.

Ho, E., & Bedford, R. (2008). Asian transnational families in New Zealand: Dynamics and challenges. *International Migration, 46*(4), 41–62.

Janes, A. (2004). The 1.5 generation. *New Zealand Listener, 194*(3349), 17–23.

Keum, J. (2000). *Confucianism and Korean Thoughts*. Jimoondang.

Kim, E., Im, H., Nahm, E., & Hong, S. (2012). Korean American parents' reconstruction of immigrant parenting in the United States. *Journal of Cultural Diversity, 19*(4), 124–132.

Kim, H. (2013). Parenting patterns of "1.5 generation Kowis" in New Zealand: "Take best of both worlds to raise the next generation." *New Zealand Journal of Asian Studies, 15*(2), 78–93.

Kim, H. (2014). *Parenting experiences of 1.5 generation Kowi parents*. Unpublished PhD Thesis. Auckland University. https://researchspace.auckland.ac.nz/handle/2292/24659

Kim, H., & Agee, M. (2019). Where are you from?: Identity as a key to parenting by 1.5 generation Korean-New Zealand migrants and implications for counselling. *British Journal of Guidance and Counselling, 47*(1), 35–49.

Kim, H. O., & Hoppe-Graff, S. (2001). Mothers' roles in traditional and modern Korean families: The consequences for parental practices and adolescent socialization. *Asia Pacific Education Review, 2*(1), 85–93.

Kim, K. (2006). Hyo and parenting in Korea. In K. Rubin, & O. K. Chung (eds.), *Parenting Beliefs, Behaviors, and Parent-Child Relationships: A Cross-Cultural Perspective* (pp. 207–224). Psychology Press.

Kong, L. (1999). Globalisation and Singaporean transmigration: Re-imagining and negotiating national identity. *Political Geography, 18*, 563–589.

Lee, J. Y., Kearns, R. A., & Friesen, W. (2009). Seeking affective health care: Korean immigrants' use of homeland medical services. *Health and Place, 16*, 108–115.

Lee, Z. (1999). Korean culture and sense of shame. *Transcultural Psychiatry, 36*(2), 181–194.

Mills, J., Bonner, A., & Francis, K. (2006). Adopting a constructivist approach to grounded theory: Implications for research design. *International Journal of Nursing Practice, 12*(1), 8–13.

Mills, J., Bonner, A., & Francis, K. (2008). The development of constructivist grounded theory. *International Journal of Qualitative Methods, 5*(1), 25.

Orellana, M. F., Thorne, B., Chee, A., & Lam, W. S. E. (2001). Transnational childhoods: The participation of children in process of family migration. *Social Problems, 48*(4), 572–591.

Park, K. (1999). "I really do feel I'm 1.5!": The construction of self and community. *Amerasia Journal, 25*(1), 139–163.

Phillips, J. (2006). History of immigration. In *Settler and Migrant Peoples of New Zealand* (pp. 20–42). David Bateman.

Rubin, H. J., & Rubin, I. S. (eds.). (2012). *Qualitative Interviewing: The Art of Hearing Data* (3rd edition). Sage.

Shim, T. Y., Kim, M., & Martin, J. N. (2008). *Changing Korea: Understanding Culture and Communication*. Peter Lang.

Statistics New Zealand. (2002). *2001 Census of Population and Dwellings: Ethnic Groups—Reference Report*. Statistics New Zealand.

Statistics New Zealand. (2014). *2013 Census QuickStats about National Highlights*. Retrieved from http://www.stats.govt.nz/Census/2013-census/profile-and-summary-reports/quicksta ts-about-national-highlights.aspx

Strauss, A. L., & Corbin, J. M. (1994). Grounded theory methodology: An overview. In N. K. Denzin, & Y. S. Lincoln (eds.), *Handbook of Qualitative Research* (pp. 273–285). Sage.

Wilkinson, S., & Kitzinger, C. (2013). Representing our own experience; Issues in "Insider" research. *Psychology of Women Quarterly, 37*(2), 261–255.

Wolf, D. L. (1997). Family secrets: Transnational struggles among children of Filipino immigrants. *Sociological Perspectives, 40*(3), 457–482.

Won, P. (2002). *Traditional Korean thought.* Inha University Press.

World Health Organisation. (2010). *Health of Migrants: The Way Forward—Report of a Global Consultation,* "Madrid, Spain, 3–5 March 2010." (2010).

Yeoh, B. S. A., Huang, S., & Lam, T. (2005). Transnationalizing the "Asian" family: Imaginaries, intimacies and strategic intents. *Global Networks, 5*(4), 307–315.

Yoon, I. J. (2006). Understanding the Korean diaspora from comparative perspectives. Paper presented at the *Asia Culture Forum 2006,* Kwangju City, Korea.

Yoon, I. J. (2005). Korean Diaspora. In *Encyclopaedia of Diasporas: Immigrant and Refugee Cultures Around the World. Diaspora Communities, 2,* 201–213.

Zhou, M. (1997). Growing up American: The challenge confronting immigrant children and children of immigrants. *Annual Review of Sociology, 23,* 63–95.

III

HEALTH AND WELL-BEING

7

Healthcare Utilization among 1.5 Generation Korean Americans

Comparison with Other Immigrant Generation Koreans and 1.5 Generation Asian Subgroups

Sou Hyun Jang

INTRODUCTION

Korean Americans comprise the fifth-largest Asian ethnic group in the United States, following Chinese, Indian, Filipino, and Vietnamese Americans (U.S. Census Bureau 2017). Researchers have found that Korean Americans have lower healthcare access and utilization rates than other Asian American subgroups (Choi 2013; Hill et al. 2006; Jang et al. 2005; Lee et al. 2014; Ryu et al. 2001; Sohn and Harada 2004). For example, Korean Americans reported having a usual source of healthcare at a much lower rate (45.2%) than Vietnamese Americans (59.8%) and Chinese Americans (78.0%) (Lee et al. 2014).

The vast majority of studies on Korean Americans' healthcare utilization have focused on those who are foreign-born. This is because foreign-born, compared to U.S.-born, Korean Americans tend to face greater barriers to accessing U.S. healthcare as they are less likely to be insured or proficient in English (Carrasquillo et al. 2000; Markova et al. 2007; Thamer et al. 1997). Researchers have largely considered foreign-born Korean Americans as one monolithic group regardless of the age at which they migrated to the United States, or how many years they have been in the United States. However, previous studies have found that foreign-born Korean Americans who came to the United States as children or adolescents show different adaptation experiences than foreign-born Korean Americans who came to the United States as adults (Hurh 1990; Park 1999). Thus, aggregating foreign-born Korean Americans into one group regardless of their immigrant generation may mask the unique health issues and needs of each subgroup.

Researchers have used different definitions for 1.5 generation, which is comprised of foreign-born Americans who migrated to the United States as children or adolescents. Some researchers broadly define 1.5 generation as those who migrated to the destination country during their primary school years (Chiang-Hom 2004). Most others have a narrower definition: foreign-born immigrants who migrated to the United States between the ages of 6 and 13 (Zhou 1997), 11 and 16 (Hurh 1990), or at age 12 or earlier (Espiritu 1994; Rumbaut and Ima 1988). In this chapter, respondents are defined as 1.5 generation if they were born outside of the United States and came to the United States at the age of 13 or earlier.

In general, 1.5 generation Americans tend to show better assimilation to the United States, including language assimilation (Portes et al. 2001) and educational attainment (Rumbaut 2004), than their first-generation counterparts. Despite the plethora of studies on assimilation and education outcomes (Akresh and Akresh 2011; Portes and Rumbaut 2001; Zhou and Bankston 1994), the relationship between assimilation and health-related outcomes, including healthcare utilization, is understudied among immigrants across different immigrant generations. Distinguishing 1.5 generation Korean Americans from other immigrant generations will help reveal their true condition of U.S. healthcare utilization and associated factors, which could inform tailored public health policy for different immigrant generation groups.

This chapter has four main objectives. First, with 1.5 generation Korean Americans as a distinctive analytic category, the primary aim is to assess whether there is a difference in the healthcare utilization rate between 1.5 generation Korean Americans and other immigrant generation Korean Americans. Second, this chapter examines whether there is a difference in the healthcare utilization rate between 1.5 generation Korean Americans and other 1.5 generation Asian American subgroups, such as Chinese, Filipino, and Vietnamese Americans. Third, applying Andersen's healthcare utilization model (1995), this chapter compares differences in predisposing (e.g., socio-demographic characteristics), enabling (e.g., health insurance and English proficiency), and need (e.g., self-reported health status) factors among different immigrant generations of Korean Americans and among different subgroups of 1.5 generation Asian Americans. Lastly, it examines whether these factors are associated with healthcare utilization among 1.5 generation Korean Americans. This chapter is not an in-depth examination but rather a brief sketch of major issues associated with healthcare utilization, focusing on 1.5 generation Korean Americans compared to related groups.

HYPOTHESES AND THEORETICAL FRAMEWORK

This chapter poses three hypotheses to examine healthcare utilization among 1.5 generation Korean Americans compared to other immigrant generation Korean Americans and 1.5 generation Asian American subgroups. Foreign-born Asian Americans have lower insurance (Huang and Carrasquillo 2008) and healthcare utilization rates (Ye et al. 2012) than their U.S.-born counterparts. Among foreign-born Americans, 1.5 generation Americans show better assimilation into U.S. society than their first-generation counterparts (Portes et al. 2001; Rumbaut 2004), which might influence their utilization of healthcare in the United States. Thus, the first hypothesis is posed as:

> *H1: The 1.5-generation Korean Americans have higher healthcare utilization than their first-generation Korean American counterparts and have lower healthcare utilization than their second-generation Korean American counterparts.*

Korean Americans are known to have lower health insurance rates than other Asian American groups. For example, Korean Americans show the highest uninsured rate (29.8%), followed by their Vietnamese (21.5%), Chinese (16.8%), Filipino (11.7%), and Japanese (7.9%), counterparts (Huang and Carrasquillo 2008). Korean Americans also have lower English proficiency than most other Asian American groups (Gee and Ponce 2010). About half of Korean Americans (46.9%) reported having limited English proficiency while 4.6 percent of Filipino, 6.5 percent of Japanese, and 33.8 percent of Chinese Americans reported so. Only Vietnamese Americans reported a higher rate of limited English proficiency (51.8%) than Korean Americans. As health insurance and English proficiency are known to be significant barriers for immigrants' healthcare utilization in the United States (Leclere et al. 1994), the second hypothesis is:

> *H2: The 1.5-generation Korean Americans have lower healthcare utilization than other 1.5-generation Asian American subgroups.*

In his healthcare utilization model, Andersen (1995) indicates that there are three main factors that influence an individual's utilization of healthcare. First, there are predisposing factors, such as age, race/ethnicity, and gender. Then there are enabling factors, including health insurance and income. Lastly, there are need factors, an individual's perceived and actual need for healthcare, which are often measured by self-reported health status. As Akresh (2009) found this model to be applicable for general immigrants in the United States, the third hypothesis is posed as:

> *H3: Predisposing, enabling, and need factors are related to healthcare utilization among 1.5-generation Korean Americans.*

DATA AND METHODS

Data

I analyzed the 2015–2016 California Health Interview Survey (CHIS) data, which had a sample size of 42,089 adults, including 471 self-reported Koreans Americans. CHIS is a random-dial telephone survey focusing on various health issues (e.g., health status, health insurance, health conditions, and healthcare access)among

California residents. Even though the data are geographically restricted, the Los Angeles metropolitan area is home to the largest number of Korean Americans in the United States (Min 2012); thus, it is meaningful to analyze the CHIS data for the objectives of this chapter.

One strength of the CHIS data is that, unlike other nationally representative health datasets (e.g., NHIS, NHANES), it was possible to distinguish Koreans from other Asian subgroups. Moreover, the two-year combined CHIS data allowed us to analyze the data by immigrant generation. More detailed information about the data is on the CHIS website (CHIS 2017). This chapter included survey participants who were eighteen years old and older and of self-reported Korean, Chinese, Filipino, and Vietnamese race/ethnicity.

Measurement

It should be noted that measurement of 1.5 generation was somewhat crude due to limited data. Since the CHIS data does not include a variable which indicates the age at which each respondent migrated, one alternative way to distinguish 1.5 generation is the subtraction of the years each respondent has lived in the United States from their age. If measured this way, the CHIS data has two variables that could be used for immigrant generation distinction: (1) years spent in the United States and (2) the percentage of life spent in the United States. Unfortunately, due to privacy concerns, the publicly available data only provides categorical values (e.g., less than 5 years, 5–9 years, 10–14 years, and 15 years or longer), not continuous values (e.g., 0–100 years), for both variables. However, one remedy to using categorical variables is using the mid-point from each categorical value as the value to be subtracted.

In this chapter, the percentage of one's life spent in the United States was used for immigrant generation distinction because this variable had higher variance than years spent in the United States. Originally, the percentage of life spent in the U.S. variable had five categories: 0–20%, 21–40%, 41–60%, 61–80%, and 81%+. The mid-point of each value (e.g., 10%, 30%, 50%, 70%, 90%) was used to categorize foreign-born participants into 1.5 generation or other/not. Of note, each respondent was assumed to have continuously spent their life in the United States since their arrival. For example, if a 40-year-old foreign-born respondent had spent 50 percent of his or her life in the United States (i.e., 20 years), he or she was not considered in 1.5 generation (40 − 20 = 20 years old at migration). If another 40-year-old foreign-born respondent had spent 70 percent of his or her life in the United State (i.e., 28 years), he or she was considered in 1.5 generation (40 − 28 = 12 years old at migration).

Healthcare utilization was measured by whether or not a respondent ever visited a doctor in the past year. Originally, the variable for number of visits had eleven categories: 0, 1, 2, 3, 4, 5, 6, 7–8, 9–12, 13–24, 25+ times. Since the original variable was a mixture of continuous and categorical values, it was recoded as a dichotomous variable: 0 = never visited a doctor; 1 = ever visited a doctor. Predisposing factors included age, gender, marital status, educational attainment, and type of employment. Enabling factors included health insurance status and English proficiency. Need factors were measured through self-rated health status.

Analysis

All statistical analyses were performed using Stata 15.0. Due to the limited number of respondents divided by ethnicity and immigrant generation, descriptive statistics were used for most of the analyses. Each analysis was conducted for 1.5 generation Korean Americans, first-generation Korean Americans, second-generation Korean Americans, and other 1.5 generation Asian American subgroups (e.g., Chinese, Filipino, and Vietnamese). A chi-squared test was conducted to examine the association between the three factors (predisposing, enabling, and need) and healthcare utilization among 1.5 generation Korean Americans. The significance level was set at $p<0.05$.

FINDINGS

Characteristics of Survey Respondents

The majority of self-reported Korean participants (n = 471) were foreign-born (n = 398, 84.5%). About 15 percent (n = 58) came to the United States when they were 13 years old or younger, which, according to the definition used in this chapter, makes them 1.5 generation Korean Americans. The remainder of foreign-born Koreans (n = 340) came to the United States after the age of 13 and were therefore categorized as first-generation Korean Americans. The U.S.-born Koreans were defined as second-generation Korean Americans (n = 73).

Table 7.1 shows the characteristics of 1.5 generation Koreans compared with other immigrant generation Koreans and other 1.5 generation Asian subgroups. In general, 1.5 generation Korean Americans' socio-demographic characteristics were more similar to second-generation Korean Americans than first-generation Korean Americans. The mean age of 1.5 generation Korean Americans was 37.6 (SD = 12.9) years old, which was younger than first-generation Korean Americans (66.7, SD = 14.9) and most other 1.5 generation Asian subgroups, such as 1.5 generation Chinese (45.2, SD = 19.0) and Filipino Americans (40.4, SD = 14.8). The mean age was similar to 1.5 generation Vietnamese Americans (36.5, SD = 9.8) and second-generation Korean Americans (37.9, SD = 17.9). Slightly more than half (55.2%) of 1.5 generation Korean Americans were female, which is a lower proportion than first-generation (60.6%) and second-generation (57.5%) Korean Americans, but a higher proportion than other 1.5 generation Asian subgroups. Considering the similarities in age and proportion of females between 1.5 generation and second-generation Korean Americans, it is noticeable that more than half (56.9%) of 1.5 generation were married while only slightly more than one-third (35.6%) of second-generation were married.

The 1.5 generation Korean Americans had a higher level of education than other immigrant generation Koreans and other 1.5 generation Asian subgroups, with the

Table 7.1 Socio-Demographic and Assimilation Characteristics, Compared to Other Immigrant Generation Korean Americans and Other 1.5 Generation Asian Subgroups (%)

	First Gen Korean	Second Gen Korean	1.5 Gen Korean	1.5 Gen Chinese	1.5 Gen Filipino	1.5 Gen Vietnamese
Age, Mean (SD)	66.7	37.9	37.6	45.2	40.4	36.5
	(14.9)	(17.9)	(12.9)	(19.0)	(14.8)	(9.8)
Female	60.6	57.5	55.2	44.4	50.6	36.4
Marital status						
Married	56.5	35.6	56.9	56.5	39.6	63.6
Living with partner	2.4	2.7	3.5	3.7	6.6	4.6
Widow/separated/divorced	33.8	9.6	-	4.6	15.4	4.6
Never married	7.4	52.1	39.7	35.2	38.5	27.3
Educational Attainment						
High school or below	37.7	23.3	22.4	12.0	27.5	20.5
Some college/AA	8.2	19.2	12.1	7.4	27.5	11.4
BA	38.8	30.1	37.9	45.4	35.2	50.0
MA/PhD	15.3	27.4	27.6	35.2	9.9	18.2
Type of Employment						
Not in labor force/unemployed	71.2	35.6	24.1	38.9	25.3	13.6
Private sector	15.0	34.3	44.8	35.2	46.2	61.4
Public sector	2.9	6.9	10.3	16.7	22.0	11.4
Self-employed	10.0	19.2	17.2	9.3	6.6	11.4
Family business or farm	0.9	4.1	3.5	0	0	2.3
English Proficiency						
Speak only English	2.9	50.7	43.1	40.7	57.1	27.3
Very well	7.1	42.5	44.8	42.6	27.5	40.9
Well	27.7	6.8	12.1	13.9	15.4	25.0
Not well	49.7	0	0	2.8	0	6.8
Not at all	12.6	0	0	0	0	-
N	340	73	58	108	91	44

Source: 2015–2016 California Health Interview Survey (CHIS).

exception of 1.5 generation Chinese Americans. More than one-third (37.9%) of 1.5 generation Korean Americans had a BA degree and more than a quarter (27.6%) had an MA or Ph.D. degree. About three-quarters (75.9%) of the 1.5 generation Korean Americans were employed, which is higher than that of first- and second-generation (28.8% and 64.4%, respectively). The higher rate of unemployment among first-generation Korean Americans is likely due to their older age. The 1.5 generation Korean Americans' employment was most concentrated in the private sector, followed by self-employed (17.2%), public sector (10.3%), and family business (3.5%). They had a higher rate of being self-employed than 1.5 generation Chinese (9.3%), Filipino (6.6%), and Vietnamese (11.4%) Americans.

In terms of English proficiency, 1.5 generation Korean Americans were slightly behind second-generation, and first-generation Korean Americans were far behind second-generation. For example, slightly less than half (43.1%) of 1.5 generation Korean Americans answered that they speak only English, compared to about 3 percent of first-generation Korean Americans and about half of second-generation Korean Americans. Among those who speak English and other languages, 56.9 percent of 1.5 generation Korean Americans reported that they speak English very well or well, compared to about one-third of first-generation Korean Americans. About two-thirds of first-generation Korean Americans reported that they speak English not well or not at all, while none of 1.5 generation nor second-generation Korean Americans answered so. The 1.5 generation Korean Americans seemed to have a similar level of language assimilation with other 1.5 generation Asian Americans, except for 1.5 generation Filipino Americans who had a higher assimilation as English is one of the official national languages of their home country.

It is widely known that foreign-born Americans tend to be healthier than their U.S.-born counterparts (Rumbaut 1997; Stephen et al. 1994). To explain this phenomenon, researchers suggest two possible explanations. On the one hand, healthier immigrants selectively chose to migrate to the destination country (Marmot et al. 1984). On the other hand, the health-related culture of the immigrant's home country plays a crucial role in buffering relatively unhealthy American health behaviors (Hummer et al. 1999; Scribner 1996). However, other studies have found that this "healthy immigrant effect" vanishes by immigrant generation, mainly because of barriers to accessing healthcare (Razum et al. 2000).

Table 7.2 suggests that the healthy immigrant effect may not be applicable to Korean Americans. In fact, Korean Americans show the opposite pattern of the healthy immigrant effect; the proportion of respondents who reported excellent or very good health status was highest among second-generation Korean Americans, followed by 1.5 generation and first-generation Korean Americans. One possible explanation for this unexpected pattern is that first-generation Korean Americans in this analysis are much older (mean age = 67) than their younger-generation counterparts (mean age = 38), suggesting that they likely have more health issues.

Half of 1.5 generation Korean Americans reported that they have excellent or very good health while the other half reported good or fair health. None answered poor health. The 1.5 generation Korean Americans reported a higher rate of excellent or

Table 7.2   Self-Reported Health Status of 1.5 Generation Korean Americans Compared to Other Immigrant Generation Korean Americans and Other 1.5 Generation Asian Subgroups (%)

	First Gen Korean	Second Gen Korean	1.5 Gen Korean	1.5 Gen Chinese	1.5 Gen Filipino	1.5 Gen Vietnamese
Excellent	9.4	30.1	17.2	25.9	19.8	22.7
Very good	16.5	27.4	32.8	34.3	23.1	25.0
Good	33.2	30.1	34.5	32.4	40.7	40.9
Fair	25.9	8.2	15.5	4.6	13.2	11.4
Poor	15.0	4.1	0	2.8	3.3	0
N	340	73	58	108	91	44

Source: 2015–2016 California Health Interview Survey (CHIS).

very good health compared to all other 1.5 generation Asian subgroups, with the exception of 1.5 generation Chinese Americans. Previous research has indicated several factors associated with immigrants' self-reported health, such as socioeconomic status (Adler and Newman 2002; Dowd and Zajacova 2007) and language assimilation (Gee and Ponce 2010; Kandula, Lauderdale, and Baker 2007; Mulvaney-Day et al. 2007; Schachter et al. 2012). Considering higher socioeconomic status and greater language assimilation to be associated with better self-reported health, 1.5 generation Korean Americans' better self-reported health status might be due to their higher educational attainment than other 1.5 generation Asian subgroups, except for 1.5 generation Chinese Americans, as well as better language assimilation than other 1.5 generation Asian Americans.

Despite 1.5 generation Korean Americans' better self-reported health status, the story is quite different when looking at their health insurance status. As shown in Table 7.3, 1.5 generation Korean Americans reported a lower insured rate (91.4%) than first- and second-generation Korean Americans (95.3% and 94.5%, respectively) and most other 1.5 generation Asian subgroups. Only 1.5 generation Vietnamese Americans (88.6%) had a slightly lower health insurance rate than 1.5 generation Korean Americans.

The insured 1.5 generation Korean Americans showed a slightly different pattern than the insured first- and second-generation Korean Americans. Most were covered by employer-based plans (70.7%); less than 15 percent purchased private insurance. On the contrary, less first- and second-generation Korean Americans had employer-based insurance or purchased private insurance. The 1.5 generation Korean Americans showed the lowest rate of Medicaid or Medicare, which suggests limited access to the public health insurance system in the United States.

Only 1.5 generation Vietnamese Americans had a lower health insurance rate (88.6%) than 1.5 generation Korean Americans. This finding is consistent with previous studies that found that Korean Americans have a lower health insurance rate than other Asian subgroups (Carrasquillo et al. 2000; Huang 2013; Shin et al. 2005; Ryu et al. 2001). Compared with other 1.5 generation Asian

Table 7.3   Health Insurance Status of 1.5 Generation Korean Americans Compared to Other Immigrant Generation Korean Americans and Other 1.5 Generation Asian Subgroups (%)

	First Gen Korean	Second Gen Korean	1.5 Gen Korean	1.5 Gen Chinese	1.5 Gen Filipino	1.5 Gen Vietnamese
Have any insurance	95.3	94.5	91.4	95.4	92.3	88.6
Type of health insurance						
Insurance covered by employer-based plans	20.9	50.7	70.7	58.3	68.1	70.5
Purchased own plan	7.9	12.3	13.8	5.6	4.4	6.8
Medicaid	46.5	26.0	10.3	13.0	15.4	13.6
Medicare	62.1	9.6	1.7	24.1	6.6	2.3
N	340	73	58	108	91	44

Source: 2015–2016 California Health Interview Survey (CHIS).

subgroups, 1.5 generation Korean Americans showed the highest insurance rate through employer-based plans or purchased private insurance. This is consistent with previous research showing that employment status is associated with immigrants' health insurance status (Buchmueller et al. 2007). Previous studies have found that self-employed Korean Americans had a lower health insurance rate than Korean Americans who work in the non-Korean private sector or the public sector (Ryu et al. 2001). Confirming these earlier findings, being self-employed and having health insurance was negatively associated among 1.5 generation Korean Americans. About 70 percent of self-employed 1.5 generation Korean Americans were insured whereas most non-self-employed Korean Americans (95.8%) were insured (p<.05).

Healthcare Utilization

As noted earlier, Korean Americans have a lower healthcare utilization rate than other Asian American subgroups (Choi 2013; Hill et al. 2006; Jang et al. 2005; Ryu et al. 2001; Sohn and Harada 2004). Table 7.4 shows that 1.5 generation Korean Americans were in between first-generation, who showed a higher healthcare utilization rate, and second-generation, who showed a lower healthcare utilization rate. Although this difference was statistically significant, as shown by a chi-squared test (p<.01), the direction of the difference was opposite of what was expected. In other words, while H1 assumed that healthcare utilization rate would increase as immigrant generation increases, it actually decreased. Thus, H1 was rejected.

Table 7.4   Healthcare Utilization of Korean Immigrants, Compared to Other Immigrant Generation Korean Americans and Other 1.5 Generation Asian Subgroups (%)

	First Gen Korean	Second Gen Korean	1.5 Gen Korean	1.5 Gen Chinese	1.5 Gen Filipino	1.5 Gen Vietnamese
Ever visited a doctor last year	86.2	72.6	77.6	81.5	84.6	75.0
N	340	73	58	108	91	44

Source: 2015–2016 California Health Interview Survey (CHIS).

The 1.5 generation Korean Americans had a lower healthcare utilization rate than both 1.5 generation Chinese Americans and Filipino Americans but a higher rate than 1.5 generation Vietnamese Americans. However, this difference was not statistically significant (p>.05). Thus, H2 was rejected.

Possible Factors Associated with Healthcare Utilization

Predisposing Factors

Among 1.5 generation Korean Americans, there were disparities in healthcare utilization by several predisposing factors. For example, 1.5 generation Korean Americans who were older, female, married, had higher education, and worked in a private company showed higher healthcare utilization rates than their counterparts. However, the results of the chi-squared test revealed that none of the predisposing factors were significantly associated with healthcare utilization among either 1.5 generation or second-generation Korean Americans. Age and employment status were significantly associated with healthcare utilization among first-generation Korean Americans. Specifically, those who are older or those who are unemployed had a higher healthcare utilization rate than their counterparts.

Enabling Factors

Figure 7.1 presents healthcare utilization by health insurance status across different ethnic and immigrant generations. Except for second-generation Korean Americans, all other groups who were insured showed much higher healthcare utilization rates than those who were uninsured. About 79 percent of insured 1.5 generation Korean Americans reported visiting a doctor in the past year, whereas only 60 percent of uninsured 1.5 generation Korean Americans reported doing so. This pattern was also found among the insured and uninsured first-generation Korean Americans (87% vs. 69%, respectively). Healthcare utilization rates by health insurance status revealed large gaps between other 1.5 generation Asian subgroups, confirming the importance of health insurance status on healthcare utilization among these groups (Jenkins et al. 1996; Miltiades et al. 2008; Stella et al. 2004).

Figure 7.2 shows that English proficiency and language assimilation were influential enabling factors for healthcare utilization among 1.5 generation Korean

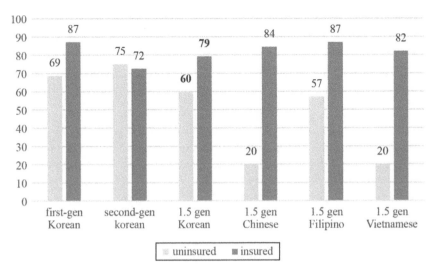

Figure 7.1 **Healthcare Utilization by Health Insurance Status by Ethnicity and Immigrant Generation (%).**

Americans, while they were not influential for second-generation who already achieved a high level of language assimilation. Interestingly, first-generation Korean American and 1.5 generation Korean Americans showed an opposite pattern of language assimilation and healthcare utilization. Among 1.5 generation Korean Americans, those who speak only English and speak only English at home showed a higher healthcare utilization rate than those who speak English well/very well or speak

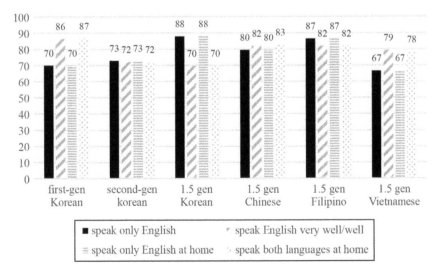

Figure 7.2 **Healthcare Utilization by Language Assimilation and by Ethnicity and Immigrant Generation (%).**

both languages at home. On the contrary, among first-generation Korean Americans, those who with a high level of English proficiency and speak both English and Korean at home had a higher healthcare utilization rate than those who speak only English or speak only English at home. In other words, among 1.5 generation Korean Americans, better language assimilation may be beneficial for healthcare utilization, whereas maintaining a connection with the native language may be more beneficial among first-generation Korean Americans.

This relationship not only varied by different immigrant generations within the same ethnicity but also by different ethnicities within the same immigrant generation. For example, 1.5 generation Filipino Americans showed a similar pattern with 1.5 generation Korean Americans, whereas 1.5 generation Chinese and Vietnamese Americans followed the same pattern as their first-generation counterparts. In other words, better English proficiency and language assimilation mattered more among 1.5 generation Chinese and Vietnamese Americans than among 1.5 generation Filipino Americans. These findings suggest that the association between language assimilation and healthcare utilization may not be always linear but depends on ethnicity and immigrant generation.

Need Factors

There were disparities in healthcare utilization by 1.5 generation Korean Americans' health status. For example, less than 10 percent of 1.5 generation Korean Americans with excellent health reported that they had ever visited a doctor, whereas 17.8 percent of 1.5 generation Korean Americans with fair health reported that they had ever visited a doctor. Self-reported health status was not significantly associated with healthcare utilization among 1.5 generation Koreans nor other immigrant generation Koreans and other 1.5 generation Asian American subgroups. Instead, 1.5 generation Korean Americans' health status was significantly associated with the number of doctor visits; those who reported worse health status were more likely to have frequent visits to the doctors than those who reported better health status.

In sum, although 1.5 generation Korean Americans show differences in healthcare utilization by most predisposing, enabling, and need factors, these differences were not statistically significant. Thus, H3 was rejected.

DISCUSSION

Considering 1.5 generation Korean Americans as a distinct subgroup, this chapter discussed their healthcare utilization rate compared to other immigrant generation Koreans and other 1.5 generation Asian American subgroups. It also described differences in predisposing, enabling, and need factors between 1.5 generation Korean Americans and other groups, and whether these factors were associated with their healthcare utilization in the United States.

Healthcare utilization among 1.5 generation Korean Americans was in between first- and second-generation Korean Americans; they showed a lower healthcare utilization rate than first-generation and a higher rate than second-generation Korean Americans. Compared to other Asian subgroups, 1.5 generation Korean Americans had a lower healthcare utilization rate, except for that of 1.5 generation Vietnamese Americans. Thus, researchers need to support the Korean community by revealing the pathways in which the U.S. healthcare system can better support Korean Americans' access to proper and timely services, while accounting for differences by immigrant generation.

There were also differences in several predisposing factors (e.g., socio-demographic characteristics), enabling factors (e.g., health insurance status, English proficiency, and language assimilation), and need factors (e.g., self-reported health status) among Korean Americans by immigrant generation. In general, 1.5 generation Korean Americans were more similar to second-generation Korean Americans than first-generation Korean Americans. Given these findings, although most previous studies grouped 1.5 generation and first-generation together, 1.5 generation should be considered as a distinctive group in health-related research.

Previous studies have found that Andersen's healthcare utilization model was applicable among immigrants (Akresh 2009) and Korean immigrants (Seo et al. 2016; Sohn and Harada 2004) in the United States. Although this chapter found disparities in healthcare utilization by predisposing, enabling, and need factors among 1.5 generation Korean Americans, they did not show any statistical significance. On the one hand, this could be due to the small number of 1.5 generation Korean Americans in the dataset. On the other hand, there could be other more relevant factors that explain healthcare utilization among 1.5 generation Korean Americans. Since the nationally representative data does not contain a large enough number of 1.5 generation Korean Americans, future studies may want to examine other related factors, beyond the factors suggested by Andersen, by using qualitative methods, such as in-depth personal interviews or focus groups.

Focusing on Korean Americans, researchers have indicated similar factors associated with their healthcare utilization, with health insurance status being the strongest associated factor (Choi 2013; Hill et al. 2006; Jang et al. 2005; Ryu et al. 2001; Sohn and Harada 2004). In addition to health insurance status, language barriers due to low levels of English proficiency are also strongly associated with healthcare utilization among Korean Americans (Gagne et al. 2014; Juon et al. 2000). The findings described in this chapter confirm that 1.5 generation Korean Americans without health insurance and with a lower level of English proficiency and language assimilation are less likely to utilize healthcare. This highlights the need for academic researchers to consider the 1.5 generation Korean Americans as having a unique level of assimilation into U.S. society, which impacts their utilization of healthcare differently than their other-generation counterparts.

This study had several limitations, mainly due to limited data. First, the 2015-2016 CHIS data has a relatively small number of Korean Americans by immigrant generation. Thus, any sophisticated statistical analysis beyond the chi-squared test was less meaningful. Moreover, the insignificant relationship between factors and healthcare utilization might also be caused by the small number of survey respondents in each group. As noted earlier, Korean Americans are often combined with other Asian Americans, and 1.5 generations are often neglected in nationally representative data. Given the findings that reveal the differences in characteristics and disparities in healthcare utilization, the nationally representative data should include more ethnic minorities and individuals from different immigrant generations for future research. Second, the method used to distinguish 1.5 generation Korean Americans was crude, as explained in the data and methods section. Lastly, there was a geographical restriction of the 2015–2016 CHIS data as it only included Koreans and other Asians residing in California, where Korean Americans reside in relatively higher densities. Korean Americans who live in an area with a lower concentration of Korean immigrants might show different characteristics of healthcare utilization as those areas would have fewer co-ethnic doctors.

This study had several strengths as well, including the comparison of various factors of healthcare utilization among Korean Americans, who were often combined with other Asian subgroups in national data. To my knowledge, this chapter describes first attempt to compare healthcare utilization among Korean Americans by immigrant generation, with a special focus on 1.5 generation Korean Americans. It highlights the need for further research on healthcare utilization among 1.5 generation Korean Americans as they have the highest educational attainment and employment rate among all Koreans but show lower insured and healthcare utilization rates than first-generation Korean Americans.

I hope this preliminary chapter contributes valuable insight into 1.5 generation Korean Americans' utilization of healthcare, and that it makes a compelling case for future studies to consider the role that immigrant generation plays in healthcare among U.S.-born and foreign-born immigrants. Furthermore, I hope this chapter inspires the research community to use large and nationally representative datasets, or enriched qualitative data, to continue the investigative work on the impact of immigrant generation on healthcare utilization. This way, we can use the data to leverage policy and systematic changes for culturally appropriate healthcare that is cognizant of the needs between immigrant generations.

REFERENCES

Adler, N. E., & Newman, K. (2002). Socioeconomic disparities in health: Pathways and policies. *Health Affairs, 21*(2), 60–76.

Akresh, R., & Akresh, I. R. (2011). Using achievement tests to measure language assimilation and language bias among the children of immigrants. *Journal of Human Resources, 46*(3), 647–667.

Andersen, R. M. (1995). Revisiting the behavioral model and access to medical care: Does it matter? *Journal of Health and Social Behavior, 36*(1), 1–10.

Buchmueller, T. C., Lo Sasso, A. T., Lurie, I., & Dolfin, S. (2007). Immigrants and employer-sponsored health insurance. *Health Services Research, 42*(1p1), 286–310.

California Health Interview Survey (CHIS). (2019). Retrieved August 28 2019 from http://healthpolicy.ucla.edu/chis/about/Pages/about.aspx.

Carrasquillo, O., Carrasquillo, A. I., & Shea, S. (2000). Health insurance coverage of immigrants living in the United States: Differences by citizenship status and country of origin. *American Journal of Public Health, 90*(6), 917.

Chiang-Hom, C. (2004). Transnational cultural practices of Chinese immigrant youth and parachute kids. In *Asian American Youth: Culture, Identity, and Ethnicity* (eds. Jennifer Lee and Min Zhou), 143–158.

Choi, J. Y. (2013). Negotiating old and new ways: contextualizing adapted health care-seeking behaviors of Korean immigrants in Hawaii. *Ethnicity and Health, 18*(4), 350–366.

De Gagne, J. C., Oh, J., So, A., & Kim, S. S. (2014). The healthcare experiences of Koreans living in North Carolina: A mixed methods study. *Health and Social Care in the Community, 22*(4), 417–428.

Dowd, J. B., & Zajacova, A. (2007). Does the predictive power of self-rated health for subsequent mortality risk vary by socioeconomic status in the US? *International Journal of Epidemiology, 36*(6), 1214–1221.

Espiritu, Y. L. (1994). The intersection of race, ethnicity, and class: The multiple identities of second-generation Filipinos. *Identities Global Studies in Culture and Power, 1*(2–3), 249–273.

Gee, G. C., & Ponce, N. (2010). Associations between racial discrimination, limited English proficiency, and health-related quality of life among 6 Asian ethnic groups in California. *American Journal of Public Health, 100*(5), 888–895.

Hill, L., Hofstetter, C. R., Hovell, M., Lee, J., Irvin, V., & Zakarian, J. (2006). Koreans' use of medical services in Seoul, Korea and California. *Journal of Immigrant and Minority Health, 8*(3), 273–280.

Huang, A. (2012). Disparities in health insurance coverage among Asian Americans. *Asian American Policy Review, 23*, 41.

Huang, K., & Carrasquillo, O. (2008). The role of citizenship, employment, and socioeconomic characteristics in health insurance coverage among Asian subgroups in the United States. *Medical Care, 46*(10), 1093–1098.

Hurh, W. M. (1990). The 1.5 generation: A paragon of Korean-American pluralism. *Korean Culture, 11*(1), 21–31.

Jacobs, E. A., Lauderdale, D. S., Meltzer, D., Shorey, J. M., Levinson, W., & Thisted, R. A. (2001). Impact of interpreter services on delivery of health care to limited-English-proficient patients. *Journal of General Internal Medicine, 16*(7), 468–474.

Jang, S. H. (2018). *Medical Transnationalism: Korean Immigrants' Medical Tourism to South Korea*. Rowman & Littlefield.

Jang, Y., Kim, G., & Chiriboga, D. A. (2005). Health, healthcare utilization, and satisfaction with service: Barriers and facilitators for older Korean Americans. *Journal of the American Geriatrics Society, 53*(9), 1613–1617.

Jenkins, C. N., Le, T., McPhee, S. J., Stewart, S., & Ha, N. T. (1996). Health care access and preventive care among Vietnamese immigrants: do traditional beliefs and practices pose barriers? *Social Science and Medicine, 43*(7), 1049–1056.

Juon, H. S., Choi, Y., & Kim, M. T. (2000). Cancer screening behaviors among Korean-American women. *Cancer Detection and Prevention, 24*(6), 589–601.

Kandula, N. R., Lauderdale, D. S., & Baker, D. W. (2007). Differences in self-reported health among Asians, Latinos, and non-Hispanic whites: The role of language and nativity. *Annals of Epidemiology, 17*(3), 191–198.

Leclere, F. B., Jensen, L., & Biddlecom, A. E. (1994). Health care utilization, family context, and adaptation among immigrants to the United States. *Journal of Health and Social Behavior, 35*(4), 370–384.

Lee, S., Choi, S., & Jung, M. J. (2014). Ethnic variation in access to health care of Asian Americans who are not US citizens: Chinese, Korean, and Vietnamese ethnic groups. *Journal of Health Care for the Poor and Underserved, 25*(2), 577–590.

Markova, T., Dean, F., & Neale, A. V. (2007). Healthcare attitudes and behaviors of immigrant and US-born women in Hamtramck, Michigan: A MetroNet study. *Ethnicity and Disease, 17*(4), 650.

Marmot, M. G., Adelstein, A. M., & Bulusu, L. (1984). Lessons from the study of immigrant mortality. *Lancet (London, England), 1*(8392), 1455.

Miltiades, H. B., & Wu, B. (2008). Factors affecting physician visits in Chinese and Chinese immigrant samples. *Social Science and Medicine, 66*(3), 704–714.

Min, P. G. (2008). *Ethnic Solidarity for Economic Survival: Korean Greengrocers in New York City*. Russell Sage Foundation.

Min, P. G. (ed.). (2012). *Koreans in North America: Their Experiences in the Twenty-First Century*. Lexington Books.

Mulvaney-Day, N. E., Alegria, M., & Sribney, W. (2007). Social cohesion, social support, and health among Latinos in the United States. *Social Science and Medicine, 64*(2), 477–495.

Park, K. (1999). "I really do feel I'm 1.5!": The construction of self and community by young Korean Americans. *Amerasia Journal, 25*(1), 139–164.

Portes, A., & Rumbaut, R. G. (2001). *Legacies: The Story of the Immigrant Second Generation*. University of California Press.

Razum, O., Zeeb, H., & Rohrmann, S. (2000). The "healthy migrant effect"—not merely a fallacy of inaccurate denominator figures. *International Journal of Epidemiology, 29*(1), 191–192.

Rumbaut, R. G. (2004). Ages, life stages, and generational cohorts: Decomposing the immigrant first and second generations in the United States. *International Migration Review, 38*(3), 1160–1205.

Rumbaut, R. G., & Ima, K. (1988). *The Adaptation of Southeast Asian Refugee Youth: A Comparative Study*. Washington, DC: US Department of Health and Human Services, Family Support Administration, Office of Refugee Resettlement.

Rumbaut, R. G., Massey, D. S., & Bean, F. D. (2006). Linguistic life expectancies: Immigrant language retention in Southern California. *Population and Development Review, 32*(3), 447–460.

Ryu, H., Young, W. B., & Park, C. (2001). Korean American health insurance and health services utilization. *Research in Nursing and Health, 24*(6), 494–505.

Schachter, A., Kimbro, R. T., & Gorman, B. K. (2012). Language proficiency and health status: Are bilingual immigrants healthier? *Journal of Health and Social Behavior, 53*(1), 124–145.

Seo, J. Y., Bae, S. H., & Dickerson, S. S. (2016). Korean immigrant women's health care utilization in the United States: A systematic review of literature. *Asia Pacific Journal of Public Health, 28*(2), 107–133.

Shin, H., Song, H., Kim, J., & Probst, J. C. (2005). Insurance, acculturation, and health service utilization among Korean-Americans. *Journal of Immigrant Health, 7*(2), 65–74.

Sohn, L., & Harada, N. D. (2004). Time since immigration and health services utilization of Korean-American older adults living in Los Angeles County. *Journal of the American Geriatrics Society, 52*(11), 1946–1950.

Son, J. (2013). Assimilation and health service utilization of Korean immigrant women. *Qualitative Health Research, 23*(11), 1528–1540.

Stella, M. Y., Huang, Z. J., & Singh, G. K. (2004). Health status and health services utilization among US Chinese, Asian Indian, Filipino, and other Asian/Pacific Islander children. *Pediatrics, 113*(1), 101–107.

Stephen, E. H. (1994). *Health of the Foreign-Born Population—United States, 1989–90* (No. 241). US Department of Health and Human Services, Public Health Service, Centers for Disease Control and Prevention, National Center for Health Statistics.

Thamer, M., Richard, C., Casebeer, A. W., & Ray, N. F. (1997). Health insurance coverage among foreign-born US residents: The impact of race, ethnicity, and length of residence. *American Journal of Public Health, 87*(1), 96–102.

U.S. Census Bureau. (2017). American Community Survey 1-Year Estimates. Retrieved from. https://factfinder.census.gov/faces/tableservices/jsf/pages/productview.xhtml?pid=ACS_15 _1YR_B02018&prodType=table.

Ye, J., Mack, D., Fry-Johnson, Y., & Parker, K. (2012). Health care access and utilization among US-born and foreign-born Asian Americans. *Journal of Immigrant and Minority Health, 14*(5), 731–737.

Zhou, M. (1997). Growing up American: The challenge confronting immigrant children and children of immigrants. *Annual Review of Sociology, 23*(1), 63–95.

Zhou, M., & Bankston III, C. L. (1994). Social capital and the adaptation of the second generation: The case of Vietnamese youth in New Orleans. *International Migration Review, 28*(4), 821–845.

8

Sexual Health Behaviors, Substance Use, and Health Care Utilization among Korean American Women

Minjin Kim and Hyeouk Chris Hahm

INTRODUCTION

One of the Health People 2020 goals is to eliminate health disparities and improve access to comprehensive health care services (US Department of Health and Human Services, 2011). Health care utilization, the use of health care services, is an important factor associated with disease prevention, early stage diagnosis and treatment, and overall health outcomes (Politzer et al., 2001). Evidence suggests that Asian immigrants face difficulties in obtaining appropriate and timely health care and have lower rates of health care access and utilization compared to the U.S.,-born population, particularly for preventive care and screening services (Lee et al., 2010; Ye, Mack, Fry-Johnson, & Parker, 2012). Major barriers are often related to lack of insurance, language barriers, discrimination, and lack of familiarity with the health care system (Hacker, Anies, Folb, Zallman, 2015; Seo, Kim, Dickerson, 2014; Seo, Kuerban, Bae, & Strauss, 2019).

Similar challenges have been documented in Korean American immigrants. For Korean American immigrants, health is not always the top priority (Fang et al., 2017; Kim et al., 2019). Instead, basic survival and their children's education are often seen as the most important asset within this community (Kim, 2002). In general, Korean American immigrants seek treatment when they are sick and the signs and symptoms of illness are not manageable (Kim, 2017), which suggests that wellness and prevention is not within the realm of their daily lives. However, there is a serious lack of data to accurately portray the health needs of this population, and people of Korean descent in the United States remain one of the most underserved and understudied minority population.

Korean populations are the fastest growing Asian subgroup in the United States. According to the Pew Research Center (2017), the Korean American population increased significantly by 48.4 percent between 2000 and 2015. As the immigration population has grown rapidly in the United States, there have been changes in the immigration generation of the Korean population in the United States. In the 1970s after the passage of the Immigration and Nationality Act of 1965, almost all Korean Americans were foreign-born immigrants (U.S. Department of Homeland Security, 2014). At the beginning of the twenty-first century, around two-thirds of the Korean American population is comprised of foreign-born immigrants (Pew Research Center, 2017). In 2015, the U.S. Census Bureau indicated that, among the foreign-born Korean population in the United States, 58 percent were U.S. citizens and 64 percent had lived in the United States for at least 10 years. Among those ages 5 and older, 58 percent reported speaking English "very well." These rapid changes have made it even more complex and difficult for researchers to understand the health and health behavior of people of Korean descent in the United States.

When examining specific health and health behaviors of Asian American immigrants, it is critical to disaggregate data by immigrant generational status (Duncan and Trejo, 2017). While several studies have examined the acculturation, health, and health behaviors of Korean Americans (Maxwell, Crespi, Alano, Sudan, & Bastani, 2012; Shin & Lach, 2014; Yu, Huang, & Singh, 2010), there has been little focused on immigrants who arrived as child or adolescents, such as the "1.5 generation," specifically on their health needs, risk behavior, and health utilization. The 1.5 generation Koreans are those who were born in Asia or a country other than the United States and came to the United States as a child or adolescent. They are a heterogeneous group, varied with citizenship and immigration status, language proficiency, and the development of cultural social networks. The 1.5 generation often does not fit into either first-generation (those who immigrate as adults) or the second generation (U.S.-born) categories (Roberge, 2009; Rumbaut & Ima, 1994). However, existing research often categorized 1.5 generation Korean Americans as foreign-born, which may mask its underlying health needs, risk behavior, and health utilization.

In this study, we define 1.5 generation as individuals who have been born in a foreign country and immigrated to the United States and grew up in the United States as a child or adolescent. We explore young 1.5 generation Korean-born immigrants' and second generation Korean Americans' acculturation, health and health behavior, and compare how these two generation groups are different or similar. We particularly examine sexual behaviors, health risk behavior, and health utilization of young 1.5 generation and second generation Korean women aged 18–35. Further, overall health care utilization (HIV testing, STI testing, physical health, mental health) among Asian Americans are disproportionately lower than other racial and ethnic groups (e.g., White, Black, and Hispanic) (Ulmer, Nerenz, & Mcfadden, 2009). To understand health risk behaviors and health utilization behaviors of young 1.5 generation and second generation Korean American women, this study aims to (1) assess the acculturation characteristics of 1.5 generation and second generation Korean American women, (2) evaluate the relationship between acculturation and sexual health behavior, substance use, and health care utilization (i.e., medical exams, HIV tests, STI tests, and gynecological exams) across the 1.5 generation and second-generation, and (3) assess the relationships between acculturation, sexual behaviors, substance use, and health utilization within the 1.5 generation group and the second generation group.

METHODS

Overview of the Study Project

Data for this study were derived from the Asian American Women's Sexual Health Initiative Project (AWSHIP), a five-year mixed methods study funded by the National Institute of Mental Health (NIMH). The data used for this chapter were collected from January 2010–August 2011. Study participants were required to meet all of the following criteria:(a) be a single (unmarried) woman; (b) be between ages 18–35; (c) have been born in a foreign country and immigrated to the United States and grew up in the United States as a child or adolescent (1.5 generation) or have been born in the United States (second generation); (d) be a current resident of the Greater Boston area; and (e) self-identify as Chinese, Vietnamese, Korean, or a mix of these ethnicities. For the purpose of this chapter, we selected only women who identified themselves as Korean.

A total of 720 Asian American women completed surveys using Computer-Assisted Self-Interviewing (CASI). Of these, 151 participants identified as 1.5 generation or second generation Korean and were included in the dataset for the purpose of this chapter. Trained research assistants provided laptop computers to each research participant and demonstrated how to use CASI, which has been shown to be effective in eliciting answers to highly sensitive questions, such as those involving substance use and HIV risk behaviors (Brown & Vanable, 2009). The survey took 45–60 minutes to complete, and participants received $20 as compensation for their time. All study protocols and procedures were approved by Boston University's Institutional Review Board (IRB).

Sample Characteristics

Of the 151 Korean American participants, the majority of participants were between 18–24 (81.3%), protestant (63.3%), and had some college or college degrees (73.2%). Among the participants, 56 participants identified themselves as 1.5 generation, while 95 participants identified as second generation (63.3%). There were no statistically significant differences between the 1.5 generation and the second generation.

Measurements

Acculturation

The Suinn-Lew Asian Self Identify Acculturation Scale (SL-Asia) is a 21-item measure, on a 5-point scale that assesses the multidimensional aspects of acculturation of Asian populations including language, ethnic media, food, friendship preferences, ethnic identification, and generational and residential status (Suinn, Ahuna, & Khoo, 1992). Total SL-ASIA scale scores reflect overall acculturation levels with high scores indicating greater acculturation.

Sexual behavior

Three variables measured sexual behavior patterns in this study (age of first sexual intercourse, condom use in past six months, and condom use at most recent sexual intercourse). Age of first sexual intercourse was assessed using the question: "how old were you the first time you had vaginal intercourse?" The responses were recoded into "under 18 years old," "18 years or older," and "not applicable." Condom use in past 6 months and at recent vaginal or anal intercourse was coded as "yes" or "no."

Substance use

Five variables were measured to assess substance use patterns (use of cigarettes, binge drinking, past year marijuana use, ever used illicit drugs, past year illicit drug use). Participants were asked "During the past 12 months, how many days did you drink alcohol?" Responses were recoded as 1 for "at least 1 day" and 0 for "none." Binge drinking was ascertained by asking "During the past 12 months, how many days did you have five or more drinks on a single occasion?" Responses were coded as 1 for "at least 1 day" and 0 for "none." "Have you ever smoked cigarettes regularly?" was asked with "yes" and "no" responses. These variables were dichotomized with "yes" and "no" responses. Past year marijuana use was ascertained by asking whether participants had used marijuana in the past twelve months. Past year illicit drug use was determined by asking whether participants had used cocaine, crystal metham-phetamine, or any other illegal drug in the past twelve months.

Health care utilization

Insurance status responses were coded as 1 for "have health insurance" and 0 for "no health insurance." Participants were asked, "How long ago did you last consult a doctor or nurse for a routine check-up?" Responses were coded as "within 1 year" or "longer than 1 year ago." Participants were asked "Has there been any time in the past 12 months when you thought you should get medical care, but you did not?" Responses were coded as "yes" or "no." Questions on whether participants had ever had a gynecologic or pelvic examination, ever had an HIV test, and ever had a STI test were asked. Responses to these questions were dichotomized with "yes" and "no" responses.

Statistical Analysis

Data analysis were conducted in SPSS (version 24.0). We used descriptive statistics and Chi-square analysis to examine the association between generations and demographic and acculturation characteristics. A series of one-way analysis of variance (ANOVA) was performed to determine the relationship between the mean acculturation score and the sexual health behavior, substance use, and health care utilization of young 1.5 generation and second generation Korean women in the Greater Boston area, considering statistical significance $p < 0.05$.

RESULTS

Demographic Acculturation Characteristics

Of the 151 participants, the majority of participants were between 18-24 (81.3%), protestant (63.3%), and second generation (63.3%). As presented in table 8.1, among the SL-ASIA survey items, location in which they were raised, community association, music preference, contact with Asia, language proficiency, language preference, feeling of pride of own ethnic group, self-identification of ethnicity, and self-reported cultural identity were statistically significant ($p < 0.05$).

Sexual Health Behavior

Nearly half of participants (48.3%) reported that they had never had sexual intercourse (table 8.2). There were no statistically significant differences between the 1.5 generation and second generation in relation to the age of first sexual intercourse. However, the age of first sexual intercourse and the acculturation was statistically significant among the 1.5 generation group ($p < 0.05$). Respondents who had first had sexual intercourse under the age of 18 had higher acculturation scores (Mean = 66.4. SD = 6.5) than those respondents who had first had sexual intercourse when they were 18 years old or older (Mean = 57.0, SD = 12.2) and those respondents who had never had sexual intercourse (Mean = 51.8, SD = 51.8). Among those who had sexual intercourse experience (n = 78), both 1.5 generation and second generation Korean women had low consistent use of condoms in the past 6 months (22.2% vs. 31.4%). There were significant differences in the consistent use of condoms at recent sexual intercourse between 1.5 generation and second generation ($p = 0.013$) participants. Compared to second generation Korean women, 1.5 generation Korean women were less likely to have used a condom at recent sexual intercourse (62.7% vs. 33.3%). Among the 1.5 generation group who had sexual intercourse experience (n = 27), those who used a condom at recent sexual intercourse had higher acculturation scores (Mean = 62.0, SD = 12.8) than those who didn't use a condom at recent sexual intercourse (Mean = 54.6, SD = 9.0).

Substance Use

As presented in table 8.3., 82.5 percent of participants reported that they drank alcohol at least one day in the past 12 months. Of these participants (n = 125), 56.8

Table 8.1 Acculturation Characteristics by Generation (N = 151)

	1.5 Generation (n = 56)		Second Generation (n = 95)		Total (n = 151)		
	N or M	% or SD	N or M	% or SD	N or M	% or SD	P-value[†]
SL-ASIA (21 items; range 21-105)	55.8	9.98	65.1	7.80			0.000*
Location raised							
Mostly in Asia	12	21.4	4	4.2	16	10.6	0.000*
Equally in Asia	11	19.6	5	5.3	16	10.6	
Mostly in US and some in Asia	16	28.6	21	22.1	37	24.5	
In US only	17	30.4	65	68.4	82	54.3	
Community association							
Almost exclusively Koreans	6	10.7	10	10.5	16	10.6	0.027*
Mostly Koreans	19	33.9	46	48.4	65	43.0	
About equally Korean and non-Korean groups	21	37.5	24	25.3	45	29.8	
Mostly non-Korean ethnic groups	6	10.7	15	15.8	21	3.9	
Almost exclusively non-Korean ethnic groups	4	7.1	0	0.0	4	2.6	
Music preference							
Only Korean music	1	1.8	0	0.0	1	0.7	0.038*
Mostly Korean	3	5.4	6	6.3	9	6.0	
Equally Korean and English	25	44.6	30	31.6	55	36.4	
Mostly English	14	25.0	46	48.4	60	39.7	
English only	13	23.2	13	13.7	26	17.2	
Contact with Asia							
Raised one year or more in Korea	33	58.9	23	24.2	56	37.1	0.000*
Lived for less than one year in Korea	3	5.4	5	5.3	8	5.3	
Occasional visits to Korea	12	21.4	50	52.6	62	41.1	
Occasional communications with people in Korea	5	8.9	10	10.5	15	9.9	
No communications with people in Korea	2	3.6	7	7.4	9	6.0	
Language proficiency							
Reading							
Read Korean better than English	4	7.1	2	2.1	6	4.0	0.001*

(Continued)

Table 8.1   Acculturation Characteristics by Generation (N = 151) *(Continued)*

	1.5 Generation (n = 56)		Second Generation (n = 95)		Total (n = 151)		
	N or M	% or SD	N or M	% or SD	N or M	% or SD	P-value†
Read both Korean and English equally well	21	37.5	12	12.6	33	21.9	
Read English better than Korean	26	46.4	71	74.7	97	64.2	
Read only English	5	8.9	10	10.5	15	9.9	
Writing							
Write Korean better than English	3	5.4	2	2.1	5	3.3	0.003*
Write both Korean and English equally well	16	28.6	7	7.4	23	15.2	
Write English better than Korean	30	53.6	71	74.7	101	66.9	
Write only English	7	12.5	15	15.8	22	14.6	
Language Preferences							
Mostly Korean, some English	3	5.4	1	1.1	4	2.6	0.003*
Korean and English about equally well	25	44.6	19	20.0	44	29.1	
Mostly English, some Korean	22	39.3	59	62.1	81	53.6	
Only English	6	10.7	16	16.8	22	14.6	
Pride							
Extremely proud	18	32.1	26	27.4	44	29.1	0.027*
Moderately proud	33	58.9	51	53.7	84	55.6	
Little pride	0	0.0	14	14.7	14	9.3	
No pride but do not feel negative toward group	4	7.1	4	4.2	8	5.3	
No pride but do feel negative toward group	1	1.8	0	0.0	1	0.7	
Self-Identification							
Asian	15	26.8	4	4.2	19	12.6	0.002*
Asian American	12	21.4	24	25.3	36	23.8	
Korean American	28	50.0	62	65.3	90	59.6	
American	1	1.8	4	4.2	5	3.3	
Refuse to answer	0	0.0	1	1.1	1	0.7	
Rate self							
Very Korean	3	5.4	2	2.1	5	3.3	0.009*
Mostly Korean	15	26.8	9	9.5	24	15.9	
Bicultural	26	46.4	48	50.5	74	49.0	
Mostly westernized	6	10.7	28	29.5	34	22.5	
Very westernized	6	10.7	8	8.4	14	9.3	

Note. †Significant difference (p < 0.05) between 1.5 generation and second generation.

Table 8.2 Sexual Health Behavior among Korean American Women (N = 151)

	1.5 Generation (n = 56)					Second Generation (n = 95)					Total (n = 151)		
			SL-ASIA					SL-ASIA					
	N	%	Mean	SD	P-value††	N	%	Mean	SD	P-value†††	N	%	P-value†
Age of first sexual intercourse													
<18 years old	10	17.9	66.4	6.5	0.000*	17	17.9	66.9	8.81	0.239	27	17.9	0.769
≥18 years old	17	30.4	57.0	12.2		34	35.8	66.0	5.30		51	33.8	
N/A	29	51.8	51.8	6.3		44	46.3	63.6	6.54		73	48.3	
Condom use past 6 months every time (n = 78)													
Yes	6	22.2	62.8	8.6	0.069	16	31.4	67.2	11.74	0.259	22	28.2	0.393
No	21	77.8	55.0	9.8		35	68.6	64.7	6.81		56	71.8	
Condom use at recent sex (n = 78)													
Yes	9	33.3	62.0	12.8	0.042*	32	62.7	64.5	6.73	0.335	41	52.6	0.013*
No	18	66.7	54.6	9.0		19	37.3	66.2	9.52		37	47.4	

Note: SD = Standard Deviation, SL-ASIA = Suinn-Lew Asian Self Identity Acculturation, N/A = Not applicable, *p < 0.05.
†Significant difference (p < 0.05) between 1.5 generation and second generation.
††Significant difference (p < 0.05) in acculturation score between the groups among 1.5 generation.
†††Significant difference (p < 0.05) in acculturation score between the groups among second generation.

Table 8.3 Substance Use among Young Korean American College Women by Generation (n = 151)

	1.5 Generation (n = 56)					Second Generation (n = 95)					Total		
			SL-ASIA					SL-ASIA					
	N	%	Mean	SD	P-value††	N	%	Mean	SD	P-value†††	N	%	P-value†
Days drink alcohol past 12 months													
At least 1 day	46	82.1	56.9	10.0	0.118	79	83.2	65.4	8.28	0.489	125	82.8	0.873
None	10	17.9	51.4	8.85		16	16.8	63.9	4.95		26	17.2	
Days binge drink past 12 months (n = 125)													
At least 1 day	25	54.3	57.8	11.61	0.538	46	58.2	66.2	8.21	0.269	71	56.8	0.673
None	21	45.7	55.9	7.91		33	41.8	64.1	8.34		54	43.2	
Days binge drink past 2 weeks (n = 125)													
At least 1 day	18	39.1	57.5	13.44	0.740	22	27.8	67.3	8.08	0.214	40	32.0	0.192
None	28	60.9	56.5	7.41		57	72.2	64.6	8.31		85	68.0	
Smoke cigarette regularly													
Yes	6	26.6	62.2	15.91	0.279	14	33.3	67.0	9.56	0.755	20	13.2	0.702
No	15	71.4	56.1	8.38		28	66.7	66.2	6.63		43	28.5	
Used marijuana past 12 months													
Yes	13	23.2	63.8	9.30	0.002*	36	37.9	67.9	6.80	0.006*	49	32.5	0.063
No	43	76.8	53.8	7.21		59	62.1	63.4	7.91		102	67.5	

Note: SD = Standard Deviation, SL-ASIA = Suinn-Lew Asian Self Identity Acculturation, *p < 0.05.
†Significant difference (p < 0.05) between 1.5 generation and second generation.
††Significant difference (p < 0.05) in acculturation score between the groups among 1.5 generation.
†††Significant difference (p < 0.05) in acculturation score between the groups among second generation.

percent of participants reported that they had engaged in binge drinking at least one day in the past 12 months. In this study, 13.2 percent of participants reported that they smoked cigarettes regularly and 32.5 percent reported having used marijuana in the past 12 months. Among those who had ever used marijuana (n = 66), 74.2 percent reported that they had used marijuana in the past 12 months. There were no statistically significant differences between immigration generational status and substance use behavior. A significant relationship between ever having used marijuana and the level of acculturation in the 1.5 generation group (p = 0.010) and the second generation group (p = 0.016). The 1.5 generation participants who had ever used marijuana had higher acculturation levels compared to those who had never used marijuana before. Similarly, the second generation respondents who had ever used marijuana had higher acculturation levels compared to those who had never used marijuana before (table 8.3.).

Health Care Utilization

As presented in table 8.4, 21.9 percent of participants reported that they had no health insurance during the time of the study. When health insurance status was compared by immigration generational status, 1.5 generation Korean American women were more than twice as likely to not have health insurance as second generation Korean American women (33.9 % vs. 14.7%, p = 0.006). About 31.4 percent of participants reported their last routine medical check-up was longer than one year ago. There was no statistically significant association between immigration generational status and the one-year routine medical check-up. However, among second generation Korean American women, respondents who reported having had their last routine medical check-up within one year had higher acculturation scores than those who reported having had their last routine medical check-up more than one year ago (p = 0.011). Moreover, 1.5 generation Korean American women were almost twice as likely as second generation Korean American women to report that they did not seek medical care when they needed to (25.0% vs. 13.7%).

With regards to ever having had a gynecological exam, almost half of participants (49%) reported that they had never had a gynecological exam; 43.8 percent of 1.5 generation Korean American women reported that they had never had a gynecological exam, compared to 51.1 percent of the second generation Korean American women. About 79.3 percent of Korean American women reported they had never seen a doctor for HIV testing and 72.2 percent reported they had never seen a doctor for STI testing. There were no significant differences between immigration generational status and reported receiving of HIV testing and STI testing. However, 1.5 generation Korean American women who reported having seen a doctor for HIV testing and STI testing had significantly higher acculturation scores than those who had never been tested for HIV and STIs (p = 0.002, p = 0.001, respectively).

Table 8.4 Health Care Utilization Behavior among Korean American College Women (n = 151)

	1.5 Generation (n = 56)					Second Generation (n = 95)					Total		
	N	%	SL Mean	SD	P-value[††]	N	%	SL Mean	SD	P-value[†††]	N	%	P-value[†]
Health insurance													
Yes	37	66.1	55.6	8.35	0.768	81	85.3	65.3	7.63	0.494	118	78.1	0.006*
No	19	33.9	56.4	12.69		14	14.7	63.8	8.84		33	21.9	
Routine medical check-up[1]													
Within 1 year	34	66.7	58.2	10.26	0.202	60	69.8	66.9	7.56	0.011*	94	68.6	0.705
>1 year ago	17	33.3	54.4	8.61		26	30.2	62.3	6.67		43	31.4	
Did not get a medical care when needed													
Yes	14	25.0	56.6	9.5	0.763	13	13.7	65.8	7.21	0.744	27	17.9	0.080
No	42	75.0	55.6	10.26		82	86.3	65.0	7.93		124	82.1	
Ever had gynecological exam[2]													
Yes	27	56.3	58.6	9.61	0.231	43	48.9	66.3	8.0	0.257	70	51.5	0.410
Never	21	43.8	55.1	9.85		45	51.1	64.4	7.08		66	48.5	
Ever HIV tested[3]													
Yes	8	14.5	66.0	8.16	0.002*	23	24.2	65.9	8.40	0.584	31	20.7	0.159
No	47	85.5	54.0	9.20		72	75.8	64.9	7.65		119	79.3	
Ever STIs tested													
Yes	12	21.4	64.8	7.64	0.001*	30	31.6	66.4	8.60	0.266	42	27.8	0.179
No	44	78.6	53.6	9.25		65	68.4	64.5	7.39		109	72.2	

Note: SD = Standard Deviation, SL = Suinn-Lew Asian Self Identity Acculturation, *p < 0.05.
[1]Fourteen missing values were excluded and the percentages are based on the number of non-missing values.
[2]Fifteen missing values were excluded and the percentages are based on the number of non-missing values.
[3]One missing values were excluded and the percentages are based on the number of non-missing values.
*Significant difference (p < 0.05) between 1.5 generation and second generation.
**Significant difference (p < 0.05) in acculturation score between the groups among 1.5 generation.
***Significant difference (p < 0.05) in acculturation score between the groups among second generation.

DISCUSSION

The present study documents important findings relating acculturation, sexual behaviors, substance use, and health care utilization across 1.5 generation and second generation young Korean women in the United States. There were a number of health risk behaviors and health utilization behaviors that were similar regardless of immigration generation differences. However, when we specifically examined the relationships among acculturation, sexual behaviors, substance use, and health utilization within the 1.5 generation and second generation group, we revealed that as this group becomes more acculturated, high risk behaviors increase, such as sexual health behaviors and substance use.

In this study, almost half of Korean American women, both 1.5 generation and second generation, had never had sexual intercourse. This shows that this population tends to delay their first sexual intercourse compared to other racial and ethnic groups (Boislard, Bongardt, & Blais, 2016), however, once they were sexually experienced, they did not report consistent condom use. Consistent condom use in the past 6 months was reported by only 22.2 percent of the 1.5 generation group and 31.4 percent of the second generation group. When we specifically examined the relationships between acculturation and sexual behaviors, less acculturated members of the 1.5 generation group were shown to have less likely had earlier initiation of sexual intercourse than those who were highly acculturated. However, less acculturated 1.5 generation group members reported that they did not use condoms during recent sexual contact and were less likely to have seen a doctor for HIV testing and STI testing compared to those who were highly acculturated in the 1.5 generation group. Prior studies of Asian immigrants indicate that less acculturated Asian American women reported more conservative rates of sexual behavior than less acculturated Asian American women (Hahm, Lahiff, & Barreto, 2006; Meston & Ahrold, 2010). In the Asian collectivist nature of cultural context, HIV- and STI-related stigma and cultural taboos may act as barriers to HIV and STI prevention. These cultural barriers may not effectively encourage Korean women to seek for HIV and STI testing services, even when they are at risk and in need of services (Hahm, Song, Ozonoff, Sassani, 2009).

Results of this study further revealed that Korean American women were at a high risk of engaging in substance use such as drinking alcohol, smoking cigarettes, and smoking marijuana, regardless of immigration generational status differences. In the United States in 2018, 12.1 percent of women, 25.1 percent of those aged 18–24 years, and 25.7 percent of those aged 25–34 years reported binge drinking (Kanny et al., 2018). The binge drinking habits of Korean American women was comparatively high (56.8%) in our sample. Consistently, studies have found heavy episode drinking among Korean Americans (Iwamoto, Takamatsu & Castellanos, 2012). Cook, Karriker-Jaffe, Bond, and Lui (2014) suggest that immigrants from strong ethnic drinking cultures, like Korea are more likely to have problematic drinking patterns after migrating to the United States, especially when they are transitioning from adolescence to adulthood. In addition, prior studies reported that those who migrated at an earlier age, especially women, may be at a higher risk of binge drinking (Li and Wen, 2015; Torres, Ro, & Sudhinaraset, 2019). The smoking rates of our sample were slightly lower (13.2%) than overall Massachusetts smoking rates (16.9%) (Centers for Disease Control and Prevention, 2019). However, the rates of marijuana use in the past 12 months in our sample (32.5%) were relatively high compared to young Asian American women in Massachusetts (26.1%) (Hahm, Augsberger, Feranil, Jang, J., & Tagerman, 2017). This study further highlights that more highly acculturated 1.5 generation and second generation Korean women were significantly associated with marijuana use in the past 12 months. This result is similar to other studies that examined the relationship between acculturation and substance use among Asian Americans (Thai, Connell, & Tebes, 2010). There is evidence that acculturative stress (Iwamoto, Grivel, Cheng, & Zamboanga, 2016; Iwamoto, Kaya, Grivel, & Clinton, 2016), depression and suicidal thoughts (Hahm, Gonyea, Chiao, & Koritsanszky, 2014), and the differences in acculturation levels between parents and children (Choi, He, & Harachi, 2008) contribute to substance use and illicit drug use among adolescents and young Asian American adults. This finding raises important questions regarding mental health utilization among Korean American women.

Perhaps the most alarming finding of this chapter is the pattern of underutilization of all types of medical and sexual health care. It is important to recognize that the samples were MA residents, and MA requires all residents to enroll in health insurance. In spite of this, 33.9 percent of 1.5 generation and 14.7 percent of second generation women reported not having insurance. Between the two groups, although second generation women had a higher proportion of health insurance than 1.5 generation, both groups had similar patterns of poor health care utilization. Specifically, in terms of medical health care utilization, one in three from both groups had had routine medical check-ups more than one year ago. Reproductive health care utilization was even worse for both groups: only about one in two had ever had gynecological exams. Less than one in four from both groups reported ever having had HIV testing and less than one in three from both groups reported ever being tested for STIs. This is consistent with a previous study (Hahm et al., 2009). This finding highlights that both the 1.5 and second generation are vulnerable groups with poor health care seeking behaviors. Notably, both groups grew up in America, thus, English language may not be the barrier for health care utilization. In addition, these women tend to have higher education levels; 90.0 percent of women were in college or had completed college education. For the majority of second generation women in particular, lack of health insurance may not be the reason for not seeking routine exams. Although there was no statistical significance of not getting medical care when needed between 1.5 generation and second generation Korean, it is important to note that 1.5 generation women were twice as likely to report that they did not get medical care when needed compared to the second generation (25.0% vs. 13.7%). This might be due to 1.5 generation members who were foreign-born facing unique acculturative stressors, such as language and health communication barriers, and not being familiar with the health care system in the United States.

IMPLICATIONS FOR FUTURE RESEARCH

Historically, scholarship on immigrant health and health behaviors has been focused on how immigrants change and adapt to the dominant American culture and how it may in turn influence their health and wellbeing. Particularly, there has been a notable emphasis on U.S.-based societal and cultural assimilation or acculturation of health behaviors. More recently, studies have begun to look at a transnational framework and combine with an assimilation-focused framework to examine the potential for ongoing influence of countries of origin and its influence on immigrant health and health behaviors among U.S. immigrants (Portes & Rumbaut, 2014; Torres, Ro, & Sudhinaraset, 2019). We suggest that future research is needed to examine health and health behaviors of 1.5 generation Koreans using both transnational and assimilationist frameworks while paying attention to heterogeneity of the 1.5 generation Koreans.

Our findings may provide contributions to advance research, policy, and intervention programs. Our study showed that the level of acculturation varies between and within the 1.5 and the second generation Korean Americans, which emphasizes the importance of considering the acculturation and immigration generational status in understanding this diverse ethnic group and to provide more comprehensive and conclusive explanations of 1.5 generation Korean Americans health, health risk behaviors and health utilization. As has been noted in previous studies, early initiation of sexual intercourse, substance use, and use of preventive health services are shaped by the acculturation process in American society (Becerra, Herring, Marshak, & Banta, 2013; Roncancio, Ward, Berenson, 2011; Thai, Connell, & Tebes, 2010). Given that nearly half of young Korean American women are engaging in high-risk drinking, almost one-third of young Korean American women use marijuana, and there is low preventive health care utilization, public health policies to reduce alcohol consumption and substance use and promote preventive health care utilization are needed in this population.

For future research, it will be important to conduct a thorough in-depth analysis on the barriers and facilitators of medical/sexual health utilization based on acculturation and immigration generational status of young Korean women in the United States. Due to the cross-sectional and retrospective design of this study, it does not lend itself to the establishment of temporal order. We suggest longitudinal designs to further understand how the temporal relationship between acculturation and cultural development may impact acculturative stress, and how it mediates the effects of sexual health and substance use problems among Korean American women.

Currently, there are limited health education intervention studies that focus on 1.5 generation Korean immigrants. One study that developed a storytelling HPV intervention in considering the cultural and generational differences among Korean American college women suggest that Korean American college women had tendency to identify themselves with the health experience stories that corresponded to their generation as the most engaging and they felt most connected to it (Kim, Lee, Kiang, & Allison, 2019). This exploratory study raises an interesting line of investigation for future research to develop comprehensive cross-cultural and cross-generational specific interventions focused on multiple health domains such as sexual health, mental health, and substance use, rather than interventions targeted to one culture, one generation, or one health domain for vulnerable young Korean American women. Moreover, researchers and health care providers must be mindful about the differences and similarities in health and health behaviors between 1.5 Korean immigrants and U.S.-born Korean Americans, and screen for the level of acculturation in primary care, counseling centers and early intervention programs to identify young Korean Americans who may be at risk for or currently experiencing sexual health risks and substance use problems. It is clear that there are a variety of opportunities for future research that takes into account acculturation and generational status of Korean Americans.

REFERENCES

Becerra, M. B., Herring, P., Hopp Marshak, H., & Banta, J. E. (2013). Association between acculturation and binge drinking among Asian-Americans: Results from the California Health Interview Survey. *Journal of addiction, 2013,* 10. doi:10.1155/2013/248196

Boislard, M. A., van de Bongardt, D., & Blais, M. (2016). Sexuality (and Lack Thereof) in adolescence and early adulthood: A review of the literature. *Behavioral Sciences (Basel, Switzerland), 6*(1), 8. doi:10.3390/bs6010008

Brown, J., & Vanable, P. (2009). The effects of assessment mode and privacy level on self-reports of risky sexual behaviors and substance use among young women. *Journal of Applied Social Psychology, 39*(11), 2756–2778.

Centers for Disease Control and Prevention. (2019). Current Cigarette Smoking among Adults in the United States. Retrieved from https://www.cdc.gov/tobacco/data_statistics/f act_sheets/adult_data/cig_smoking/index.htm.

Choi, Y., He, M., & Harachi, T. W. (2008). Intergenerational cultural dissonance, parent-child conflict and bonding, and youth problem behaviors among Vietnamese and Cambodian immigrant families. *Journal of Youth and Adolescence, 37*(1), 85–96. doi:10.1007/s10964-007-9217-z

Cook, W. K., Karriker-Jaffe, K. J., Bond, J., & Lui, C. (2015). Asian American problem drinking trajectories during the transition to adulthood: Ethnic drinking cultures and neighborhood contexts. *American journal of Public Health, 105*(5), 1020–1027. doi:10.2105/AJPH.2014.302196

Duncan, B., & Trejo, S. J. (2017). The complexity of immigrant generations: Implications for assessing the socioeconomic integration of Hispanics and Asians. *Industrial & Labor Relations Review, 70*(5), 1146–1175. doi:10.1177/0019793916679613

Fang, C. Y., Ma, G. X., Handorf, E. A., Feng, Z., Tan, Y., Rhee, J., Miller, S. M., Kim, C., & Koh, H. S. (2017). Addressing multilevel barriers to cervical cancer screening in Korean American women: A randomized trial of a community-based intervention. *Cancer, 123*(6), 1018–1026. doi:10.1002/cncr.30391

Hacker, K., Anies, M., Folb, B. L., & Zallman, L. (2015). Barriers to health care for undocumented immigrants: A literature review. *Risk Management and Healthcare Policy, 8,* 175–183. doi:10.2147/RMHP.S70173

Hahm, H. C., Augsberger, A., Feranil, M., Jang, J., & Tagerman, M. (2017). The asso-ciations between forced sex and severe mental health, substance use, and HIV risk behaviors among Asian American women. *Violence Against Women, 23*(6), 671–691. doi:10.1177/1077801216647797

Hahm, H. C., Gonyea, J. G., Chiao, C., & Koritsanszky, L. A. (2014). Fractured identity: a framework for understanding young Asian American women's self-harm and suicidal behaviors. *Race and Social Problems, 6*(1), 56–68. doi:10.1007/s12552-014-9115-4

Hahm, H. C., Lahiff, M., & Barreto, R. (2006). Asian American adolescents' first sexual intercourse: Gender and acculturation differences. *Perspectives on Sexual and Reproductive Health, 38*(1), 28–36.

Hahm, H. C., Song, I., Ozonoff, A., & Sassani, J. (2009). HIV testing among sexually expe-rienced Asian and Pacific Islander young women. *Women's Health Issues, 19*(4), 279–288.

Iwamoto, D., Takamatsu, S., & Castellanos, J. (2012). Binge drinking and alcohol-related problems among U.S.-Born Asian Americans. *Cultural Diversity and Ethnic Minority Psy-chology, 18*(3), 219–227.

Iwamoto, D. K., Grivel, M., Cheng, A., & Zamboanga, B. (2016). Asian American and White college students' heavy episodic drinking behaviors and alcohol-related problems. *Substance Use and Misuse, 51*(10), 1384–1392.

Iwamoto, D. K., Kaya, A., Grivel, M., & Clinton, L. (2016). Under-researched demograph-ics: heavy episodic drinking and alcohol-related problems among Asian Americans. *Alcohol Research: Current Reviews, 38*(1), 17–25.

Kanny, D., Naimi, T., Liu, Y., Lu, H., & Brewer, R. (2018). Annual total binge drinks consumed by U.S. adults, 2015. *American Journal of Preventive Medicine, 54*(4), 486–496.

Kim, E. (2002). The relationship between parental involvement and children's educational achievement in the Korean immigrant family. *Journal of Comparative Family Studies, 33*(4), 529–540.

Kim, M., Lee, H., Kiang, P., & Allison, J. (2019). Development and acceptability of a peer-paired, cross-cultural and cross-generational storytelling HPV intervention for Korean American college women. *Health Education Research, 34*(5), 483–494.

Kim, M., Lee, H., Kiang, P., Aronowitz, T., Sheldon, L. K., Shi, L., Kim, S., & Allison, J. (2019). HPV vaccination and Korean American college women: Cultural factors, knowl-edge, and attitudes in cervical cancer prevention. *Journal of Community Health, 44*(4), 646–655. doi:10.1007/s10900-019-00634-9

Kim, M., Lee, H., Kiang, P., & Kim, D. (2017). Human Papillomavirus: A qualitative study of Korean American female college students' attitudes toward vaccination. *Clinical Journal of Oncology Nursing, 21*(5), E239–E247. doi:10.1188/17.CJON.E239-E247

Li, K., & Wen, M. (2015). Substance use, age at migration, and length of residence among adult immigrants in the United States. *Journal of Immigrant and Minority Health, 17*(1), 156–164. doi:10.1007/s10903-013-9887-4

Lee, S., Martinez, G., Ma, G. X., Hsu, C. E., Robinson, E. S., Bawa, J., & Juon, H. S. (2010). Barriers to health care access in 13 Asian American communities. *American Journal of Health Behavior, 34*(1), 21–30. doi:10.5993/ajhb.34.1.3

Maxwell, A. E., Crespi, C. M., Alano, R. E., Sudan, M., & Bastani, R. (2012). Health risk behaviors among five Asian American subgroups in California: Identifying interven-tion priorities. *Journal of Immigrant and Minority Health, 14*(5), 890–894. doi:10.1007/s10903-011-9552-8

Meston, C. M., & Ahrold, T. (2010). Ethnic, gender, and acculturation influences on sexual behaviors. *Archives of Sexual Behavior, 39*(1), 179–189. doi:10.1007/s10508-008-9415-0

Pew Research Center. (2017). "Koreans: Data on Asian Americans." Pew Research Center's Social & Demographic Trends Project. Retrieved from https://www.pewsocialtrends.org/fact-sheet/asian-americans-koreans-in-the-u-s/.

Politzer, R. M., Yoon, J., Shi, L., Hughes, R. G., Regan, J., & Gaston, M. H. (2001). Inequality in America: The contribution of health centers in reducing and eliminating disparities in access to care. *Medical Care Research and Review, 58*(2), 234–248. doi:10.1177/107755870105800205

Portes, A., & Rumbaut, R. (2014). *Immigrant America: A Portrait.* University of California Press.

Pyon, T. (2012). Understanding 1.5 generation Korean Americans: Considering their diversity and educational experiences. 재외한인연구, *28*, 85–122.

Roberge, M. A. (2009). Teacher's perspective on generation 1.5, in *Generation 1.5 in College Composition: Teaching Academic Writing to US-Educated Learners of ESL,* edited by Roberge, Siegal, and Harklau, pp. 3–24. New York: Routledge.

Roncancio, A. M., Ward, K. K., & Berenson, A. B. (2011). Hispanic women's health care provider control expectations: The influence of fatalism and acculturation. *Journal of Health Care for the Poor and Underserved, 22*(2), 482–490. doi:10.1353/hpu.2011.0038

Rumbaut, R. G. (1994). The crucible within: Ethnic identity, self-esteem, and segmented assimilation among children of immigrants. *International Migration Review, 28* (4), 748–794.

Seo, J., Kim, W., & Dickerson, S. (2014). Korean immigrant women's lived experience of childbirth in the United States. *Journal of Obstetric, Gynecologic and Neonatal Nursing, 43*(3), 305–317.

Seo, J., Kuerban, A., Bae, S., & Strauss, S. (2019). Disparities in health care utilization between Asian Immigrant women and non-Hispanic white women in the United States. *Journal of Women's Health, 28*(10), 1368–1377.

Shin, C. N., & Lach, H. W. (2014). Acculturation and health of Korean American adults. *Journal of Transcultural Nursing, 25*(3), 273–280. doi:10.1177/1043659614523454

Song, Y., Hofstetter, C., Hovell, M., Paik, H., Park, H., Lee, J., & Irvin, V. (2004). Acculturation and health risk behaviors among Californians of Korean descent. *Preventive Medicine, 39*(1), 147–156.

Suinn, R., Ahuna, C., & Khoo, G. (1992). The Suinn-Lew Asian self-identity acculturation scale: Concurrent and factorial validation. *Educational and Psychological Measurement, 52*(4), 1041–1046.

Thai, N. D., Connell, C. M., & Tebes, J. K. (2010). Substance use among Asian American adolescents: Influence of race, ethnicity, and acculturation in the context of key risk and protective factors. *Asian American Journal of Psychology, 1*(4), 261–274. doi:10.1037/a0021703

Torres, J. M., Ro, A., & Sudhinaraset, M. (2019). Reconsidering the relationship between age at migration and health behaviors among US immigrants: The modifying role of continued cross-border ties. *Advances in Medical Sociology, 19*, 17–45.

Ulmer, C., McFadden, B., & Nerenz, D. R. (eds.). (2009). *Race, Ethnicity, and Language Data: Standardization for Health Care Quality Improvement.* National Academies Press (US).

U.S. Department of Health and Human Services. (2011). *Access to Health Services.* Washington (DC): DHHS. Retrieved from http://www.healthypeople.gov/2020/about/history.aspx

U.S. Department of Homeland Security. (2014). *Yearbook of Immigration Statistics, 2013.* Lawful Permanent Residents Supplemental Table 1. Retrieved from http://www.dhs.gov/yearbook-immigration-statistics

Ye, J., Mack, D., Fry-Johnson, Y., & Parker, K. (2012). Health care access and utilization among US-born and foreign-born Asian Americans. *Journal of Immigrant and Minority Health, 14*(5), 731–737. doi:10.1007/s10903-011-9543-9

Yu, S. M., Huang, Z. J., & Singh, G. K. (2010). Health status and health services access and utilization among Chinese, Filipino, Japanese, Korean, South Asian, and Vietnamese children in California. *American journal of Public Health, 100*(5), 823–830. doi:10.2105/AJPH.2009.168948.

IV

TRANSNATIONALISM AND ENTREPRENEURSHIP

9

Navigating In-Betweenness

How 1.5 Generation Immigrant Entrepreneurs Recombine Resources from Both Worlds

June Y. Lee and Edison Tse

INTRODUCTION

Immigrant entrepreneurs have been taking a growing share of the overall entrepreneurship activities in the United States. According to the Kauffman Index Report, immigrants are twice as likely to become entrepreneurs than native-born Americans (Kauffman Index, 2017). For instance, 13 percent of new entrepreneurs were immigrants in 1997, and this percentage increased to 29 percent by 2014. Moreover, more than 40 percent of the Fortune 500 companies in 2010 were founded by immigrants or children of immigrants (Partnership for a New American Economy, 2011). Migration serves as cross-border investment and trade (Gould, 1994; Leblang, 2010), while the entrepreneurship activities of high-skill immigrants can be attributed to the creation of jobs and wealth at the regional or national level (Kerr & Kerr, 2020; Lee & Lee, 2020; Saxenian, 2005, 2006). Though prior research has examined migrant entrepreneurship, the multi-faceted perspective of this discipline requires greater attention. Understanding the complexity of various dimensions of immigrant entrepreneurship such as ethnicity, generation, gender, and types of entrepreneurship activities becomes critical because these dimensions subsequently influence one's entrepreneurial motives, decision-making processes, and performance.

The larger body of immigrant entrepreneurship literature focuses on the self-employment of certain ethnic groups such as Gujarati-speaking Indians who own motels, Yemenis who own grocery stores, or Koreans who own dry-cleaning services (Kerr & Mandorff, 2019; Thomas & Ong, 2015), but another stream of immigrant entrepreneurship literature emphasizes the high-technology entrepreneurship activities of immigrant entrepreneurs (Lee & Eesley, 2018; Lee & Lee, 2020;

Saxenian, 2006). One main difference between self-employment and high-technology entrepreneurship activity is the economic and social impact of these activities that boosts job creation, level of innovation, social mobility, and wealth creation. Identifying entrepreneurship opportunity is based on how well entrepreneurs are integrated in the institutional contexts of the host and home countries—the intergenerational aspect.

One dimension, in particular, deserves more attention: the 1.5 generation of immigrants and their entrepreneurship activities. The term "1.5 generation" refers to individuals who immigrated to their host country before or during their adolescent or formal socialization years (Hurh, 1990; Lee & Cynn, 1991; Rumbaut & Ima, 1988). As the fastest-growing segment of the immigrant population, 1.5 generation immigrants play an integral role in bridging the home and host countries. Compared to the second and third generation of immigrants, 1.5 generation immigrants are not only more cognizant of the institutional cultural and social norms but also better positioned to recombine resources that are considered as valuable and rare and not easily imitated and substituted. Through the advancement of technology, 1.5 generation immigrants are able to identify cross-border opportunities and utilize financial, human, and operational resources in multiple institutional contexts.

In this paper, we extend the existing literature of immigrant entrepreneurship by focusing on a particular group of immigrant entrepreneurs: the 1.5 generation of immigrant entrepreneurs as boundary-spanning intermediaries. Through an in-depth, inductive case study of four new ventures established by 1.5 generation immigrant entrepreneurs in the San Francisco Bay Area, this study demonstrates the importance of opportunity identification, acceleration and growth, and resource recombination in both home and host countries. This study contributes to the immigrant and international entrepreneurship literature by providing a rich context of high-skill1.5 immigrant entrepreneurs.

IMMIGRANT ENTREPRENEURSHIP
AND 1.5 GENERATION

The field of immigrant entrepreneurship is interdisciplinary, as has been covered by researchers from geography, migration, sociology, management, and international businesses over recent decades (Kerr & Mandorff, 2015; Lee, 2018; Lee & Lee 2020; Saxenian, 2005, 2006; Thomas& Ong, 2015). However, there has been a significant rise in interest by those in management and entrepreneurship, especially as the flow of talent and cross-border ideas has begun to create notably increased economic value and wealth creation with the advancement of technology and infrastructure. Yet, multi-faceted immigrants and their entrepreneurship experiences are often treated as a homogenous entity, as *immigrants,* and that deserves more detailed attention by entrepreneurship scholars.

In the early years of immigrant entrepreneurship literature, the first-generation immigrant research primarily studied the self-employment and business activities of minority communities and ethnic groups. These studies documented their immigrant experiences, including challenges such as language, cultural, and socioeconomic barriers to integrate into their host country. Consequently, ethnic communities tend to operate businesses in a similar sector, as immigrant entrepreneurs relied on ethnic networks, resources, and financial capital. For instance, as of 2016, 80 percent of the dry cleaners in the state of New York are owned by Korean American immigrants who immigrated to the United States in the 1970s and 1980s, according to the Korean American Dry Cleaners' Association of New York. Kerr & Mandorff (2015) found that seventeen out of twenty-five ethnic groups demonstrated this pattern of a high concentration of one ethnic group dominating a business sector through socializing, from recreational to religious settings, where job-related networks, knowledge, and skills have been transferred within an ethnic community.

However, one way to segment immigrant entrepreneurship is by analyzing through inter-generations (i.e., first-generation vs. second-generation). Rusinovic (2008) compared transnational embeddedness of first- and second-generation immigrant entrepreneurs in the Netherlands and discovered that embeddedness of transnational networks is less active for second-generation compared to first-generation immigrant entrepreneurs. Beckers and Blumberg (2013) also highlighted the intergenerational aspects of immigrant entrepreneurship and having different "transnational capital." More specifically, a higher level of social-cultural integration of second-generation immigrant entrepreneurs does not necessarily lead to better entrepreneurship activities.

The 1.5 generation immigrant entrepreneurs are transnational and boundary-spanning by nature. By the definition of 1.5 generation immigrants, these entrepreneurs were born in their home country but have spent a significant amount of time in the host country, often adolescent and formal socialization years through schooling and work experiences (Lee, 2018). Their "in-between" experiences are different from those of the first generation who immigrated to the host country after their identity was completely shaped by the values and culture of the home country. As a connector and a bridge, 1.5 generation entrepreneurs have been immersed in the two cultures, languages, and socioeconomic systems of both the home and host country, and this has certainly accelerated with technology and the internet in recent years. As a result, they are fully aware of the institutional contexts of these two countries and are capable of conducting cross-border business activities and transactions. This allows them to uniquely position themselves to take advantage of the best of both worlds. For instance, they are able to lower operational and hiring costs, learning costs, and fundraising costs by tapping into their home and/or host countries. This is aligned with prior literature on transnational entrepreneurship where transnational entrepreneurs are immigrant entrepreneurs who conduct cross-border business activities, and during this process, they discover and execute business opportunities across multiple borders (Chen & Tan, 2008; Portes, Haller, & Guranizo, 2002; Saxenian, Motoyama, & Quan, 2002). It is worth pointing out that not all immigrant entrepreneurs are assumed to be transnational, even though they are more likely to conduct cross-border business activities compared to native-born entrepreneurs.

This study aims to better understand how 1.5 generation immigrant entrepreneurs utilize cross-border resources and networks through various entrepreneurship stages. This chapter is organized as follows. In the next section, we introduce our research methodology and case study settings. Then, we present our findings by presenting three common themes that we identified from the case study. Finally, we conclude by highlighting our theoretical and practical contribution to the field of immigrant entrepreneurship and present opportunities for future studies.

METHOD

In this study, we use an inductive in-depth case study combined with a historical-archival method to examine how new ventures incorporated by 1.5 generation immigrant entrepreneurs utilize their networks and resources from both home and host countries during the entrepreneurship process. A case study methodology is most applicable for underexplored topics that seek rich insights and narratives and where specific hypotheses are not presented to test through empirical data (Yin, 2017). In this study, a case study methodology was used to explore emerging themes and propose specific hypotheses that can be deductively analyzed in future studies (Eisenhardt, 1989; Yin, 2017). The context of this exploratory case study is technology-oriented firms founded by 1.5 generation Korean American immigrant entrepreneurs in the San Francisco Bay Area. We chose to study firms established by 1.5 generation Korean Americans because South Korea—the home country of the founders—is considered one of the most technologically advanced and digitally connected countries in the world. According to the Pew Research Center, South Korea has a 95 percent smart phone penetration rate and a 97 percent internet usage rate as of 2019. Since 2013, the Korean government has had a strong push toward entrepreneurship as job and wealth creation, social mobility, and economic growth. The historical growth of relying on large business groups has been slowing down, and the country has recognized that it is no longer scalable and competitive. Thus, significant capital and investments—both private and public sectors—have been allocated to entrepreneurship in order to develop infrastructure and ecosystems in the past decade. This strategic decision, often referred to as the Creative Economy Initiative, has attracted Korean American immigrants to return either temporarily or permanently to take advantage of opportunities that are available in both home and host countries. Yet, prior research on Korean American immigrant entrepreneurship has focused on low-skilled self-employment (Kim & Hurh, 1985), and this Korean ethnic group is relatively under-served compared to other large communities such as Chinese or Indian Americans. Recent years have seen growing examples of successful new ventures by Korean American immigrants, including Fitbit, Gusto, LegalZoom, Luxe, MyFitnessPal, Noom, and the Honest Company.

Unlike deductive studies that look at random sampling, this study strategically selected four specific firms that share the following characteristics. First, at least one co-founder of the founding team is a 1.5 generation Korean American immigrant entrepreneur. The exact time period of immigration to the United States and reasons for their immigration vary, ranging from seeking a better quality of life to the pursuit of improved educational or professional opportunities. Regardless of the reason for their immigration to the United States, these 1.5 Korean American immigrant entrepreneurs, as founding members, are in a position to make strategic decisions.

Next, all the firms are technology firms rather than low-skilled or self-employment entrepreneurship opportunities. In other words, their business values are being created and delivered through technology, and technology serves as the core of their product or services, business operations, and business model. This also implies that these ventures are funded through private investments such as angel investors, venture capitalists, government grants, and corporate venture capital funds rather than self-funded or business loans through commercial banks. The role of high-skill, high-tech Korean American immigrant entrepreneurs has been growing, with direct economic impacts on job and wealth creation.

Lastly, these new ventures are still operating and headquartered in the San Francisco Bay Area—often referred to as Silicon Valley. This region has the largest high-skilled and technology-oriented Korean American immigrant entrepreneur population in the United States. The Korean government announced the launch of Korea Innovation Center, a government-run accelerator with strategic partnerships from private sectors, and selected four strategic foreign locations: San Jose, Washington DC, Berlin, and Beijing. The San Francisco Bay Area, which spans from San Francisco to San Jose, has very active Korean American science and engineering communities.

We purposefully decided to restrict this study to the Silicon Valley because this region has the largest high-tech, high-skill Korean American immigrants in the United States and thus provided more cases from which to select and analyze. Prior literature on immigrant entrepreneurship demonstrates that high-skill immigrants can create clusters of knowledge, networks, and entrepreneurship activities (Lee & Lee, 2020; Saxenian, 2006). The data has been collected through primary and secondary sources. We conducted interviews with 1.5 generation Korean American immigrant entrepreneurs and/or collected historical and archival data through the ABI/INFORM database using firm name and founder's name in Korean and English, then triangulated with secondary resources such as firm websites, press releases, social media posts, and newspaper articles in Korean and English. Moreover, we attended conferences, seminars, and networking events where these firms or their investors have participated. The purpose of this multi-layered approach is to better understand the holistic representation of these firms.

FINDINGS

Based on the analysis and findings, we present three themes that emerged regarding how 1.5 Korean American immigrant entrepreneurs strategically mobilize their networks and resources at different stages of their entrepreneurship process: (1) opportunity identification and venture formation, (2) resource acquisition and

Table 9.1   Description of Case Study Firms

	Case 1	Case 2	Case 3	Case 4
Year founded	2017	2015	2013	2012
Number of co-founders	Two	One	Two	Two
Primary reasons for immigration	Education	Education	Education	Education
Industry	Biotechnology	Analytics	Healthcare	Consumer goods
Funding status	Seed	Seed	Series B	Series D
Funding raised	$4 million	$1 million	$22 million	$192 million
Firm size (number of employees)	11-50	11-50	11-50	251-500
Headquartered	Palo Alto, California	Palo Alto, California	San Francisco, California	San Francisco, California
International markets entered	South Korea	None	South Korea, Japan	South Korea, Hong Kong, Taiwan, China

Source: Compiled by the authors (2019).

recombination, and (3) growth and internationalization. We also highlight the institutional perspectives of South Korea and the San Francisco Bay Area, including the contexts of social, economic, and political factors that influenced the firm's decision-making process and strategy. Table 9.1 summarizes the main characteristics of the firms and founding team and their cross-border entrepreneurship activities.

Leveling the Playing Field by Tapping into Cross-Border Networks and Resources

Since the beginning of their entrepreneurship process, firms founded by 1.5 generation Korean Americans have actively engaged their networks and resources from both home and host countries. The way in which these resources were recognized and added values varies. For instance, one firm (case 1) had two co-founders who were 1.5 Korean American immigrant entrepreneurs. These co-founders met during their postgraduate studies at Stanford University, and they knew from the inception of the ideation that their university and personal networks from South Korea and the United States would be tapped. Though they realized it was not strategically possible to simultaneously operate in two countries on day one, due to regulatory requirements of the medical industry in which they were operating, they also knew that South Korea would still serve as an important institutional resource. When describing the early stage of their venture, one highlighted the importance of the social and political climate in the home country. In 2013, the Korean government launched the Creative Economy Initiative, where it acknowledged that the country was no longer able to rely on Korean business groups such as Samsung, LG, and Hyundai to drive the country's economic growth and job and wealth creation. Thus, the government has launched several entrepreneurship initiatives such as government-run accelerators with public-private sector partnerships, grant opportunities, and pitch competitions in order to foster more entrepreneurship and innovation activities. The two co-founders recognized that it would be a great time to utilize resources available in South Korea, particularly for those investors who were seeking to access scientific discoveries and top talents in Silicon Valley (case 1). Consequently, approximately half of their first round of seed funding came from Korean investors, and the other came from investors in the United States. Furthermore, they applied for and successfully received multiple Korean government grant opportunities and awards in order to overcome the liability of newness and foreignness in the United States. Their continuous involvement and engagement led them to open a satellite office in Seoul with a few personnel. At the same time, the co-founders also participated in two accelerators in Palo Alto through their university and venture capitalists, which helped them become more qualified and capable entrepreneurs (case 1). They described the main benefits of participating in these accelerators as operational support, access to potential investors, and skill sets development. Additionally, they utilized their university and personal networks to be mentored and get advised on grant application and fundraising vetting processes.

Another firm (case 2) was founded by a 1.5 Korean American immigrant entrepreneur who initially moved to the United States for his MBA degree. When he was attending undergraduate school in South Korea, he was a founding member of a new venture, and his firm went public in 2000, shortly after he graduated. Through this experience, he built his networks and reputation in the entrepreneurship sector and has been serving as an advisor, angel investor, and mentor both in South Korea and the United States. Even prior to the launch of his firm, he traveled back and forth to speak at conferences and panel sessions. He has maintained strong ethnic ties and played an active role in the entrepreneurship ecosystem in South Korea as a way to give back to his home country and contribute to the society by sharing his views and experiences from Silicon Valley (case 2). He decided to launch his data analytics software company after completing his MBA and working at one of the major Silicon Valley firms for a decade. As a 1.5 generation Korean American immigrant, he had to get H1B work visa sponsorship and eventually earn his green card in order to start his firm. When he experimented with a business opportunity, it was natural for him to tap into a community of entrepreneurs and investors in both Korea and the United States. He applied for a top-tier three-month accelerator program in Seoul, where his firm received $50,000 (USD) in addition to receiving mentorship, office space, technical assistance, and legal resources. Upon returning to the United States, the firm raised $1 million (USD) in seed funding after successfully building the product and securing a set of customers (case 2). This strategic decision to recombine valuable and rare resources from both home and host countries allowed the firm to develop competitive advantages compared to other firms.

Similar patterns were observed in other firms outside of our selected cases, where 1.5 generation Korean American immigrant entrepreneurs were well-versed in understanding the institutional settings of both South Korea and the United States, particularly in early years of their new venture in order to increase their probability for survival. Not only were they able to speak the language, utilize ethnic networks, and understand the cultural norms, they also accessed opportunities provided by both public and private sectors—which were not easily spelled out for second- or third-generation immigrant entrepreneurs to take advantage of. For instance, the government websites, policy reports, press releases, and announcements of entrepreneurship programs are written in Korean, and conferences and seminars are provided in Korean as well. In fact, this sentiment was echoed by other entrepreneurs and investors, and the ability to access opportunities in South Korea is not easily replicable or substitutable. In return, these firms are able to mitigate the liability of newness in the host country, the United States, through their capabilities to combine resources when possible.

Home-Bound Internationalization

Firms actively recombined resources from both home and host countries, not only during the initial phase of new ventures, but also through business operations and expansion. These firms, founded by 1.5 generation Korean American immigrant entrepreneurs, are "internationalized" to the home country as their first "abroad" office (cases 1, 2, 3). In fact, three out of four cases had their first "abroad" office in Seoul to assist their manufacturing and back-end operations functions. In the case of one firm (case 4), it originally launched in South Korea and then relocated its headquarters office to San Francisco while reincorporating its Seoul office as a foreign subsidiary. It later opened three additional offices in Hong Kong, Taiwan, and Singapore. In other words, all four firms had business activities in the home country, and their first satellite office was Seoul.

One rationale for home-bound internationalization to South Korea was to minimize the liability of foreignness. Prior literature on internationalization highlights the importance of understanding the institutional contexts in order to overcome the liability of foreignness (Zaheer, 1995, 2002). Because 1.5 generation Korean American immigrant entrepreneurs are able to understand the cultural, social, and economic contexts in which their firms operate, they have a lower barrier to enter their home country as part of the internationalization strategy.

One firm (case 3) we analyzed offers smart home hardware devices that monitor indoor air quality, dust levels, and other helpful health-related information, and provides personalized recommendations. Initially, its Seoul office focused on the manufacturing process of the hardware, but it has expanded to the Korean market with a different firm strategy. For instance, it entered the South Korea market with a B2B strategy by partnering with government agencies, hospitals, schools, and large business groups, whereas it entered the U.S. market with a B2C strategy by selling hardware to individual customers through online marketplaces such as Amazon (case 3). It highlighted that due to the market characteristics of South Korea, such as being a relatively small market compared to the United States, densely populated around the capital, high internet penetration rate, and strong interests in new technology tools, B2B was a more suitable business model. In contrast, the United States is a big market with a highly segmented market; therefore, every region has unique characteristics, and the strategy in Silicon Valley might not work well in other parts of the United States. Thus, the firm decided to pursue B2C as an entry point. It now has a marketing and sales team in the Seoul office for the Korean market (case 3).

Case 4 shows a similar pattern of home-bound internationalization with a different localized strategy in South Korea. In the beginning, case 4 started in South Korea as an e-commerce platform selling its own K-beauty cosmetic products. Once it was accepted by an accelerator in San Francisco, the founding team relocated to the United States and incorporated a new headquarters in San Francisco. The Korean office serves as a foreign subsidiary, and it internationalized to China, Taiwan, Hong Kong, and Singapore in recent years. Operating in the highly competitive cosmetic and beauty industry, it decided that B2C is more appropriate for the Asian markets, whereas it shifts to an online-to-offline business model in the United States with strategic partnerships with major cosmetic brands such as Sephora.

This phenomenon of home-bound internationalization of new ventures is a relatively under-researched area in the transnational and immigrant entrepreneurship literature. It is also a strategy that 1.5 generation immigrants are uniquely positioned to exploit due to their ability to understand the institutional contexts of both the home and host countries. Entry into a foreign market needs to be supported by localization that reflects the behaviors and understanding of local users, competitors, and other major stakeholders such as government agencies. We observed that there are varying degrees of home-bound internationalization, from setting up manufacturing facilities and back-end operations to reduce operating and transaction costs (case 1, 2), to treating the home country as an equally significant market to invest and operate to generate revenues and complement the primary market, which is the United States. In the latter case, firms established products, engineering, marketing, sales, and legal teams (case 3, 4).

Reconceptualizing 1.5 Generation Immigrant Entrepreneurs as Boundary-Spanning Intermediaries

While analyzing the entrepreneurship experiences of these 1.5 generation immigrant founders, we noticed that they go beyond the status-quo of immigrant entrepreneurs. More specifically, firms founded by 1.5 generation immigrant entrepreneurs were not necessity-based, self-employment, unlike prior literature on the first-generation Korean American immigrant entrepreneurs. These entrepreneurs found a technology-based opportunity, often through their work experiences or postgraduate studies. Because of their personal immigrant experiences, they were highly motivated to succeed by obtaining a university education from top universities in the United States, and, in some cases, postgraduate degrees that would differentiate them from other entrepreneurs.

At the same time, they acknowledged the challenges of being an immigrant or minority in the United States. For instance, one of the 1.5 generation entrepreneurs described that she was the only female during multiple investor meetings. Another entrepreneur recalled that he was often the only minority in a room full of investors, and he noticed this dynamic immediately upon entering the meeting room. Yet, all of them had an optimistic and positive attitude and outlook regarding their experience that their identity is a unique asset and advantage that differentiates them from other native-born entrepreneurs or immigrant entrepreneurs without connections to their ethnic communities. These firms were also actively supported by the Korean entrepreneurship and greater ethnic communities in Silicon Valley that invited them to present their work at professional gatherings, conferences, workshops, and through media outlets.

The transnational experiences of the 1.5 generation Korean American entrepreneurs are unique, given the institutional and socioeconomic factors of their home country, South Korea. All four cases began their ventures in the midst of the Creative Economy Initiative, in which there was a strong push by the Korean government to encourage entrepreneurship activities to create economic growth and mobility. Though the degree to which these firms recombined resources and international networks varies, they all credited their current progress to their connections with South Korea and their ability to access talents, investors, accelerators/incubators, government resources (e.g., grants, co-working space, legal and accounting assistance), and manufacturing and back-end operations facilities. Half of the cases (cases 3, 4) are treating the Korean market as a strategically important international market to operate, increase market share, and be fully present. While other firms rely on the home country resources heavily to overcome the initial liability of newness and foreignness in the United States (cases 1, 2), these 1.5 generation immigrant entrepreneurs were able to serve as boundary-spanning intermediaries.

CONCLUSION

This study aims to provide insights into how new ventures founded by 1.5 generation Korean American immigrant entrepreneurs recombine resources from both home and host countries to gain competitive advantages during various stages of their entrepreneurship process. In the initial stage of new ventures, firms heavily utilized resources from their home country such as personal and professional networks through university and family ties, participation in top-tier incubators and accelerators, government grants and other public-sector resources (e.g., free co-working office space, accounting, legal assistance), and participation in pitch competitions. Once firms were able to survive and overcome the liability of newness in the United States, they actively sought private investment opportunities through angel investors, venture capitalists, and large corporations in the home country in addition to being covered by major media outlets such as newspapers, magazines, and TV stations. Furthermore, these firms were able to strategically establish offices in the home country in order to reduce transaction costs by setting up back offices or manufacturing facilities and recruiting talent such as engineers, designers, and salespeople to support the headquarters in the United States, and/or expanding the Korean market.

We acknowledge that this study on 1.5 generation immigrant entrepreneurs is exploratory in nature, and there exists a need to develop a much fuller investigation into these behaviors and the role of different generations and its implications. Future studies can investigate how immigrant founder's different generations influence their decision-making and resource utilization across home and host countries, using a larger data set such as a survey. For instance, do second- or third-generation immigrant entrepreneurs have any competitive advantages compared to native-born non-immigrant American entrepreneurs? Can these later-generation immigrant entrepreneurs still access cross-border resources from their home country?

This study extends the current literature on immigrant entrepreneurship by providing a generation-specific aspect and provides valuable practical lessons for immigrant entrepreneurs, investors, and policymakers in both home and host countries. Prior studies on immigrant entrepreneurship have looked at low-skilled or self-employment entrepreneurship activities of, primarily, first-generation immigrants as they experience cultural, social, and language barriers in the United States (Kim & Hurh, 1985). More recent studies have highlighted the growing entrepreneurship activities of international students and immigrants in high-technology industries and their competitiveness, without specific focus on the generational aspect (Lee, 2018; Lee & Eesely, 2018; Lee & Lee, 2020, Tung, 2008). As far as we are aware, this is one of the first entrepreneurship studies that focused on firms incorporated by the 1.5 generation Korean American immigrants in a high-technology industry. The 1.5 generation immigrants are better positioned to access cross-border networks, knowledge, and resources, particularly in their respective home countries. This competitive advantage leads firms to be more resilient in early stages of their ventures. Moreover, they span institutional boundaries between home and host countries while serving as a bridge that potentially creates economic values in both home and host countries.

REFERENCES

Beckers, P., & Blumberg, B. F. (2013). Immigrant entrepreneurship on the move: A longitudinal analysis of first-and second-generation immigrant entrepreneurship in the Netherlands. *Entrepreneurship and Regional Development*, 25(7–8), 654–691.

Brzozowski, J., Cucculelli, M., & Surdej, A. (2014). Transnational ties and performance of immigrant entrepreneurs: The role of home-country conditions. *Entrepreneurship and Regional Development*, 26(7–8), 546–573.

Chen, W., & Tan, J. (2008). Roots and wings: Glocalized networks and transnational entrepreneurship. Academy of Management Proceedings (Vol. 2008, No. 1, pp. 1–6). Briarcliff Manor, NY: Academy of Management. In *68th Annual Meeting of the Academy of Management, AOM 2008*.

Eisenhardt, K. M. (1989). Building theories from case study research. *Academy of Management Review, 14*(4), 532–550.

Gould, D. M. (1994). Immigrant links to the home country: Empirical implications for US bilateral trade flows. *The Review of Economics and Statistics*, 302–316.

Hurh, W. M. (1990). "The Korean Frontiers in America: Immigration to Hawaii, 1896-1910", by Wayne Patterson (Book Review). *Journal of American Ethnic History, 10*(1), 144.

Kauffman. 2017. "Startup Activity Swings Upward for Third Consecutive Year, Annual Kauffman Index Reports." Accessed May 1, 2019. https://www.kauffman.org/newsroom/2017/05/startup-activity-swings-upward-for-third-consecutive-year-annual-kauffman-index-reports

Kerr, S. P., & Kerr, W. (2020). Immigrant entrepreneurship in America: Evidence from the survey of business owners 2007 & 2012. *Research Policy, 49*(3), 103918.

Kerr, W. R., & Mandorff, M. (2015). *Social Networks, Ethnicity, and Entrepreneurship* (No. w21597). National Bureau of Economic Research.

Kim, K. C., & Hurh, W. M. (1985). Ethnic resources utilization of Korean immigrant entrepreneurs in the Chicago minority area. *International Migration Review, 19*(1), 82–111.

Leblang, D. (2010). Familiarity breeds investment: Diaspora networks and international investment. *American Political Science Review, 104*(3), 584–600.

Lee, J. C., & Cynn, V. E. H. (1991). Issues in counseling 1.5 generation Korean Americans. In C. C. Lee & B. L. Richardson (eds.), *Multicultural Issues in Counseling: New Approaches to Diversity* (pp. 127–140). American Association for Counseling.

Lee, J. Y. (2018). *Transnational Return Migration of 1.5 Generation Korean New Zealanders: A Quest for Home*. Lanham, MA: Rowman & Littlefield Publishing Group.

Lee, J. Y., & Lee, J. Y. (2020). Female transnational entrepreneurs (FTEs): A case study of Korean American female entrepreneurs in Silicon Valley. *Journal of Entrepreneurship and Innovation in Emerging Economies, 6*(1), 67–83.

Lee, Y. S., & Eesley, C. (2018). The persistence of entrepreneurship and innovative immigrants. *Research Policy, 47*(6), 1032–1044.

Lin, X. (2010). The diaspora solution to innovation capacity development: Immigrant entrepreneurs in the contemporary world. *Thunderbird International Business Review, 52*(2), 123–136.

Partnership for a New American Economy. 2011. The "New American" Fortune 500: A Report by the Partnership for a New American Economy. Accessed September 12, 2019. https://www.newamericaneconomy.org/sites/all/themes/pnae/img/new-american-fortune-500-june-2011.pdf

Portes, A., Haller, W. J., & Guarnizo, L. E. (2002). Transnational entrepreneurs: An alternative form of immigrant economic adaptation. *American Sociological Review*, 278–298.

Rumbaut, R. G., & Ima, K. (1988). The Adaptation of Southeast Asian Refugee Youth: A Comparative Study. Final Report to the Office of Resettlement.

Rusinovic, K. (2008). Transnational embeddedness: Transnational activities and networks among first-and second-generation immigrant entrepreneurs in the Netherlands. *Journal of Ethnic and Migration Studies, 34*(3), 431–451.

Saxenian, A. (2005). From brain drain to brain circulation: Transnational communities and regional upgrading in India and China. *Studies in Comparative International Development, 40*(2), 35–61.

Saxenian, A. (2006). International Mobility of Engineers and the Rise of Entrepreneurship in the Periphery (No. 2006/142). WIDER Research Paper.

Saxenian, A., Motoyama, Y., & Quan, X. (2002). *Local and Global Networks of Immigrant Professionals in Silicon Valley.* Public Policy Institute of California.

Thomas, W. F., & Ong, P. M. (2015). Ethnic mobilization among Korean dry-cleaners. *Ethnic and Racial Studies, 38*(12), 2108–2122.

Tung, R. L. (2008). Brain circulation, diaspora, and international competitiveness. *European Management Journal, 26*(5), 298–304.

Yin, R. K. (2017). *Case Study Research and Applications: Design and Methods.* Thousand Oaks, CA: Sage publications.

Zaheer, S. (1995). Overcoming the liability of foreignness. *Academy of Management Journal, 38*(2), 341–363.

Zaheer, S. (2002). The liability of foreignness, redux: A commentary. *Journal of International Management, 8*(3), 351–358.

Zolin, R., & Schlosser, F. (2013). Characteristics of immigrant entrepreneurs and their involvement in international new ventures. *Thunderbird International Business Review, 55*(3), 271–284.

10

Female Transnational Entrepreneurs (FTEs)

Transnationalism, Gender, and Identity

June Y. Lee and Jane Yeonjae Lee

INTRODUCTION

Increasingly, studies of entrepreneurship and migration have examined the role of immigrant entrepreneurs in revitalizing and diversifying the economy of the host society.[1] Transnational skilled entrepreneurs have been characterized as being more capable of building international networks and collaborations between their home and host societies. These studies focus on the technically oriented entrepreneurs and produce a single grand narrative about a particular migrant group that transfers knowledge and becomes a technical pioneer in their home society. In this chapter, we scrutinize a group of first and 1.5 generation Korean American female transnational entrepreneurs (FTEs) living in Silicon Valley and build a nuanced understanding about the diversity and complexity of being transnational entrepreneurs (TEs). Through a multi-layered qualitative approach, the study illustrates the contesting ways in which the first and 1.5 generation female immigrants adapt to live in a transnational social field.

Between 1995 and 2005, immigrant entrepreneurs started 52 percent of all new Silicon Valley companies. In 2012, these companies, which are concentrated in California, employed 560,000 workers and generated $63 billion in sales (Bluestein, 2015). According to a study by the Kauffman Foundation, immigrants are nearly twice as likely to become entrepreneurs compared to U.S.-born citizen. In fact, 51 percent of all U.S. start-ups valued at $1 billion or higher have at least one immigrant founder (Anderson, 2016). The most recent examples include Instagram, Uber, Slack, SpaceX, and Palantir Technologies. Such tendencies make it imperative to examine the context in which immigrant entrepreneurs are being motivated to form and grow their ventures.

Against this backdrop, this chapter examines how female ethnic minorities in Silicon Valley developed their entrepreneurial motives and performances in relation to the region's entrepreneurial ecosystem, family and transnational networks, and gender and ethnic identities. In particular, we focus on first and 1.5 generation Korean American female immigrants who have mostly immigrated following their spouses after completing their tertiary education, or during their teenage years to study in the United States. Our subjects have little to no prior entrepreneurial experience and limited access to their host society's networks and resources.

Conceptually speaking, the chapter seeks to learn from the body of literature on transnationalism that aims to understand the transnational social fields across national borders (Glick-Schiller et al., 1992). While the traditional debate has focused on "who" benefits from the ethnic entrepreneurs, the current literature directs the question away from "brain gain" and toward "brain circulation." It does so by recognizing the contemporary skilled immigrants as TEs whose personal lives are connected between their host and home societies and who are bringing benefits to multiple players and societies across national borders (Saxenian, 2004; Shin and Choi, 2015). Moreover, 1.5 generation skilled immigrants are known to be the "ideal" type of global talent, as they hold the bi-cultural and bilingual skills with commitments to their home and host nations (Lee, 2019). This chapter sheds light on a newly emerging segment of TEs—a group of highly skilled Korean American FTEs. From there, it builds a nuanced understanding of how transnational connections shape the FTEs' entrepreneurial motives and performances that are also complicated by gender and ethnic identities.

The rest of the chapter is structured as follows. First, we examine the existing literature on transnational entrepreneurship and how we aim to approach our study theoretically. Second, we discuss the context of Korean immigrant entrepreneurs in the United States and in Silicon Valley to situate our study. Third, we discuss the research methodology that is framed by a qualitative approach aimed at understanding the complex picture of the entrepreneurial motives and experiences of Korean female immigrant entrepreneurs. Next, we present the findings of our study in three different themes: (1) the motivations, (2) the minority status of female and ethnic identities, and (3) the transnational social field. Finally, we conclude by discussing theoretical and practical implications, along with limitations and opportunities for further research.

TOWARD A NUANCED UNDERSTANDING OF TRANSNATIONAL ENTREPRENEURSHIP

This chapter argues that the discourses around TEs of building connections and making contributions between their host and home countries are limited in depicting the complex entrepreneurial trajectories. This section discusses the theoretical development of TE and the limitations of the current scholarship. It also argues that the studies of TE need to be aligned with the questions of minority entrepreneurship and entrepreneurial motivation. This must be done to scrutinize the processes behind entrepreneurship and to understand the complexities of FTEs' motives, their experiences, their performances, and the role of ethnic and gender identities.

Taking a transnational approach to study migrant entrepreneurship means understanding the FTEs' everyday experiences from a transnational angle. It also means investigating how and to what extent transnational connections shape and affect the everyday lives of immigrant entrepreneurs. With the rise of information and communication technologies (ICT) and multinational companies (Kivisto, 2001), along with the increasing mobilities of people, skills, and ideas (Urry, 2005), TEs are better positioned to take advantage of both worlds. We follow the definition of transnationalism by Basch, Glick-Schiller, and Szanton Blanc (1996), which defines the concept as:

> Process by which transmigrants, through their daily activities, forge and sustain multi-stranded social, economic, and political relations that link together their societies of origin and settlement, and through which they create transnational social fields that cross-national borders. (Basch et al., 1994:6)

Presumably, transnational connections shape the immigrant entrepreneurs' lives in various ways, from their initial decision-making processes to stay in the United States to the ways in which they operate their businesses as well as their future projections of their start-ups. Transnational entrepreneurship advances the understanding of skilled migrants who bring "brain circulation" (Saxenian, 2004; Shin and Choi, 2015) instead of brain gain or brain loss as they move. Such characteristics of transnational entrepreneurship should be differentiated from the traditional concept of ethnic entrepreneurship, which simply refers to the ethnic connections and networks within the host society as "a set of connections and regular patterns of interaction among people sharing common national background or migration experiences" (Waldinger et al., 1990: 3). The concept of ethnic entrepreneurship is limited in explaining the current situation of transnational migrants who become entrepreneurs on the global setting and those whose everyday lives are connected between their host and home society and between more than two countries (Drori et al., 2009).

Studies of transnational entrepreneurs have illustrated that, with their cross-border networks and resources, TEs add great economic value to their host and home societies (Light, Zhou, & Kim, 2002; Min, 1990). Silicon Valley has been studied as the ultimate destination for new ventures, with a mature ecosystem of entrepreneurs, investors, accelerators, incubators, universities, and established firms (Kenney, 2000). It has also been of interest as a place where ethnic entrepreneurship has played a vital role in providing the maturity and diversity of the region's entrepreneurial ecosystem. Saxenian (2002a) provides descriptive views of the role ethnic entrepreneurs played in Silicon Valley, primarily focusing on the community of ethnic (e.g., Indian and Chinese) engineers and scientists and how they have contributed to the growth of the region since the 1980s. Park (1996, 2009) suggests that Koreans and Korean Americans played a significant role in the development of the high-tech industry in Silicon Valley during the 1990s through the transnational flow of capital, complications over visas, and the linkage to global production and trade of high-technology products and services.

Although TE has developed an important set of scholarship and questions around the transnational flows of recent skilled entrepreneurs, it lacks diversity (e.g., gender, generational difference, and different identity politics) within the group. For instance, immigrant entrepreneurs experience greater liability of foreignness as they navigate the unfamiliar social, cultural, and legal aspects of a host country. Lee and Eesley (2018), for example, discovered that Asian Americans have a higher rate of entrepreneurship compared to white Americans based on the alumni survey of Stanford University. However, non-American Asians (i.e., foreign-born international students) have a substantially lower, about 12 percentage points, start-up rate compared to that of Asian Americans. This study emphasizes the importance of institutional and structural support for first-generation immigrant entrepreneurs. Also, studies focusing specifically on entrepreneurship of female and ethnic minorities have been sparse (Drori et al., 2009). Nevertheless, they require further attention because gender- and ethnic-biased innovations in particular exist that reflect such entrepreneurs' own identities (Leung, 2011; Greene et al., 2003).

Additionally, the current studies on TE require further interrogation on entrepreneurial motivations. Studies on entrepreneurial motives have argued that an entrepreneur takes advantage of information asymmetry when identifying entrepreneurial opportunities (Burton et al., 2002; Shane, 2000; Shane & Venkataraman, 2000; Armour & Cumming, 2006). This information asymmetry stems from one's knowledge and prior experience (e.g., through education, career history, and network). Most of these studies have been analyzed in the self-response survey settings (Hsu et al., 2007). On the contradictory side, a few scholars have argued the notion of "accidental entrepreneurs" or "leisure-time invention," wherein entrepreneurs accidentally discover an idea then share it with others to experiment and receive feedback before fully assessing its commercial market values (Davis et al., 2013; Shah & Tripsas, 2007). During this process, the context in which these individuals are exposed becomes important. These diverging views highlight the complexity of entrepreneurial motives and how such complexity is not holistically reflected in the current literature on entrepreneurial motives and identification of opportunities. The studies of transnational entrepreneurship need to be closely aligned with these studies on entrepreneurial motives to depict the diversities and complexities of TE motivations.

Informed by the theoretical development of TEs that is aligned with questions of minority entrepreneurship and complexities of entrepreneur motives, this chapter seeks to examine the different trajectories of the Korean American FTEs. It pays particular attention to how their transnational connections, entrepreneurial motives, life-course decisions, ethnicity, gender, and complex identities and attitudes might come together in the formation of new economic and social spaces. This chapter will advance the field of international political economy and transnational entrepreneurship across the Asia Pacific region from a rarely existing ethnographic angle.

STUDY METHODS

This study[2] took a multi-layered qualitative approach to understand the phenomenon of FTEs, with a focus on individual trajectories and narratives. Between April 2017 and October 2018, the authors conducted semi-structured interviews with fourteen Korean FTEs based in Silicon Valley. The interview protocol consisted of three sections. First, the study participants were asked to explain the reasons for their immigration to the United States and their background, including their personal, educational, and professional history and experiences. Second, they were asked why they decided to become entrepreneurs in Silicon Valley. This included their trajectories and experiences of running their start-ups and their plans related to their companies. Lastly, they were asked to reflect on their particular experiences based on their identities and to consider how they positioned themselves in the Silicon Valley ecosystem and with the transnational Korean diasporic community. These questions were purposefully left open-ended, so the study participants could freely share their thoughts and experiences. The interview narratives were complemented by participatory observation of company visits, which took place between April 2017 and October 2018. The authors also attended workshops and seminars, some of which were organized by the study participants themselves. These participatory observations were particularly important in examining the role of social groups and communities in the study participants' entrepreneurial lives. They were also important in understanding how the study participants engage and interact with the Korean American entrepreneur communities in Silicon Valley. The results were triangulated with secondary resources from newspaper articles, social media channels, and official company websites. This multi-layered qualitative approach was appropriate for this study because the exact number of female FTEs in Silicon Valley is unavailable and hence the explorative nature of the research.

The study participants were recruited through a snowball sampling method. Firstly, around twenty-seven Korean female entrepreneurs were identified as potential study participants based on the authors' personal networks and by identifying Korean female names from various online communities. Then the study participants were carefully selected based on a number of different criteria (e.g., the types of their venture, their length of stay in the United States, their marriage status, the stage and progress of their venture, and various other personal factors). This theoretical sampling approach is consistent with inductive case study methodology in contrast to random sampling for deductive, empirical studies (Eisenhardt & Graebner, 2007). Considering that the study is exploratory in nature, the authors wanted to make sure it captured the vast diversity of the situations in which these FTEs are situated. At the same time, this research selected only first-generation immigrants and a small number of 1.5 generation Korean immigrants (i.e., those who were born in South Korea and moved to the United States at a relatively young age). It excluded second-generation Korean entrepreneurs because their immigrant trajectories and identities would be vastly different. Out of the fourteen study participants, nine of them moved to the United States during their tertiary education and five moved after getting married. We did not particularly analyze the findings by comparing the different experiences between first and 1.5 generation immigrants, as they all seem to share similar experiences based on where they were situated (i.e., Silicon Valley and the connection to South Korea). However, the subtle differences are discussed in the results and discussion sections.

Interviews were mostly conducted in Korean and were later transcribed and translated into English. Most of these interviews took place at the offices, meeting rooms, co-working spaces, or residence of the study participants. The interviews, on average, lasted two hours, with follow-up communications including emails and in-person meetings. Discourse analysis was used to find several common themes from an exploratory approach (Wood & Kroger, 2000). A number of occurring themes were identified after the first five interviews, and by using those keywords, we looked for a common structure of narratives as well as complexities of the individual stories. By employing discourse analysis as our analytical lens, we attempted to de-contextualize their norms, values, and perceptions, and how their experiences have been produced through shared sociological and cultural understanding (Wood & Kroger, 2000).

KOREAN AMERICAN FTES IN SILICON VALLEY: MOTIVES, EXPERIENCES, AND PERFORMANCES

In this section, we discuss the ways in which FTEs perform their entrepreneurial roles within Silicon Valley and their transnational social field. We also examine what kinds of factors influence and shape their motives and experiences as entrepreneurs. Our findings suggest that there are three different mechanisms at play. First, the ecosystem of Silicon Valley plays a major role as an environmental factor which motivates, shapes, and sustains Korean American FTEs' ventures. Second, FTEs' minority status as women and ethnic entrepreneurs stands as a challenge, but sometimes this challenge is reverted as opportunities for ventures. Third, some of the FTEs' challenges are overcome by their transnational linkages between their home and host countries, and their "in-between" identities and belongingness. Such links provide them with more opportunities and resources at both ends of their transnational social field. As will be discussed in the following sections, these three mechanisms are interrelated and are certainly not separate patterns.

Entrepreneurship Motivations

The study participants indicated that being located in Silicon Valley and having access to the knowledge, resources, institutional supports, and networks (i.e., being situated within the so-called "Silicon Valley ecosystem") was an important factor in motivating the migrant entrepreneurs to start their own businesses. Out of the fourteen Korean American FTEs we studied, four intended to become entrepreneurs prior to moving to the United States. They chose to come to Silicon Valley because they were interested in and curious about the "entrepreneurial spirit" and/or wanted to join the workforce or attend a university in the area to learn about entrepreneurship. On the flipside, the remaining ten study participants never thought of becoming entrepreneurs and moved to the Silicon Valley mainly because of their spouses' work, intra-company transfer, better quality of life, and/or postgraduate education, without any intention of starting a new venture. Yet, being exposed to the Silicon Valley environment, coupled with various other factors (e.g., experiencing difficulty in finding a job that matched their educational background, work and life balance after giving birth, and being empowered by others around them), they gradually gained courage and built their skills to start a new business. For all the study participants, it was clear they could not have achieved success in their entrepreneurial businesses had they been living in a different city.

Silicon Valley's ecosystem is composed of important parts and stakeholders that play synergetic roles with each other. Such players include serial entrepreneurs, accelerators, incubators, a vast diversity of venture capitalists, law firms, universities, and established firms that are aided and supported by the maturity of the system and the growing workforce in the area (Kenney, 2000). One of the study participants had prior work experience at a large, established firm in South Korea with an engineering and marketing background. Even with her previous work experience, she did not have any prior resources or knowledge of starting her own venture, but her first foot in the door of an accelerator proved a life-changing experience for her:

> I participated in a beauty tech accelerator, which was a three-week intensive startup accelerator program. In the morning, we had guest lectures and workshops run by investors, entrepreneurs, and other relevant people. In the afternoon, we worked on our start-ups and received lots of coaching especially related to pitch deck, such as what to write, how to present, what to focus on, what to avoid, and so on. This was really helpful. They also assigned us to a set of mentors and advisors. On the very last day, we had a demo day where we pitched our start-up in front of a group of investors and participants. I also met several Korean investors who expressed interest in my company. This accelerator also helped out with in corporation, registration, legal assistance, and filing for patents. Because they also have incentives to make our start-up successful, they regularly check in with us to share any connections and make introductions to their networks. We also give them updates on a regular basis. (Participant 6, aged 40)

Through her first experience at an accelerator, this FTE was able to find mentors and advisors for her start-up, and she learned all the right skills to launch her venture. She also noted that this kind of three-week intensive course, where you can meet real practitioners working in the entrepreneurial arena, is not easy to join. Moreover, she was surprised by the practicality and value of the workshop. The success of her story is not unique, but it resembles many of the existing stories in Silicon Valley. Nevertheless, it should also be noted that the study participant had immense working experience in large corporations. Hence, she had a firm idea of her business model and had support from her ethnic networks (e.g., the Korean investor she met at the accelerator and through her husband, who already had a number of his own networks in Silicon Valley).

Another participant also indicated that being able to participate in various accelerators and incubators in Silicon Valley was a huge asset for providing the launch pad for her businesses. While looking for her next course of action during her postdoctoral training in Silicon Valley, she met another recently graduated Korean doctoral student who shared a similar vision with her. They both had interests in developing a product which would provide individualized healthcare service, and they decided to co-create their medical service product. Prior to launching this product, they had the opportunity to be involved in two different accelerators: one led by venture capitalist and one led by the university where they met. While the venture capital accelerator was relatively easier to join, the university-led accelerator was highly selective, and they had to go through a series of application procedures to get into the program. For this study participant, finding the right investors with a basic knowledge and understanding of medicine and medical care was important, and it was through the business partners' participation in accelerators that they were exposed to many different types of mentors and venture capitalists:

> Both of the accelerators provided useful workshops, networks, and a community that really supports each other. They try to help out and sit down and discuss and foster ideas. One of the best things about joining the university-led accelerator was that one of their limited partners had a medical background and had a high success rate in their operation model. We raised over $3.5 million from 12 investors, and many of these investors were introduced [through] the two accelerators we participated in, along with our personal networks from schools and other communities. (Participant 10, aged 36)

The story of Participant 10 illustrates that the value of venture capitalists in Silicon Valley is not simply the large amounts of monetary opportunities but also their wealth of knowledge, experience, networking, and other intangible assets (e.g., strategic planning and providing vision). Similar to Participant 6, the success of Participant 10's entrepreneurial performance in fundraising and developing her product was a combination of different factors (e.g., being exposed to the mature and diverse venture capitalists who also built networks for her and her business partners, having access to her own ethnic networks within the United States and South Korea, and having access to networks through her university). Almost all of the advisory board and current employers were selected through the participants' networks, and they see that having the right people to work with is the biggest asset of their company.

There is a common saying that Silicon Valley has its own "spirit" and "mentality" that also results in its entrepreneurial success. While the definition of the term can be diverse and can also consist of both positive and negative connotations (i.e., working too hard, long work hours for start-ups has become normative), the study participants defined the Silicon Valley spirit based on its difference from what they encountered through their cultural and social upbringing in South Korea. More specifically, the study participants indicated that in South Korea, being an entrepreneur is not seen as being "successful" as it is in Silicon Valley. The positive norms and values associated with being an entrepreneur in Silicon Valley were something they continuously encountered over time. In South Korea, starting one's own venture is seen as a huge risk, and only through education and parental guidance does one gain a social norm and value to take a risk-free career path (i.e., becoming a doctor, lawyer, or working for the government). Several of the study participants shared a similar view:

> Koreans tend to be risk-averse compared to other ethnic groups. I'm not sure what it is about the Korean culture, but Chinese and Indians like to take risks. They are not afraid to bring their product into a bigger market, and their thinking is just at a different scale. They are also firm believers that things will work out, and they make it happen by [continuing to push] forward. I think that's a typical Silicon Valley mentality that Koreans don't have. (Participant 9, aged 40)

> Koreans grow up in a very competitive environment, and they are afraid of failures, whereas Americans focus more on the positive aspects rather than the negative ones. I think having this positive outlook is the most important skill a CEO should possess. (Participant 4, aged 41)

Most of the study participants stated that being surrounded by those "risk-takers" who have a positive outlook toward failure and seeing failure in entrepreneurship as an option were both important aspects of the Silicon Valley spirit and mentality. All of the study participants who were first-generation migrants and had been brought up in a competitive work and educational environment in South Korea saw this cultural difference as a learning curve in their lives which also affected and motivated their entrepreneurial endeavors.

Minority Entrepreneurs: Experiences of being Women and Immigrant Entrepreneurs

As much as our study participants have been relatively privileged in their lives for having the opportunities to be well educated, gain U.S. permanent residency through their spouses or work, and be exposed to the vast entrepreneurial resources of Silicon Valley on their path toward becoming successful entrepreneurs, they are also considered minority entrepreneurs and are underprivileged. In particular, they experience different power dynamics for being women and immigrant entrepreneurs in their host society. This section discusses how the Korean American FTEs perform and mobilize their gender and ethnic identities. Their narratives suggest that there are different types of challenges faced by women and ethnic minority entrepreneurs, yet most of the FTEs navigate their way to overcome and leverage their minority identities as resources and opportunities.

The studies of minority entrepreneurship for women and ethnic migrants have illustrated that entrepreneurship provides social and economic mobility for those who experience low advancement in their corporate career due to discrimination and poor adjustment (Heilman and Chen, 2003). Specifically, scholars have also argued that a particular entrepreneurial behavior of women founders requires further scrutiny (Greene et al., 2003). They also maintain that there is a particular gender-biased innovation, and gender role identities often become resources for business innovations and performances (Leung, 2011). Indeed, many of the participant FTEs innovated their products and services based on their personal experiences of being a female, a mother, and an immigrant. One Korean American FTE explained how she came up with her product idea while living as a working mother:

> My first start-up was an online marketplace to offer a pool of after-school programs such as summer camps and extracurricular activities for kids. The idea came from my personal difficulties and challenges that I faced while being a working parent. I often wondered why information on those programs for kids was not readily available in an online platform in this digital era. (Participant 9, aged 40)

For Participant 9, the difficulty in finding the information on available after-school programs was also due to the fact that she did not have the time and access to socialize with other parents at her children's school. This was due to lack of time after her work but also because it was difficult for her to easily talk to other American parents or the teacher due to language and cultural barriers. She also felt strongly that a knowledge-sharing system of after-school programs was lacking in general and that any parent of any background would appreciate the online platform. Initially, she pursued this idea as a side project while maintaining her full-time career as a senior software engineer at one of the renowned high-technology firms in Silicon Valley. Upon realizing sufficient interests and market values, she decided to quit her successful career. She began by reaching out to organizations that were offering after-school programs and summer camps while creating a website to on-board these organizations.

Another Korean American FTE also gained her motive to start her own business based on her personal experience with being both an ethnic minority and a mother in the host society. After moving to the United States with her husband and working for a number of different firms, she had her first child and took a few years off from work. She realized that it was difficult for her to get back to the workforce after the gap years, especially when competing with young professionals with more adaptive skills and competitive backgrounds. After realizing that a large number of female immigrants' situations might be worse than hers, with even greater barriers to joining the workforce in their host society, she decided to launch a non-profit to help and empower women at the margins. She specifically targeted doubly margin-alized female ethnic migrants who have stepped out of the workforce during their childbearing period and helps them fill in the gap and continue working or find new jobs, should they wish to.

Being women and ethnic minority entrepreneurs whose daily lives and social networks did not surround the participant FTEs with other young professionals, educators, or venture capitalists, they often found it difficult to find the right infor-mation and be connected. Only a small number of them had access to university or professional networks, and the rest had to find their own way to start their ventures. Especially for the FTEs who wanted to become entrepreneurs for economic and social mobility reasons after being out of the workforce for many years, it was even harder to build networks and gain resources to start their own businesses. However, in some cases, the study participants successfully leveraged the networks of their spouses or family members to advance their enterprises. One of the participants said:

> I was looking for a pro-bono lawyer who was willing to assist with the initial setup and incorporation of my start-up. I searched online and had some free consultations with lawyers, but I didn't know if they were trustworthy. Around that time, I was volunteering at my son's elementary school and getting to know other parents. I learned that my son's friend's father is a well-known partner at a law firm in Palo Alto. I got connected with his law firm, and they were really helpful in explaining different legal structures, roles and responsibilities of board members and advisors, how to set up board structure, et cetera. (Participant 1, aged 37)

Despite the challenges and difficulties of being female immigrant entrepreneurs, our study participants were optimistic and persistent about the unique values they were able to create in their respective industry and market segments. They echoed the sentiment that being a female entrepreneur could even be an advantage in the current climate, given the nascent but significant efforts to level the playing fields for female entrepreneurs:

> It is a great time to be a female founder. There are tons of platforms dedicated to female founders and entrepreneurs. Time is now. I feel I have to fully take advantage of the opportunities that are opening up right now . . . I went to all initiatives and forums that you can possibly find in San Francisco related to being a female founder . . . and there are a lot. Some are more like therapy sessions (laughs), but in some sessions, you can actually get tangible advice on the product. (Participant 6, aged 40)

Participant 6 has witnessed shifts in the entrepreneurial landscape over the past decade, wherein more emphasis and dialogue have taken place in an effort to level the playing field for female and minority entrepreneurs. Many of the study participant FTEs felt more passionate and enthusiastic about such trends where they increasingly see conferences, workshops, bootcamps, and venture capital funds committed to raising awareness of female and minority entrepreneurship.

Performing the Hybrid Identities across Their Transnational Social Field

"Transnational social field" refers to a boundary-free social space where a transnational migrant maintains his or her transnational flows and ongoing relationships between the society of immigration and the society of origin through activities such as exchanges of goods or information and contacts between home and host societies (Faist, 2000; Garcia, 2006). Those who are living in this transnational social field are aware of the opportunities and availabilities of social and economic entities, and such knowledge and awareness of the alternative opportunities influences the choices within the daily lives of transnational migrants (Lee, 2018). Our findings suggest that the Korean American FTEs are aware of their status as transnational migrants and are able to utilize the opportunities, resources, and values from both ends of their transnational

social field. This is especially more prevalent among the 1.5 generation study participants because of their strong connections through education in the United States.

Some of our participant FTEs identified themselves as possessing an understanding
of the different technological trends, an "insider's knowledge" of how the business is
run, and the cultural and social norms of both of their host and home societies. Hence,
they are well-positioned to combine their knowledge and create and re-create their
businesses between Korea and the United States. Often, entrepreneurial motives stem
from critical assessments of products and services that are working well in one context
and subsequent re-contextualization or localization of these products and services in
another context. For instance, Participant 2 introduced an iOS app in 2008 shortly
after the release of the first iPhone. The app she and her co-founder created was a
virtual community for teens with avatars and accessories in addition to chat and mes-
saging capability. She highlighted that this product was not new from her perspective
because she could see that some features came from a very similar Korean product that
was introduced almost a decade prior. Nevertheless, this product went viral and the
start-up got acquired by one of the largest game publishers.

Furthermore, about half of our study participants made a strategic decision to set
up a second office in South Korea to mobilize financial, human, and operational
resources more efficiently. Because South Korea is an institutionally familiar place
for these TEs, the learning curve for setting up operations and building legitimacy
is relatively easier compared to someone who is completely foreign to the Korean
market system. Moreover, they can leverage their existing ethnic networks and
resources from their personal, university, and family connections. Also, several study
participants explained that they could hire highly qualified engineers and designers
at a relatively lower cost compared to the market rate in Silicon Valley.

> There are two reasons to open a branch in Korea: cost and efficiency. Engineering talents
> are considerably cheaper in Korea, with an abundant supply of early career profession-
> als or new grads who are looking for opportunities. They are also used to working very
> hard, in line with the Korean norms, and often can get work done overnight [in US
> time] because of the time zone difference. Front-end and UI/UX design work done in
> Korea is high-quality and outstanding, and I would prefer to run operations from the
> Korea branch. On the other hand, establishing headquarters in the US makes sense for
> the purpose of attracting US-based investors and building a leadership team that under-
> stands these investors and the trends at large in the industry. The core engineering team
> should be based in the US because then they are to provide vision and technical expertise
> for the product. Finally, and perhaps most importantly, our user base is in the US, so
> I think it's appropriate to start here [in the US], where it is easier to meet co-founders,
> investors, and mentors. (Participant 5, aged 38)

Having a satellite office in South Korea also provided an occasion for the TEs to
visit their family and friends and foster and maintain their social and family connections in South Korea. Several study participants expressed that they frequently
travel back and forth between South Korea and the United States to meet colleagues,
investors, and business partners while catching up with family members and friends,
a practice which sustained their transnational social field:

I don't even know what time zone I am in, frankly. I was up all night working while Face Timing with my husband, who is in South Korea. Half of our seed-round investors were from Korea, and the other half were from here, so we were constantly traveling back and forth and communicating through texts and emails. (Participant 10, aged 36)

Many of our study participants mentioned that they are aware that recent South Korean government policies have become lenient toward start-up companies. For instance, setting up offices and job creation in South Korea qualifies them to apply for government grants and participate in start-up competitions with prizes that consist of office space, cash, and operational and support services (e.g., legal, accounting, strategic partnership). Though the effectiveness and payoffs of these start-up-friendly government policies are yet to be assessed, FTEs emphasized that they would like to utilize the available resources and opportunities across both home and host countries.

Our study participants also highlighted that running their ventures within their transnational social field and being immersed in both home and host societies intensified their sense of belonging and connectedness to South Korea and the Korean ethnic community in Silicon Valley. Participant 2 stated:

I am now able to give back to my Korean community with my success, but until recently, I did not have much interaction with the Korean community. I benefited significantly more from the relationships I built over time in San Francisco. Since 2015, I have been a mentor of [US accelerator] and helped [US accelerator] launch a Korean investment fund. I led a Series A program in Seoul to help [US accelerator] set up an infrastructure with a framework, processes, teams, organisation to see if [US accelerator] could do more in the Korean entrepreneurship ecosystem. (Participant 2, aged 39)

A similar sentiment was echoed by several other study participants in one way or another. For instance, Participant 10 mentioned that she would like to eventually go back to South Korea or find a job where she can travel between South Korea and the United States. From that participant's point of view, Silicon Valley attracts the smartest talents from around the world, but South Korea is a small country with its entrepreneurship ecosystem yet to be developed and fostered. Through her postdoctoral and start-up experiences in Silicon Valley, she hopes to become an investor, mentor, and advisor to help Korean start-ups in the future. This case study illustrates that there is a potential for some of the FTEs to return home and bring impact to their home country's economic landscape through skills gained overseas (Potter & Conway, 2008; Lee, 2011).

CONCLUSION

This study explored the particular experiences and trajectories of Korean American FTEs in Silicon Valley. While the previous Korean American TE studies focused broadly on low-skilled self-employment or young professionals with an engineering or science degree, our paper added a specific "gendered" trajectory of FTEs whose entrepreneurial motives and performances are influenced and shaped by a number of different individual and structural factors (e.g., gender, family role, immigrant status, ethnic identity, transnational networks and resources, and the ecosystem of Silicon Valley).

We find that the group of Korean American FTEs plays a vital role in a number of different ways. Within the service sector, they provide services initially targeting the Korean community but gradually expand their ventures beyond the Korean community. What differentiates them from the previous first-generation Korean immigrants' service sector industry (e.g., owning a grocery store, dry cleaning business, or hair salon) is that their business model and growth trajectory resembles that of other start-ups in Silicon Valley. More specifically, FTEs in the service sectors are utilizing social media platforms and online advertisements to reach out and digitally market to their users. They are also offering a strong online presence to provide customer support and reduce other operating costs, and they are analyzing data to better understand their users. Because these FTEs are well connected to their home country, they can provide the most recent "trendy" style and insights of services (e.g., beauty, fashion, cosmetics, food) that are well-suited for Koreans and others who are interested in exploring Korean-influenced services. With their transnational connections between South Korea and the United States, these FTEs possess and apply different types of skillsets compared to that of the service sector industry built by Korean Americans in the 1980s and 1990s.

The FTEs in our study also play a critical role in influencing the entrepreneurship landscape of both home and host country. For instance, a number of participants indicated that they would like to someday return to South Korea, expand their ventures to South Korea, become an investor, and/or serve in some capacity impacting and cultivating start-ups and small/medium enterprises in South Korea. Consequently, their learning and experiences from Silicon Valley are valuable. FTEs are well-positioned to pinpoint clear differences between how start-ups operate in South Korea and the United States and to identify opportunities to intervene in the Korean market. As Saxenian (2007) has famously documented in her book, the technically skilled transnational migrants can be more influential and significant in growing their home country's ICT firms than could policy intervention or multinational enterprises located elsewhere. In the case of South Korea, it would not be so much about growing the high-tech industry and bringing "new technical skills" because South Korea is already advanced in its ICT and high-tech firms. Rather, it would be much more about how transnational skilled migrants can intervene in diversifying and decentralizing the economy and giving more opportunities to small/medium enterprises.

This chapter contributes to the field of transnational entrepreneurship and female entrepreneurship. First, this study provides a gendered perspective of TEs by further focusing on the intersection of female and TEs, which is a relatively under-researched area. Second, this study further segments immigrant entrepreneurs from the perspectives of the first-generation and 1.5 generation immigrants. First-generation and 1.5 generation immigrant entrepreneurs face a different setup of challenges in order to overcome the liability of foreignness in their host countries, compared to second- and third-generation immigrants. Finally, this study provides a new context and example of transnational entrepreneurship by looking at a group of recent Korean American entrepreneurs in Silicon Valley. The majority of prior studies on transnational entrepreneurship treated Asian Americans as one group, although each ethnic group is heterogeneous, and the specific social and cultural contexts play an important role.

This study is not without its limitations. Foremost, the role of the wider Korean American transnational entrepreneur community in Silicon Valley requires further attention. Despite its economic growth and prosperity, South Korea has a relatively underdeveloped start-up environment and infrastructure compared to that of other developed countries; however, the general interests in start-ups have increased immensely over the past decade in the hopes of decentralizing the economy. Moreover, South Korea is considered one of the most technologically advanced and digitally connected countries in the world. As a result, many young, technically skilled individuals who wish to start their own ventures relocate to Silicon Valley, seeking a fairer, more competitive, and more resourceful environment. The role this wider group of Korean American transnational entrepreneurs—that includes both female and male entrepreneurs—plays in the Silicon Valley would be worthwhile to examine, as these migrant entrepreneurs bring particular skills and knowledge to the region and could serve as an example for other ethnic groups.

This chapter has provided a nuanced understanding of TEs through a case study of Korean American FTEs in Silicon Valley and has explored the vital role they play within their transnational social field. The study has depicted the different ways in which the FTEs utilize the resources and networks of their host and home societies and overcome their minority status to become successful entrepreneurs. Through a qualitative approach, this study has attempted to open up the complex stories of the entrepreneurial endeavors and calls for a better interrogation of understanding transnational and minority entrepreneurship that are interlinked to one's ethnic, gendered, and transnational identities. Moreover, we argue that the conceptualizations of the first and 1.5 generation Korean Americans' entrepreneurship and identities should further be expanded beyond the conflicts and hardship to be aligned with transnational opportunities under the new power dynamics and cosmopolitan endeavors.

NOTES

1. This chapter was originally published in *Journal of Entrepreneurship and Innovation in Emerging Economies*, Vol. 6, Issue 1 Copyright 2020 © SAGE Publications India Private Limited, New Delhi. All rights reserved. Reproduced with the permission of the copyright holders and the publishers, SAGE Publications India Pvt. Ltd, New Delhi.

2. This research and the consent to carry out the fieldwork have been approved by the institutional review board of the first author.

REFERENCES

Anderson, S. (2016). Immigrants and Billion Dollar Startups. Retrieved from http://nfap
.com/wp-content/uploads/2016/03/Immigrants-and-Billion-Dollar-Startups.NFAP-Policy
-Brief.March-2016.pdf

Armour, J., & Cumming, D. (2006). The legislative road to Silicon Valley. *Oxford Economic Papers*, 58, 596–635.

Bluestein, A. (2005). The Most Entrepreneurial Group in America wasn't born in America. *Inc.* Retrieved fromhttp://www.inc.com/magazine/201502/adam-bluestein/the-most-en trepreneurial-group-in-america-wasnt-born-in-america.html

Congress.gov. (2010). H.R.5193-Startup Visa Act of 2010. Retrieved from https://www.con gress.gov/bill/111th-congress/house-bill/5193

Davis, L. N., Davis, J. D., & Hoisl, K. (2013). Leisure time invention. *Organization Science*, 24(5), 1439–1458.

Drori, I., Honig, B., & Wright, M. (2009). Transnational entrepreneurship: An emergent field of study. *Entrepreneurship Theory and Practice*, 33(5), 1001–1022.

Eisenhardt, K. M., & Graebner, M. E. (2007). Theory building from cases: Opportunities and challenges. *Academy of Management Journal*, 50, 25–32.

Faist, T. (2000). *The Volume and Dynamics of International Migration and Transnational Social Spaces*. Oxford: Oxford University Press.

Garcia, D. (2006). Mixed marriages and transnational families in the intercultural context: A case study of African-Spanish couples in Catalonia. *Journal of Ethnic and Migration Studies*, 32(3), 403–433.

Glick-Schiller, N., Basch, L., & Szanton-Blanc, C. (1992). Transnationalism: A new analytic framework for understanding migration. In N. Glick-Schiller, L. Basch, & C. Blanc (eds.), *Towards a Transnational Perspective on migration: Race, Class, Ethnicity, and Nationalism Reconsidered* (pp. 1–24). New York, NY: New York Academy of Sciences.

Greene, P., Hart, M., Gatewood, E., Brush, G.,& Carter, N. (2003). Women entrepreneurs: Moving front and center: An overview of research and theory. *Coleman White Paper Series*, 3(1), 1–47.

Kauffman Foundation. (2017). Startup Activity Swings Upward for Third Consecutive Year, Annual Kauffman Index Reports. Retrieved from https://www.kauffman.org/newsroom/20 17/05/startup-activity-swings-upward-for-third-consecutive-year-annual-kauffman-index -reports

Kenny, M. (2000). *Understanding Silicon Valley: The Anatomy of an Entrepreneurial Region*. Stanford, CA: Stanford University Press.

Kim, D. Y. (2006). Stepping-stone to intergenerational mobility? The springboard, safety net, or mobility trap functions of Korean immigrant entrepreneurship for the second genera-tion. *International Migration Review*, 40(4), 927–962.

Kim, K. C. & Hurh, W. M. (1985). Ethnic resources utilization of Korean immigrant entre-preneurs in the Chicago minority area. *International Migration Review*, 19(1), 82–111.

Kivisto, P. (2001). Theorising transnational immigration: A critical review of current efforts. *Ethnic and Racial Studies*, 24(4), 549–577.

Klepper, S. (2010). The origin and growth of industry clusters: The making of Silicon Valley and Detroit. *Cities and Entrepreneurship, Journal of Urban Economics*, 67(1), 15–32.

Lee, J. Y. (2011). A trajectory perspective towards return migration and development: The case of young Korean New Zealander returnees. In R. Frank, J. Hoare, P. Kollner, & S. Pares (eds.), *Korea: Politics, Economy and Society* (pp. 233–256). Danvers, MA: Brill.

Lee, J. Y. (2016). Korean Americans: Entrepreneurship and religion. In I. Miyares, & C. Airriess, (eds.), *Contemporary Ethnic Geographies in America* (2nd edition, pp. 285–302). Rowan & Littlefield Publishing Group.

Lee, J. Y. (2018). *Transnational Return Migration of 1.5 Generation Korean New Zealanders: A Quest for Home*. Lanham, MD: Lexington Books.

Lee, J. Y. (2019). The peripheral experiences and positionalities of Korean New Zealander returnees: Skilled return migrants and knowledge transfer. *Asian Survey*, 59(4), 653–672.

Lee, Y. S., & Eesley, C. (2018). The persistence of entrepreneurship and innovative immigrants. *Research Policy*, 47(6), 1032–1044.

Leung, A. (2011). Motherhood and entrepreneurship: Gender role identity as a resource. *International Journal of Gender and Entrepreneurship*, 3(3), 254–264.

Min, P. G. (1990). Problems of Korean immigrant entrepreneurs. *International Migration Review*, 24(3), 436–455.

Park, E. J. W. (1996). Asians matter: Asian Americans and the high technology industry in Silicon Valley. In B. O. Hing (ed.), *The State of Asian America: Immigration Policies* (pp. 155–177). Los Angeles, CA: LEAP Publications.

Park, E. J. W. (2009). Korean Americans and the U.S. high technology industry: From ethnicity to transnationalism. In E. Y. You, H. Kim, K. Park, & M. D. Oh (eds.), *Korean American Economy & Community in the 21st Century* (pp. 293–314). Los Angeles, CA: Korean American Economic Development Center.

Potter, R., & Conway, D. (2008). The development potential of Caribbean young return migrants: making a difference back home. In T. van Naerssen, E. Spaan, & A. Zoomers (eds.), *Global Migration and Development* (pp. 213–230). New York, NY: Routledge.

Saxenian, A. (2002a). Silicon Valley's new immigrant high-growth entrepreneurs. *Economic Development Quarterly*, 16(1), 20–31.

Saxenian, A. (2002b). Transnational communities and the evolution of global production networks: The cases of Taiwan, China, and India. *Industry and Innovation*, 9(3), 183–202.

Saxenian, A. (2004). The Silicon Valley connection: Transnational networks and regional development in Taiwan, China, and India. In A. D'Costa, & E. Sridharan (eds.), *India and the Global Software Industry* (pp. 164–192). New York, NY: Palgrave Macmillan.

Saxenian, A. (2006). *The New Argonauts: Regional Advantage in a Global Economy*. Cambridge, MA: Harvard University Press.

Survey of Business Owners (SBO)-Characteristics of Businesses: 2007 Tables. Retrieved from https://www.census.gov/data/tables/2007/econ/sbo/2007-sbo-characteristics-of-businesses .html

Shah, S. K., & Tripsas, M. (2007). The accidental entrepreneur: The emergent and collective process of user entrepreneurship. *Strategic Entrepreneurship Journal*, 1(1–2), 123–140.

Shane, S., & Venkataraman, S. (2000). The promise of entrepreneurship as a field of research. *Academy of Management Review*, 25(1), 217–226.

Shin, G. W., & Choi, J. N. (2015). *Global Talent: Skilled Labor as Social Capital in Korea*. Stanford, CA: Stanford University Press.

Waldinger, R. D., Aldrich, H., & Ward, R. (1990). *Ethnic Entrepreneurs: Immigrant Business in Industrial Societies*, Vol. 1. Sage Publications, Inc.

Wood, L., & Kroger, R. (2000). *Doing Discourse Analysis: Methods for Studying Action in Talk and Text*. Thousand Oaks, CA: Sage Publications.

Yoon, I. J. (1997). *On My Own: Korean Businesses and Race Relations in America*. Chicago, IL: University of Chicago Press.

Index

About the Editors and Contributors

Su C. Choe is originally from South Korea. She completed the BA in international studies and anthropology at City College of New York. Su organized her undergraduate senior thesis on the shift of female sexuality in Korean women's history, highlighting the change of Korean women's ability to express their sexuality throughout Korea's various social changes. Su was awarded the June Nash award for her undergraduate thesis. Continuing her research interests in social changes, gender, and sexuality, Su earned MA in anthropology from Georgia State University. While working as a fully funded research and teaching assistant during the graduate program, Su completed her MA thesis on a cross-generational study between first-generation Korean-American mothers and 1.5-generation Korean-American daughters in Duluth, Georgia. This ethnographic research revealed how the social changes such as the processes of modernization in South Korea and immigration to the United States affect the women's intimate experiences and construct their understandings of love, marriage, and the creation of the self and family. Su's research interests broadly focus on social changes, transnationalism, immigration, gender, sexuality, and intimacy, with a focus on Korean and Korean-American cultures.

Alicia Corts is an assistant professor of theater. Her research investigates identity formation and performance in virtual spaces. Her work has been published in *Theatre Journal, Theatre Symposium*, and *Ecumenica*, and she has book chapters in the edited volumes *The Immersive Internet, The Retrofuturism of Cuteness*, and the forthcoming *Opera in the Digital Age*. Alicia is also a professional director, having worked in Chicago, New York, and Minneapolis. She is also a member of the Stage Directors and Choreographers Society, a professional union of directors.

Hyeouk Chris Hahm is a professor and researcher at Boston University, School of Social Work. She dedicates to reducing health disparities among Asian American populations with a particular emphasis on building empirical evidence of health risk behaviors (e.g., self-harm, suicide, and HIV risk behaviors). Funded by NIMH grants (K01 and R34), Hahm has developed and tested theoretical framework that explains suicide behaviors among Asian American women. Further, she developed culturally grounded interventions: AWARE (Asian American Women's Actions in Resilience and Empowerment) and Youth AWARE, which has been implemented in colleges and high schools. Hahm is a recipient of a research mentor award at Boston University and innovator's award from Asian Women for Health. She is the editor of *Asian American Parenting: Family Processes and Interventions* (Springer, 2017) and served as guest editor for a special issue of the *American Journal of Orthopsychiatry* in 2018–2019. Hahm is an author of more than fifty peer-reviewed journal publications and has given 200 professional talks locally, nationally and internationally. She is an editorial board member for the *Journal of Youth and Adolescence* in the United States and the *Journal of Korean Mental Health* in South Korea. Hahm is a fellow of the Society for Social Work and Research (SSWR), where she currently serves on the nominating committee.

Sou Hyun Jang is an assistant professor in the Department of Sociology at Sung kyun kwan University (SKKU), Seoul, South Korea. She received her PhD in Sociology from The Graduate Center of the City University of New York (CUNY). Before joining SKKU, she worked as a post-doctoral fellow in the Department of Health Services at the University of Washington and the Fred Hutchinson Cancer Research Center. Her research interests include transnational healthcare behaviors and social determinants of health disparities. She is the author of *Medical Transnationalism: Korean Immigrants' Medical Tourism to South Korea* (Lexington Books, 2018), which examines how Korean immigrants' medical transnationalism is related to their barriers to healthcare in the United States and other fields of transnationalism. Her previous works focusing on medical transnationalism appeared in Social Science and Medicine, *American Journal of Health Behavior, Journal of Immigrant and Minority Health*, and *International Journal of Health Services*.

Hyeeun Kim is a lecturer of counseling (School of Social Practice) at Laidlaw College and adjunct lecturer of Pastoral Care and Christian Formation at Knox College in New Zealand (NZ). She moved to NZ as an international student in 1994 and is now married with two children. She worked with young people and their families for many years as an ordained Presbyterian minister, experienced counselor, and clinical supervisor. With her knowledge and experiences as a researcher, educator, consultant, pastor, counselor, and migrant, she has worked with various organizations and government agencies. As an advocate for migrants in NZ, she is often invited to speak about migration and its related mental health issues at various workshops, conferences and to tertiary education providers. Her doctoral research was a study of 1.5 generation Korean-New Zealanders' experiences as parents and the influences on their parenting, which was nominated for the Vice-Chancellor's Prize for Best Doctoral Thesis.

Jane Yeonjae Lee is a research associate in the Department of Geography at Kyung Hee University. Her research revolves around transnational skilled migrants, ethnic communities, mobilities, urban environmental politics, and smart urbanism for socially marginalized groups. Her work on migration, mobilities, and cities has been published in *Health and Place, Asian Survey, Journal of Ethnic and Migration Studies, New Zealand Geographer, Transactions of the Institute of British Geographers, Geography Compass*, Elgar Handbook on Medical Tourism and Patient Mobility, and Contemporary Ethnic Geographies in America. She is the author of *Transnational Return Migration of 1.5 Generation Korean New Zealanders: A Quest for Home* (2018).

June Y. Lee is an assistant professor in the Department of Entrepreneurship, Innovation, Strategy and International Business at University of San Francisco School of Management. Her research focuses on how the institutional environment influences cross-border entrepreneurship activities. She received her PhD and MS in Management Science and Engineering from Stanford University and AB in Mathematics and Economics from Bryn Mawr College.

Minjin Kim is an assistant professor in the College of Nursing at University of Cincinnati. She is a transcultural implementation nurse scientist dedicated to developing technology-based interventions and advancing implementation science to address health disparities and promote health equity among racial and ethnic minorities and immigrants. She has contributed to several community-based participatory research projects to develop and test culturally appropriate interventions related to the prevention of hepatitis B and HPV-associated cancers, particularly among Asian Americans. Her recent research works revolve around cross-cultural and cross-generational storytelling interventions to promote HPV vaccination for both men and women and mental health and stigma around COVID-19.

Edison Tse is an associate professor in the Department of Management Science & Engineering at Stanford University. He is also the Director of Asia Center of Management Science and Engineering, which has the charter of conducting research on the growth of emerging economy in Asia and establishing research affiliations with Asian enterprises, with a special focus in China, Korea and India. In 1973, he received the prestigious Donald Eckman Award from the American Automatic Control Council in recognition of his outstanding contribution in the field of Automatic Control. In 2003, he received the Golden Nugget Award from General Motors R & D and Planning. In 2008, he received the Dean's Award for Industry Education Innovation from School of Engineering, Stanford University. He had served as an Associate Editor of the IEEE Transactions of Automatic Control, and a co-editor of the *Journal of Economic Dynamics and Control*, which he co-founded. He had been the academic director of many Chinese Executive Leadership Programs under Stanford Center of Professional Development (SCPD) from 2004 to 2015. Since 2003, he dedicated his research effort in dynamic entrepreneurial strategy and transformation of Chinese production economy to innovation economy. He wrote a book in Chinese entitled "源创新" on this theory and published in China in 2012. A second edition of this book, with new chapters incorporating some experiences of practicing the theory in China, was published in 2016 by China CITIC Press with a new title "重新定义创新 (Redefine Innovation)." He is now working on the extension of this theory to developing countries. His main thesis is that innovation is cultural dependent. Successful innovation in a developing country must be synergistic to its culture, its political, social, and economic environment.

Professor Edison Tse received his BS, MS, and PhD in Electrical Engineering from Massachusetts Institute of Technology.

Irene Yung Park was born in South Korea and migrated to Argentina with her family at the age of 3. She obtained her bachelors' degree in History in Buenos Aires, graduating with the gold medal from the Catholic University of Argentina and the gold medal from the National Academy of History. She completed her formation in Italy, obtaining a MA and PhD in Theology and a MA in Philosophy with dissertations on Modernity and Secularization in Contemporary Theology, and on Scholastic Metaphysics, respectively. Her research interests and publications have revolved around topics related to religion and culture, democracy and global citizenship education, cultural identity and, lately, to ethnicity and transnationalism in Korean migrant communities. She is presently a lecturer at Underwood International College, Yonsei University, and a PhD candidate in Sociology at the Graduate School of Korean Studies, Korea.